MIND, HISTORY, AND DIALECTIC

The Philosophy of R. G. Collingwood

MIND, HISTORY, AND DIALECTIC

THE PHILOSOPHY OF
R. G. Collingwood

LOUIS O. MINK

INDIANA UNIVERSITY PRESS
Bloomington / London

CONTENTS

PREFACE   *vii*

Chapter 1 · Introduction   *1*
  1 · Collingwood as a Systematic Philosopher, 1
  2 · Affinities with Pragmatism and Existentialism, 7
  3 · The Problem of Interpretation, 12
  4 · The Idea of Dialectic, 16

PART I: THE IDEA OF DIALECTIC

Chapter 2 · The Dialectic of Experience   *27*
  1 · Collingwood's Pentateuch of Forms of Experience:
       A Summary, 27
  2 · The Doctrine of the "Concrete Universal," and Its
       Consequences, 48
  3 · The Dialectic of Ethical Systems, 53
  4 · The Unresolved Problem of Speculum Mentis, *55*

Chapter 3 · The Dialectic of Concepts   *59*
  1 · From the Dialectic of Experience to the Dialectic
       of Concepts, 59
  2 · Formal Logic and Collingwood's "Logic," 61
  3 · Philosophical Method and the "Overlap of Classes," 62
  4 · The Scale of Forms, 66
  5 · The Change in Collingwood's Idea of Dialectic, 73

Chapter 4 · The Dialectic of Mind   *79*
  1 · Collingwood's Moral Philosophy, 79
  2 · Collingwood's Theory of Mind: The Levels of
       Practical Consciousness, 82
  3 · Collingwood's Theory of Mind: The Levels of
       Cognitive Consciousness, 92

v

4 · *Abstraction and Freedom, 106*
5 · *Beyond Realism and Idealism, 111*
6 · *From the Dialectic of Experience to the Dialectic of Mind, 113*

PART II: THE DIALECTIC OF IDEAS

Chapter 5 · *The Logic of Thought*   *121*

    1 · *Why Collingwood's "Logic" Is Not Logic, and His "Metaphysics" Is Not Metaphysics, 121*
    2 · *The "Logic of Questions and Answer," and Some Criticisms of It, 123*
    3 · *"Logic" or Hermeneutics?, 131*
    4 · *The Theory of Absolute Presuppositions, 139*
    5 · *Absolute Presuppositions as A Priori Concepts, 144*
    6 · *Absolute Presuppositions and the Dialectic of Mind, 151*

Chapter 6 · *The Grammar of Action: History*   *157*

    1 · *Objections to Collingwood's Account of Historical Knowledge, 157*
    2 · *The Second Objection: Does Collingwood's Theory Ignore the Real Motivations and Causes of Human Action?, 162*
    3 · *The First Objection: Can Collingwood Account for the Effects of Natural Events in Human History?, 170*
    4 · *The Third Objection: Does Collingwood's Theory Leave Nothing for History but Biography?, 173*
    5 · *The Fourth Objection: How Can the Criterion of Historical Truth Possibly Be A Priori?, 183*
    6 · *The Fifth and Sixth Objections: How Can Historical Explanations Claim Certainty? And How Can Understanding What Happened Leave Nothing to Be Explained?, 187*

Chapter 7 · *The Rhetoric of Civilization: Art*   *195*

    1 · *The Origin and Relevance of Collingwood's Philosophy of Art, 195*
    2 · *"Art Is Expression": Collingwood's Account of the Genesis and Expression of Emotion, 199*
    3 · *"Art Is Imagination": Artistic Creation and Communication, and a Correction of Collingwood's Thesis that Art Is Knowledge, 215*
    4 · *"Art Is Language": Collingwood's Final Synthesis Between Expression and Imagination, 226*

Chapter 8 · *Conclusion: The Philosophy of Philosophy*   *239*

    1 · *The Philosophy of Philosophy as Part of Philosophy Itself, 239*
    2 · *Collingwood's Constitutions for the Kingdom of Knowledge, 241*
    3 · *Collingwood's Philosophy of Philosophy, 244*

NOTES   *258*

INDEX   *269*

PREFACE

I AM AWARE THAT A BOOK ABOUT AN INDIVIDUAL PHILOSOPHER, and especially about one who has not been canonized, will seem like a revised doctoral dissertation. But this one is not. I wrote a dissertation once, but it had nothing to do with Collingwood, nor he with it. This book is the outcome of many interests, of whose genesis I am as ignorant as any man is of the secret history of his own mind. It seems to me, however, that my original preoccupation with Collingwood—in direct disobedience of his repeated injunction to his readers to think their own thoughts rather than searching further into his—came about because I approved his enterprise of applying philosophy to the human vocations of art, religion, science, history, and philosophy itself, and at the same time was provoked by the repeated discovery that his views were too incisive to dismiss and too unclear to adopt. In the end I have not tried to assess what is living and what is dead in the philosophy of Collingwood, so much as to point out that what many critics have felt is dead was never there at all, and what almost all have failed to discern is living and always was.

Some philosophers have descendants and others have disciples: some, that is, leave as their legacy a new way of thinking which goes on to find its own course in students whose greatest fidelity to their master is to apply their understanding of his way to the criticism of his beliefs. Others leave only a comprehensive vision which may sustain its disciples but leaves them nothing to do. Whitehead and Wittgenstein are examples of the former, Bergson and Santayana of the latter. At one time I thought that Collingwood was a second-rate example of the latter; if he had few disciples, he clearly had no descendants. But it now seems very likely that he belongs to the first class, with the possibility of descendants yet to come. I do not know who they may be, but I think that I know what they will do. They will be engaged in conceptual analysis not unlike other modern forms of conceptual analysis but not so isolated, in principle and in practice, from the panorama of the human past, from the rich diversity of contemporary cultures, and from the perplexities of individual experience in art, religion, the privacies of thought, and the publicity of action. They will search out the a priori elements in experience and the empirical genesis of thought. They may try, although they will surely fail, to make the scope of philosophy as wide as life itself, and this attempt would at least be not unwelcome in a time when some of the descendants of Socrates try, although they too will fail, to make the scope of philosophy as narrow as an academic department.

Collingwood, however, did not ask either for descendants or for disciples. He was a vain man, but he wished, it seems, not to be revered but to be right. And this was an ironic wish when to his own knowledge and belief no one is ever finally right. This conviction did not deter him from issuing his "interim reports" and may even have liberated him from paralyzing caution. At least it sometimes seems to me that the arrogance and dogmatism with which he has been charged by his critics were most often the joyful wisdom of a man who is prepared to be wrong, as perceived by observers who are not. At any rate, my concern has been not to defend but to understand, although in such matters it is perhaps true that *tout comprendre, c'est tout pardonner.*

It is a strange experience to spend any considerable amount of time exploring the chambers, corridors, and cul-de-sacs of another man's mind, and I do not mean his "unconscious" but rather the connections of his ideas and the development of his fragmentary intellectual systems. Here, as elsewhere, it is difficult to know the dancer from the dance, and often oneself from the dancer. One cannot but admire the elegance of C. D. Broad's saying, after he had completed his monumental examination of McTaggart's philosophy, that he understood McTaggart's ideas better than anyone "but God, if He exist, and McTaggart, if he survive." I cannot say this of Collingwood. There are other interpretations of Collingwood incompatible with the one argued in this book, most notably that by Alan Donagan in his book *The Later Philosophy of R. G. Collingwood*. I am much in debt to this work for sharpening the many points with which I would disagree. All of them, if I am not mistaken, reflect the fact that I regard Collingwood as a "dialectical" philosopher and Donagan's book does not. I have made no effort to catalogue the points of disagreement, since they will be apparent enough to anyone whose interest extends to comparing interpretations.

Grateful acknowledgment is also due to Sir Malcolm Knox for illuminating in an incomparable way certain points in Collingwood's development; to Robert S. Cohen and Stephen D. Crites for reading the entire manuscript, quite differently but equally severely; to the tutors and students of the College of Social Studies of Wesleyan University for their contentious criticisms of Chapter 6 and other sections; to Wesleyan University for its generous policy of sabbatical leaves, without which I would never have attained the fourth level of consciousness; and not least to my wife and children, for keeping me from being puzzled by everything at once.

No bibliography has been included in this book, although most of Collingwood's philosophical works are referred to in one place or another, with full citations except for the major and most frequently cited books. A number of Collingwood bibliographies are now readily accessible. The first bibliography, chronologically arranged, of both his philosophical and historical writing appeared in *Proceedings of the British Academy,* XXIX (1943), pp. 474–75 (philosophical) and pp. 481–85 (historical). Some items omitted from that bibliography of philosophical works were listed in the Editor's Preface to *The Idea of History* (p. vii), and the corrected listing is reproduced as Appendix I to Alan Donagan's *The Later Philosophy of R. G. Collingwood.* A selected bibliography of both philosophical and historical works appears in *R. G. Collingwood,* by E. W. F. Tomlin (London: Longmans, Green and Co., 1953), and a more complete bibliography, alphabetically arranged and including many of the critical essays on Collingwood's philosophy, is appended to the collection by William Debbins of Collingwood's *Essays in the Philosophy of History* (Austin: University of Texas Press, 1965).

The most recent bibliography, containing the most complete list of works about Collingwood, is in William M. Johnston's *The Formative Years of R. G. Collingwood* (The Hague: Martinus Nijhoff, 1967).

In the essay which follows, Collingwood's ten philosophical books are cited, by abbreviations, in the text. Except as noted, all were published by or for Oxford University Press. In the order of their writing, they are:

RP   *Religion and Philosophy* (London: Macmillan and Co., 1916)

SM   *Speculum Mentis* (1924)

OPA *Outlines of a Philosophy of Art* (1925). Reprinted, complete, in *Essays in the Philosophy of Art* by R. G. Collingwood, ed. Alan Donagan (Bloomington: Indiana University Press, 1964).

EPM *An Essay on Philosophical Method* (1933)

IN   *The Idea of Nature* (written 1933–34, published 1945)

IH   *The Idea of History* (written 1936–39, published 1946)

PA   *The Principles of Art* (1938)

A   *An Autobiography* (1939)

EM   *An Essay on Metaphysics* (1940)

NL   *The New Leviathan* (1942). This book, unlike Collingwood's other books, is divided into paragraphs numbered 1.1, 1.11, . . . 1.2, . . . etc.; and citations of this book are therefore to the numbered paragraphs rather than to pages.

MIND, HISTORY, AND DIALECTIC

The Philosophy of R. G. Collingwood

CHAPTER I

Introduction

*When a man is proud because he can understand
and explain the writings of Chrysippus, say to
yourself, If Chrysippus had not written obscurely,
this man would have had nothing to be proud of.*
—Epictetus, *Enchiridion*

1 · Collingwood as a Systematic Philosopher

NOT MANY ACADEMIC PHILOSOPHERS IN THIS CENTURY HAVE reached an audience wider than a corporal's guard of their own colleagues, and if one were to name the English-speaking philosophers who have been widely read among non-philosophers three names would appear in surprising conjunction: Dewey, Russell, and Collingwood. On academic philosophy itself Collingwood's influence, with scattered exceptions, has been negligible. Yet nine of his philosophical books—all, in fact, except his first book—remain in print twenty-five years after his death. Although he never aimed to be a "popular" philosopher like the now-forgotten C. E. M. Joad, Collingwood wrote his books not for his professional colleagues but for an educated public; and he seems to have found not only an audience but one which is interestingly diverse and quietly growing. Historians have read *The Idea of History* who have not opened another philosophical book since they were undergraduates, and critics and theorists of the arts are as familiar with *The Principles of Art* as with any work of aesthetics in our time. And although Collingwood was not a theologian, he has been rather more widely known in theological schools than in departments of philosophy. So many people have called Collingwood an "unduly neglected" thinker that he is coming to be surely the best known neglected thinker of our time.

It is easier to account for the indifference to Collingwood by his philosophical colleagues than for the continued interest in him by a wider audience. Alone among the Oxford philosophers of his generation, it was his fate to carry the banner of systematic philosophy onto a field whence all but he had fled. In the quarter-century spanned by his major work, philosophy was rapidly changing character in the English-speaking world, and nowhere was the change more definite than at Oxford. When Collingwood arrived at Oxford as a student in 1907, the idealism of T. H. Green and F. H. Bradley was already being replaced by the realism of Cook Wilson and Prichard, and the high tide of realism in the 1920's was succeeded in the next decade by analytical philosophy. Independent by temperament, Collingwood took no part in this change, and as a result he stood alone, looking more and more like a familiar of all the devils which were being industriously exorcised. To those who noticed that he had translated Croce, he appeared to be Croce's English disciple. To others he looked like the last epigone of British Hegelianism. To still others he seemed a survival of a pernicious Kantianism which would not down.

The truth is that Collingwood was a systematic philosopher in a time which had little use for philosophical systems. To a considerable degree, however, he shared his colleagues' suspicion of the grandiose systems of the nineteenth century. Like the systematic philosophers of the tradition, he was concerned to articulate the categories of experience in their full range and complexity, and to accommodate aesthetic, religious, and political experience as well as the more familiar philosophical problems of perception, logical inference, and ethical judgment. But like philosophical analysts, he never reached a conclusion on an issue merely by deducing what he ought to think about it from general principles already formed. As a result, the corpus of his work makes up neither a system nor a series of analyses of particular problems. After *Speculum Mentis,* which was an early attempt at a system in the classical sense, each of his books must be seen as the discussion of a specific set of questions in the context of a *possible* system. His books are, as it were, not parts of a system but fragments of systems. Each one seems to belong to some intellectual scheme which includes but goes beyond it, and the feeling that in discussing art or history or religion one is focusing one's attention on a specific area but not cutting off, as with blinders, one's sense of its relation to other areas, gives each book a particular weight and authority. On the other hand, among the books there are *prima facie* inconsistencies of doctrines and methods. The *sense* of interrelationship is not easily and smoothly transformed by the reader into an understanding of systematic connections. One does not expect consistency in a collection of *obiter dicta,* however brilliant; but Collingwood's often memorable and provocative views carry with them the promise of being more than isolated insights and then seem to abjure their own promise as they fall to fighting with each other. As a consequence, Collingwood's work to an unusual degree calls for interpretation. The very lucidity and straightforwardness of his style have tended to conceal this need. I have never heard an historian complain that he could not understand *The Idea of History;* yet I am convinced, and much of this essay is designed to show, that unless this book is interpreted in the light of the continuity of Collingwood's ideas developed through his other books, *The Idea of History* is certain to be misunderstood—creatively misunderstood, perhaps, but it is a minor merit of a book that it is subject to interesting misinterpretations. The same could be said of his other books, not excepting his own autobiography.

Henry James has a story about a writer whose books were discovered to be parts of a grand design which could not be suspected by anyone reading a single book; in the image which gives its name to James's story, they were parts of a "figure in the carpet." The metaphor is singularly apposite to Collingwood's series of books, at least in the sense that each book needs some interpretative background provided by one or more of the others. This is not because he kept in mind a single complex system which he parcelled out bit by bit, but because his thinking went through a process of development and change in which earlier stages were modified but not entirely superseded by later ones, a process which is itself an illustrative example of the notion of dialectical change which was one of his own leading ideas. Almost certainly he was not aware of this, and we can understand it better than he, since we can read his books together as he never did. His *Autobiography* is of no help on this point, since it is a reconstruction of the past entirely from the standpoint of his interests and recollections at the time of its writing in 1938; and he seems not even to have reread his own earlier books for this purpose (cf. A, 56).

One example may suffice, for the moment, of the way in which his books implicate, although they do not refer to, each other. The philosophical chapters of *The Idea of History* have generally been thought to overintellectualize history unconscionably. Collingwood says there that "all history is the history of thought," and seems to mean by this that the historian can understand, in some honorific sense of "understand," *only* those historical actions which resulted from processes of deliberate reflection and calculation. But in *The Principles of Art* (written in 1937, between the original draft of *The Idea of History* in 1936 and its partial revision in 1939), Collingwood develops in detail a philosophical psychology which makes the connection between emotion and thought much closer and more continuous than it is commonly believed to be, and thereby makes clear that what he means by "thought" in *The Idea of History* is much broader in scope than the ratiocinative process his critics have taken it to be.

Because he wrote for a "public" and because he believed that a technical vocabulary conceals presuppositions which partly prejudge any issue formulated in that vocabulary (EPM, 201–208), Collingwood never availed himself of the systematic philosopher's privilege of coining neologisms or advancing stipulative definitions—a procedure which if it does not clarify at least does not mislead. But although this admirable self-denial enhances the grace of an already limpid style, it enormously increases the difficulty of tracing out the figure in the carpet whose arabesques lead from book to book. Terms shift their meaning from context to context, not like terms in common language but in fact as covertly technical terms given temporary rather than permanent jobs. The term "philosophy" itself assumes such protean forms that, as T. M. Knox has observed (IH, xv), Collingwood apparently regarded philosophy as identical with whatever he was most interested in at the time. (But since he regarded philosophy as "thought about thought," this attitude is not merely a *parti pris*.)

The discussion of Collingwood's books as a single series may therefore be of some use in correcting misinterpretations and in sketching a framework within which those who have been primarily interested in one part of the figure in the carpet (as historians have been familiar with *The Idea of History*) may at least discern its position in the larger outline. And this outline is both logical, because Collingwood was a systematic philosopher, and historical, because he never thought of himself as having a system but issued a series of "interim reports" (cf. EPM, 198) of his progress toward one. The provision of a coherent interpretation of Collingwood which takes both of these factors into account is, I believe, more illuminating than a study of the historical sources and affinities of his ideas. Such a study would be by no means irrelevant: Collingwood devoted much time and thought to the study and teaching of the history of philosophy, and his own work can even be seen as a mosaic of theses, problems, and methods whose provenance can be traced. It could hardly be otherwise, in view of the fact that he regarded the history of philosophy not as a record of philosophical doctrines to be accepted or refuted but as a series of problems about what philosophers have meant, to be solved by interpreting what they have said as answers to questions which we ourselves must reconstruct and think through. But Collingwood cannot be identified with any "school" although he learned something from many. His conception of philosophy itself is Socratic, and his repeated insistence that "philosophical reasoning leads to no conclusions which we did not in some sense know already" (EPM, 161), as well as his view that dialectical controversy reveals principles of antecedent but unrecognized agreement (NL, 24.59), are principles which Socrates would have claimed as his own; but at the same time the Socratic-Platonic ontology of Forms is entirely alien to Collingwood. His solution of the mind-body problem (in *The New Leviathan*) is Spinozist, as is also the genetic account of moral concepts (e.g., "goodness is . . . bestowed upon whatever possesses it by mind's practical activity in the form of desire," NL, 11.68), but his doctrine of the spontaneity of consciousness (PA, 207–208) is the antithesis of Spinoza's determinism. Kant's method of transcendental deduction is ubiquitous in Collingwood, and not only in the Kantian form of his primary question about history, "How is historical knowledge possible?" But Kant's fundamental distinctions between understanding and reason, between analytic and dialectic, between the theoretical and the practical, are as thoroughly abrogated by Collingwood as they were by Hegel. In fact, if Collingwood can be associated with any single figure in the history of philosophy that one would be Hegel, although even then only by virtue of Collingwood's brief but illuminating reinterpretation of Hegel in *The Idea of History,* which disposes of the clichés that Hegel's dialectic was a mechanical instrument grinding out historical inevitability, and that Hegel thought that political history ended with the Prussian state and the history of philosophy with himself. (A student who had read Collingwood before reading Hegel remarked to me with wit that he found himself regarding Hegel as a neo-Collingwoodian.) The similarities between Collingwood and his older friend Croce have been widely remarked, although the differences between them are generally ignored. And it has not been noticed, I believe, that the modern philosopher most influential on Collingwood's later thought —perhaps the only one—was Whitehead. There are no particular affinities between the metaphysical scheme of *Process and Reality,* which is subjected to sympathetic but astute criticism in *The Idea of Nature,* and any of Collingwood's leading ideas. But there is a remarkable resemblance between Collingwood's mature view that the course of scientific thought reflects the logical efficacy of absolute presuppositions which have a finite historical career, and Whitehead's thesis, in *Science and the Modern World,* that the fundamental concepts of modern science have given rise, in the development of science from the seventeenth century to the present, to results which can no longer be intelligibly interpreted in terms of those concepts, and which call for a new set of metaphysical concepts. Collingwood is no more a rival of Whitehead's than history is a rival of science. He regarded Whitehead as a "progressive" metaphysician, that is, one engaged in trying to state the presuppositions of modern science rather than in defending as eternal truths the presuppositions of outmoded science. But he believed himself to be pursuing a different, although related, aim: "the chief business of twentieth-century philosophy is to reckon with twentieth-century history" (A, 79; "twentieth-century history" does not mean the historical events of our century but its new historical consciousness, the "idea" of history). One can imagine that in Collingwood's view *Science and the Modern World* exhibits an historical consciousness in reflecting on science; and it is thus an important datum for Collingwood's own reflection on the historical consciousness and its implications.

This is the merest sketch of Collingwood's philosophical progenitors, and it could be indefinitely elaborated in numbers and in detail (I have not mentioned, for example, Vico or Dilthey, although Collingwood's debt to the former is as great as to Kant and to the latter as great as to Croce).[1] But an historical study of "influences" is in the case of Collingwood very likely to be unilluminating, because it begs the question of interpretation. It would be misleading to construct a genealogy of Collingwood's ideas as if it were evident what those ideas are. If there is a figure in the carpet, it is at least not obvious; but even its possibility is a warning against the habit, no less common now than it was among Collingwood's colleagues, of lifting a sentence from its context and assuming that it must mean what we would mean by it if it ever entered our heads to say such a thing.

2 · *Affinities with Pragmatism and Existentialism*

Once the figure is discerned, however, it reveals hitherto unnoticed affinities between Collingwood's thought and other types of recent philosophy with which he has never been identified and of which he himself had no knowledge. We may well pause here to take note of these, since the argument of the following chapters is not designed to prove nor to discuss in detail a thesis which nevertheless, I am convinced, it supports: that the themes most explicit in Collingwood's later work but discoverable throughout the whole career of his thought are those commonly associated with *pragmatism* and *existentialism*. In a very general way, this may account for the fact that philosophers have found in Collingwood a provocativeness not easy to dismiss as merely a matter of style or manner, while non-philosophers have endured his philosophical arguments in the feeling that they carry significance beyond the intramural disputes of professional philosophers. Both pragmatism and existentialism have touched nerves of modern thought and culture. If they have been, as is often said, less philosophical theories than expressions of secular faiths and doubts, they have at least been relevant to the problematic human condition; and they have been not merely expressions of it but proposals of ways of thinking about it. It is these ways of thinking which bear some comparison with Collingwood's ideas.

Collingwood's few references to pragmatism are brief and unilluminating. He never distinguishes among different theories of pragmatism or instrumentalism, and, apart from one uncomplimentary reference to William James's *Varieties of Religious Experience* (A, 93) and a footnote in *Religion and Philosophy* (1916), he never mentions any other pragmatist by name, not even the English pragmatist F. C. S. Schiller. As early as *Speculum Mentis,* he dismissed the "babblings of pragmatism," which, he said, "analyses the abstract concept of science and jumps to the conclusion that the analysis applies to knowledge in general" (SM, 182). But despite his clearly very superficial understanding of a pragmatism which was at its apogee in the United States during his own career, he was nevertheless in unsuspected agreement on many points.

The first sentence of *Speculum Mentis* is "All thought exists for the sake of action" (SM, 15); and the final chapter of his *Autobiography* is entitled "Theory and Practice." Now it may be as much of an occupational disease among dons to believe that their ideas have practical consequences as to insist that they need no such justification. But the fact is that Collingwood combatted as fiercely as Dewey any radical or categorical distinction between thinking and acting, between the theoretical and the practical. What we call thinking and what we call acting Collingwood regarded as stages of a single and continuous process. The intimate connection of thought and action he sometimes stated in a different way, for example, in the metaphor of thought as the "Inside" of action and action as the "Outside" of thought, a metaphor which is basic to his description of the historical understanding of actions by the re-enactment of the thoughts of which they are the "Outside." This has often misled critics who supposed that Collingwood regarded mind as a sort of Cartesian mental substance inhabiting a physical body and having properties which are introspectable but not otherwise observable. But this is exactly what Collingwood wished to reject: he regarded mind not as an entity but as an activity, with functions all of which are actively expressed; his account of mind (as we shall see in detail in Chapter 4) is, like that of the pragmatists, genetic and functional. In *The New Leviathan* he boldly attributed a kind of primacy to the practical over the theoretical with the broad claim that the root conceptions of theoretical (in his terminology, "scientific") thinking have their origin in the different ways in which men become aware of themselves as agents acting in concrete situations.

Along with the rejection of a radical distinction between thought and action, and all of the consequences of that rejection, Collingwood also shares with pragmatists the conception of knowing as an active process of inquiry rather than as the discovery and possession of a body of truths, and also a distaste for formal logic insofar as that claims to exhaust the possible patterns of inferential thinking. What Collingwood called his "logic"—namely, his logic of question and answer—is in fact, as in the case of Dewey, not a *formal* logic but a theory of inquiry. Some of its more remarkable principles—for example, that all propositions are answers to questions, and that they are not true or false but "right" or "wrong" in the sense that they help or fail to help us get ahead in the process of inquiry—are intelligible only as characteristic of a pragmatic, rather than of a correspondence, coherence, or semantic conception of truth.

Pragmatism has been widely represented as a philosophy of scientific method; Collingwood's comment on it in *Speculum Mentis* reflects this opinion. However, it should not require argument that, while pragmatism, especially in the forms of it represented by Peirce and Dewey, was partisan to natural science against the still lively opposition from dogmatic philosophy and theology, pragmatism itself is not "scientific" but historical and genetic; it regards systems of knowledge, social institutions, and concepts of value as arising—and perishing—in the transactions of men with nature and with each other, and seeks to ease the process of change through understanding how past ways of solving problems become formalized as habits of mind and thereby inhibit the attack on new problems. Collingwood could readily have acknowledged as a statement of his own theory of absolute presuppositions Dewey's observation in his *Logic:* "Failure to examine the conceptual structures and frames of reference which are unconsciously implicated in even the seemingly most factual inquiries is the greatest single defect that can be found in any field of inquiry." [2] And, with a slight demurrer at the use of "mind" as an entity-word (and this is an objection which would be withdrawn after an examination of Collingwood's naturalistic theory of mind), Dewey could readily have agreed with the summation of *Speculum Mentis:* "For the life of mind consists of raising and solving problems, problems in art, religion, science, commerce, politics, and so forth. The solution of these problems does not leave behind it a sediment of ascertained fact, which grows and solidifies as the mind's work goes on. . . . When the problem is fully solved the sediment of information disappears and the mind is left at liberty to go on" (SM, 317). Anyone who supposes that science is the slow but steady addition of law to law, historical knowledge of fact to fact, and art of technique to technique, will not be able to agree with this statement, but for the same reason he will have little sympathy for that philosophical pragmatism which is ironically misinterpreted as enshrining common sense when in reality it calls common sense radically into question.

It may seem even more surprising to associate Collingwood with contemporary existentialism. Certainly many of the themes of existentialists and philosophers of existence—anxiety, inauthenticity, paradox, the ontology of non-Being, the exaltation of subjectivity, and the use of phenomenological method—are not to be discovered in Collingwood even by the most acrobatic feats of intuitive interpretation. To some extent, however, this is due to the fact that existentialist thought has developed a self-generating mode of discourse which energizes its participants as it baffles its critics; and Collingwood was as remote from the existentialist style as was Rudyard Kipling. (The real affinities between existentialism and pragmatism are also obscured by such differences of language.)

The most important point at which Collingwood's views make contact with those familiar in recent existentialism is the question of freedom. This is also a point on which the figure in the carpet may escape notice. In *The New Leviathan* Collingwood treats freedom as the consciousness of alternative courses of action, in the sense that such consciousness is not a disclosure that there is an objective situation of choice but actually is *constitutive* of choice as a real possibility. The consciousness that one is choosing among alternative objects completely transforms the situation in which one (as an observer might say) chooses, but is not conscious of oneself as choosing. This view apparently identifies "freedom" with a high order of reflective awareness—in fact, with what in Chapter 4 we shall call "fourth-level consciousness"; but as "thought" is connected with "emotion" as well as distinguished from it, so all of the higher mental functions are dialectical transformations of lower functions; and in *The Principles of Art,* which is mainly concerned with the lower functions of feeling and imagination, freedom appears as the spontaneity of consciousness in every activity at every level. What this means requires an exposition of ideas yet to be made, but it is at least evident that Collingwood shares the existentialist rejection of the notion that human experience can be exhaustively understood and explained in terms of the causal determinants of experience.

A corollary of this rejection is the principle that there is no fixed or determinate human "nature" as is claimed or presupposed by views otherwise as widely divergent as classical rationalism and stimulus-response psychology. This is the principle which connects Sartre's formula that "existence precedes essence" ("essence" here meaning a human nature invariant through time and distinguishable from its individual exemplifications) and Ortega's assertion that "Man has no nature; he has only a history." Similarly Collingwood holds that "human nature, if it is a name for anything real, is only a name for human activities. . . . The historical process is a process in which man *creates for himself this or that kind of human nature* by re-creating in his own thought the past to which he is heir" (IH, 226; italics added).

There are other correspondences. What Collingwood calls the "corruption of consciousness," the failure of the attempt to become conscious of and acknowledge our emotions, corresponds to the existentialist category of inauthenticity, or what Sartre has called *la mauvaise foi*. Collingwood is very much more willing than existentialists commonly are to explore the logic of abstract concepts, but like them he enters a general caveat against confusing the clarity and logical form of abstractions with objectivity; his criticism of Hegel states briefly what Kierkegaard had said—to put it mildly—at length: "Hegel aims at building up the concrete out of abstractions; not realizing that, unless the concrete is given from the start, the abstractions out of which it is to be built up are not forthcoming" (NL, 33.89). And for Collingwood "concrete" means the unique and the individual. Both his view of history and his ethical theory are *prima facie* open to the same objections which one encounters in the criticism of *Existenzphilosophie*. In ethics he holds that the most rational conception of duty is that of individual and unique agents in individual and unique situations; both agent and situation transcend general principles and general descriptions by which they can be compared with other agents in other situations. In history he holds that historical knowledge is "wholly a reasoned knowledge of what is transient and concrete" (IH, 234). The resemblance here is not coincidental: the consciousness of duty is elsewhere explicitly identified with "historical thinking" (NL, 18.52). But it is usually thought—to many it appears self-evident—that although all events are in a sense transient and concrete and all decisions are in a sense personal and unique, events can be explained and decisions can be judged only to the extent that they are instances of general principles of explanation (e.g., causal laws) or justification (e.g., rules of conduct). We can explain an event or justify an action, it seems, only to the extent that it falls under concepts. To the extent that it falls under concepts it is not "individual" or "unique"; to the extent that it is individual or unique, it is unintelligible by any rational criteria.

Such a case against Collingwood is strong; but my present purpose is not to assess its merits nor to consider what might be said on his behalf but rather to bring out the point that his affinities with existentialism are made more evident by the fact that both are subject to the same criticisms. Of course, the logical incompatibility between rationality on the one hand and uniqueness and transience on the other is assumed in the criticisms but explicitly questioned by Collingwood. His position, although differing in many particulars, is not unlike that of Jaspers on the "fundamental problem of reason and Existenz": "Philosophy, wherever it is successful, consists of those unique ideas in which logical abstractness and the actual present become, so to speak, identical." [3]

It would be wholly unprofitable to raise and impossible to settle the question whether Collingwood is an "existentialist" or a "pragmatist." The significance of such affinities as can be discerned is to indicate that the figure in the carpet also has a ground. Thinking of any sort takes place against a background of concepts and concerns, and with thinking of any originality the background is richer and more varied than can be detected by anyone whose perspective on the origin and transformation of ideas is shallow. The difficulty with the theory of *Weltanschauungen* is that, like the eye in vision, one's own *Weltanschauung* is an instrument, not an object of thought. Only in historical perspective, after it has done its work, can it be seen how it has done so. We do not have a name to describe or an articulated theory to explain the movement of thought which transformed, after the First World War, what we call, in its earlier forms, "Romanticism." But I think it is likely that the future historian of our time will see Collingwood along with pragmatists and existentialists as tributaries of a common stream. For the present, the possibility alone may help to bring into relief, in the chapters which follow, certain themes and emphases which no coherent interpretation can neglect.

3 · The Problem of Interpretation

Collingwood's published work was of three types, each intended for a different audience. The first group includes his archaeological studies in the history of Roman Britain, the second, a handful of articles and reviews addressed to philosophers and printed in professional journals, and the third, and most important, his ten philosophical books, including his *Autobiography* and the two post-humous volumes, *The Idea of History* and *The Idea of Nature*. Collingwood also translated volumes by the Italian philosophers Benedetto Croce and Guido de Ruggiero and was the author of a charming description of a sailing journey through the Mediterranean, *The First Mate's Log.* The only one of Collingwood's books to be taken seriously by his professional colleagues was the *Essay on Philosophical Method,* published in mid-career in 1933. Yet he did not regard his books as popularizations but as his major contribution in philosophy; and he addressed them to a "public" interested in the application of philosophical argument to problems (political, aesthetic, religious) of civilized life, an interest which he accused his professional colleagues of having abandoned for "minute philosophy."

Collingwood's first published writing was his book *Religion and Philosophy* (1916). During the next eight years he wrote several articles on philosophy of religion and philosophy of history, and also two books, never published, one an early version of his "logic of question and answer" and the other an analysis of "process or becoming." The manuscripts of both were destroyed after he wrote the *Autobiography* (A, 99, n. 1). In 1924 he published *Speculum Mentis,* an attempt at a "system" in which he discusses art, religion, science, history, and philosophy as modes of experience. During the following years he continued to write on this wide range of subjects, including the small book *Outlines of a Philosophy of Art* in 1925. Most of his "professional" articles were written during this time. A new period began with the publication in 1933 of the *Essay on Philosophical Method.* His intention at that time was to carry out applications of the method of analysis prescribed in this book: *The Idea of Nature,* published in 1945 after his death, was mainly written in 1933–34, and *The Idea of History,* also posthumously edited and published in 1946, was largely written in 1936. However, it was *The Principles of Art,* published in 1938, which in the *Autobiography* of 1939 is called "the second in my series," and the *Essay on Metaphysics,* published in 1940, one year after the *Autobiography,* which appeared as "Volume II" of his "Philosophical Essays." *The New Leviathan* appeared in 1942, a year before his death in 1943. During the final decade, only two published articles were not later incorporated in the manuscript of the published books. From an active career which spanned little more than two decades, his ten books contain most of the relevant and available evidence for an interpretation of his work and an assessment of it.

As I have already suggested, however, there can be no assessment of Collingwood apart from an interpretation of him; and there can be no interpretation which does not suggest or explicitly state some classification of his books by the themes central to his thinking at different stages or by the nodal points of change in his views. Collingwood's own attempt at a history of his own opinions in the *Autobiography* is unfortunately of little direct help. For one thing, he traces the conception of almost all of his original views—of those, at least, which he mentions at all—to the years during and immediately after the First World War. The one exception is the "new conception of history" (A, 110): that all history is the history of thought, and is known by the re-enactment in the historian's mind of the thought which he is studying. Collingwood says (A, 107, 115) that this was the conclusion of a train of thought which covered twenty years and was not complete until about 1930. But it has seemed completely incredible to his interpreters that this "train of thought" was "complete" as early as 1930.

For another thing, Collingwood is mainly concerned in the *Autobiography* to reconstruct the course by which he arrived at his "rapprochement between history and philosophy," and in so doing he says a great deal about history but very little about philosophy. And in particular he has nothing to say about the theories and arguments in the *Essay on Philosophical Method,* their origins or their relation to his later views and interests. And finally, of course, the *Autobiography* was itself succeeded by both the *Essay on Metaphysics* and *The New Leviathan,* both of key importance in any interpretation. The *Autobiography,* like Augustine's *Retractations* or Nietzsche's *Ecce Homo,* complicates the problem of interpretation rather than providing independent and authoritative evidence. And on the basis of the common evidence of the published work, there exist already two different and incompatible interpretations. Since I shall propose yet a third, it may be useful here to summarize these interpretations so far as they are exemplified in "periodizations" of Collingwood's work.

One periodization, by Collingwood's student, friend, and editor, T. M. Knox, appears in the Editor's Introduction to the posthumous *The Idea of History;* the second is developed and argued in detail by

Alan Donagan in his *The Later Philosophy of R. G. Collingwood.* These classifications agree in omitting reference to Collingwood's short book *Outlines of a Philosophy of Art* (1925), and in regarding both *Religion and Philosophy* and *Speculum Mentis* (corroborated by Collingwood's own judgment in his *Autobiography*) as juvenilia. This leaves the seven books beginning with the *Essay on Philosophical Method* (1933) and ending with *The New Leviathan* (1942).

In Knox's judgment, these seven books fall into two groups, the first consisting of the *Essay on Philosophical Method, The Idea of Nature* (written between 1933 and 1937, and revised mainly in 1939 and 1940; published posthumously in 1945), and *The Idea of History* (written mainly in 1936, supplemented in 1939 and partially revised in 1940; published posthumously in 1946), and the second consisting of the *Autobiography,* the *Essay on Metaphysics* and *The New Leviathan,* with *The Principles of Art* belonging partly to the first and partly to the second of these two groups.

Chronologically, the break between these two groups falls in the years 1936–37. In Knox's opinion, the break marked a radical shift in Collingwood's understanding of the relation between philosophy and history: in the earlier period he still distinguished them as independent forms of thought, each with its own problems and methods; in the latter group, and especially in the *Essay on Metaphysics,* he assimilated philosophy to history, yielding to a radical skepticism about the possibility of solving philosophical problems. Whereas until 1936 he still believed in the possibility of metaphysics as a separate study, by 1938 he was saying that metaphysics is (and in fact always has been) exclusively an historical inquiry into the absolute presuppositions of past thinkers. And Knox has not been alone in believing that the brilliant promise of the *Essay on Philosophical Method* was sadly distorted and dissipated after 1937 in the *Autobiography* and the two books which followed it. The true Collingwood, in this view, is the middle Collingwood, whose powers slowly failed and whose grasp of the logic of his own views escaped him after the *Essay on Philosophical Method.*

In Donagan's interpretation, on the other hand, Collingwood's repeated attempts to characterize philosophy and its relations to and differences from history and science can be dismissed as "muddled and confused"; but out of this lifeless husk there emerged an original and highly developed philosophy of mind, which is defensible in its own right and in addition was a remarkable anticipation, like nothing else of its time, of interests and views now common in English and American philosophy. The main outlines of this philosophy of mind are contained in four books: *The Idea of Nature, The Idea of History, The Principles of Art,* and *The New Leviathan;* these comprise "the later philosophy of Collingwood." [4] But in addition, Collingwood himself gave two different interpretations of this philosophy of mind, an "idealist" interpretation in the *Essay on Philosophical Method,* and an "historicist" interpretation in the *Autobiography* and in the *Essay on Metaphysics.* In Donagan's view, not the *Essay on Philosophical Method* (which even for Knox is "little more than an introduction to a philosophy not yet written" [IH, xxi]) but *The New Leviathan* is Collingwood's chef d'oeuvre.

The thesis which I wish to propose in this essay, that Collingwood's leitmotif throughout the entire corpus of his work was a continuous examination of the possibility and nature of dialectical thinking (and that, quite consistently, the apparent changes in his views are themselves dialectical transformations), suggests an entirely different periodization of his work. [5] Like Knox and Donagan, I regard *Religion and Philosophy* as the least illuminating of his works; in that book he was attempting to exemplify a notion of systematic philosophy which he never abandoned, but he had not yet connected the idea of system with the idea of dialectic. But unlike Knox and Donagan, I regard *Speculum Mentis* as in certain ways the most illuminating of his books, because it is his first attempt to give content to an emerging idea of the formal characteristics of dialectical patterns and is necessary to an understanding of his later and more subtle dialectic (in a way which exactly parallels Knox's judgment that *Speculum Mentis* contains the germ of his later "scepticism and dogmatism") (IH, xi). And the *Essay on Philosophical Method,* I shall argue, *is* Collingwood's dialectical logic, produced by reflection on the kind of thinking exemplified but not discussed ("shown" but not "said") in *Speculum Mentis.*

4 · The Idea of Dialectic

Collingwood first lectured on moral philosophy in 1919 and continued to lecture annually "with constant revision" during "almost the whole remainder" of his tenure at Pembroke College, that is, until 1934 (A, 149). The *Essay on Philosophical Method,* Knox has testified, is an expansion of Collingwood's introduction to these lectures. Now Collingwood's moral philosophy was quite explicitly dialectical: in it he illustrated and applied the *Essay*'s logic of the "overlap of classes" with respect to the concepts of feeling, appetite, desire, and will, and the concepts of their associated values, which are, respectively, pleasure, satisfaction, happiness, and good. Moreover, his dialectical moral philosophy is substantially confirmed in what Donagan has described as Collingwood's philosophy of mind in *The New Leviathan,* as it is also complemented by the theory of imagination in Book II of *The Principles of Art.* The latter is an analysis of the developmental stages of consciousness by which rational thought emerges from undifferentiated feeling through intermediate levels of consciousness and imagination; this exactly parallels, in the former, the analysis of the emergence of rational will from undifferentiated feeling through levels of appetite and desire. There is much to be explicated and assessed in this philosophy of mind; the point of present relevance is that its development between 1933 and 1941 is a smoothly continuous and internally consistent fulfillment of the program of the *Essay on Philosophical Method.* It is Collingwood's theory of the *dialectical* nature of mind, as it reveals itself through action and imagination and is reflected upon in ethics, aesthetics, and logic.

But at the same time, Collingwood continued, as he had in *Speculum Mentis,* to regard mind as something which reveals itself not only in individual action and expression but in corporate culture, in the institutions of which science as well as politics are examples. And so, as on one hand he was pursuing an analysis of the dialectical nature of mind, on the other he was making a dialectical analysis of the products of mind. The form which the latter takes is a history of the development of fundamental concepts, guided by the principle that in the history of thought such fundamental concepts change in the mode of what Hegel called *Aufhebung,* by retaining but at the same time transforming their own past. The analysis of the dialectical nature of mind itself results in a philosophical theory; the dialectical history of concepts is a project. The former can be produced only by the reflection of an individual thinker; the latter is too vast a project for any single person to encompass. Nor of course did Collingwood claim to do so. But he contributed chapters to the project and laid out its principles of method: the chapters are *The Idea of Nature, The Idea of History,* and the *specimina philo-*

sophandi in Part III of the *Essay on Metaphysics;* the principles of method are discussed in the first two parts of the latter book.

That remarkable, obscure, and deathless book, Hegel's *Phenomenology of Mind,* is at least two different books both written in the same words (like an allegory whose interpretation is itself an allegory of which the allegory is an interpretation): it is an analysis of the ontogeny of individual consciousness from the most rudimentary sensation to the most sophisticated thought, and at the same time it is a history of Western civilization seen as a drama enacted by the ideas which have formed it. Whether Collingwood knew, when he wrote *Speculum Mentis,* that he was trying to do the same thing as Hegel there is no way of knowing; but it is impossible to read that book without realizing that he was, and that it was a bold but unsuccessful attempt. For the rest of his life, I believe, he was preparing to rewrite *Speculum Mentis* (and he himself described his later books as "interim reports"). In the *Essay on Philosophical Method* he attempted to give a formal description of its logic. In his lectures on moral philosophy, in *The Principles of Art,* and in *The New Leviathan* he concentrated on the analysis of individual consciousness; in *The Idea of Nature, The Idea of History,* and the *Essay on Metaphysics* he attempted to understand Western civilization through the history of its fundamental ideas—and not less urgently as his despair increased over the future of that civilization. But in the process he showed why *Speculum Mentis* could not be rewritten after all.

The reason is itself a philosophical reason, and like all philosophical reasons it will seem simple and self-evident to some and hopelessly obscure to others. It is that we think forward but understand backward. Thinking is a venture, which may succeed or fail; understanding is the consolidation of success achieved. Some philosophers do the first, and do not pause for the second, like tank divisions outracing their source of supplies; others specialize in the second and shrink at the thought of the first, like infantry replacements tidying up and making comfortable the trenches which they have taken over. Collingwood tried—he seems to have been driven—to do both, and fortunately (since he never profited from, and for most of his life simply ignored the criticism of others) he was his own best, as well as his most nagging and irritating critic.

There is, surely, a difference between philosophical analysis and speculative thinking. Philosophical analysis is the elucidation of the concepts and conceptual systems which are implicit in thought and attempts at thought; speculative thinking is the attempt to move from the concepts and conceptual systems implicit in one's own thought to other and novel concepts and conceptual systems. Philosophical analysis clarifies; speculative thinking, in the first instance, confuses, because it casts off from familiar moorings with no certainty of arriving at a destination which will provide the solid moorings of the future. Some such adventures stand out as landmarks of thought, and their success has been so widely accepted that it is easy to forget that by standards of analytic clarity they were risky enterprises indeed. The concept of inertia is so much a part of even our half-educated habits of thinking that it is difficult to re-create the state of mind of a Kepler who could not entertain it even hypothetically. And when Einstein redefined the concept of "simultaneity" so that two events might be *neither* simultaneous or non-simultaneous, the confusion of fellow-scientists and laymen alike resulted from what seemed a gratuitous rejection of a necessary truth.

Now Collingwood engaged in both philosophical analysis and speculative thinking; nor did he—and nor can anyone—always separate them in practice. But his procedure was dialectical in both cases. His philosophical analysis was a study of the dialectical logic of concepts as they have functioned in thought (e.g., the historical development of the concept of nature, or of history); these concepts and conceptual schemes implicit in thought he called "absolute presuppositions." His speculative thinking was an attempt to construct a dialectical system of concepts adequate both to understanding how contemporary experience is given structure by *our* absolute presuppositions, and to eliminating the gaps and incoherence which result from the "strains" in our system of absolute presuppositions. But each of these activities transforms the other: the history of concepts shows that philosophical thinking, even when successful, is always superseded. The history of ideas, like a *commedia dell'arte,* is made up as it goes along by the actors who enact it. On the other hand, speculative thinking, as it edges forward new conceptual possibilities, creates new problems which only then can yield up the secret of their histories to philosophical analysis. As in riding a bicycle, one must keep going not to fall. Hence one must always be preparing to rewrite *Speculum Mentis,* but can never do so. Most of the difficulties in understanding Collingwood stem from a failure to see how these twin enterprises—thinking forward and understanding backward—interact in Collingwood's own thought.

There was, I believe, only one moment of true conversion, or tergiversation, in Collingwood's thought, and that occurred much earlier than his critics and interpreters have supposed. According to Knox, the breaking point came with the abandonment of his belief in the *philosophia perennis* and the concomitant distraction into historicism after the *Essay on Philosophical Method*. According to Donagan, the turning point occurred at roughly the same time but consisted of the development of a theory of mind and of language which Collingwood himself muddled by imposing on it interpretations which themselves had not broken free of his juvenile opinions. But if one regards the development of Collingwood's thought as a dialectical process exemplifying his own repeated reliance on dialectical patterns, the moment of *kairos* came, not in mid-career, but much earlier: between *Religion and Philosophy* and *Speculum Mentis*. The latter is a dialectical essay; the former is not. In the earlier book, as Collingwood said in a retractation in *Speculum Mentis* (108, n. 1), he failed to distinguish between "implicit" and "explicit," and therefore treated religion, theology, and philosophy as identical. (This means that he had been treating religion and even philosophy as instances of what in *Speculum Mentis* he called "scientific," not "philosophical," thought.) They are, however, radically distinguished in *Speculum Mentis:* religion as the second form of experience, theology as one exemplification of the third ("science"), and philosophy as the fifth and highest. But they also belong to a series such that each form of experience makes explicit what is only implicit in lower forms. The logic (if I may use that term) of *implicit* and *explicit* is the structure of a scale of forms, of the relation of thought and action, of the "inside" and "outside" of historical events, of expressive and intellectualized language, and of the series of mental functions whose relations constitute the dialectic of mind. And, in general, Collingwood's later philosophy makes explicit what is implicit in the earlier. It is in this sense that it is "dialectical."

No single philosophical idea has such an honorable history or is in such low regard as the concept of dialectic. Its beginnings go back to that pre-history of Western philosophy which survives only in enigmatic fragments. With Socrates it became a model of philosophical discourse, and Plato both preserved it in the style of dialogue and gave its name to the program of postgraduate studies by which his philosopher-kings would achieve "a comprehensive view of the mutual relations and affinities which bind all the sciences together."[6] In the medieval success of scholasticism it became a universal method, and at the hands of Hegel it created a new language of philosophy which presided over European thought for almost a century and is still viable. But today, although it survives in the literature of existentialism and occasionally elsewhere among philosophers, it is primarily identified with Marxism-Leninism, where as a form of theoretical dogmatism it has come into not undeserved disrepute. One must always explain, it seems, that the dialectic of Socrates is not identical with the "dialectic" which Lenin claimed to have "plucked like a jewel from the garbage of idealism." Yet even so they are not unrelated, although one will look in vain for an account of their connection which is both historically informed and analytically perspicacious.

The political associations which have given "dialectic" the effect of a thoughtless and divisive slogan are not much more unnerving than the philosophical uses which, at least as they have been eagerly misinterpreted by critics, have brought it into disregard. Most of these uses reflect the fact that the term does not fit comfortably into the vocabulary of English nouns, among which it gives the appearance of being an hypostatized idea, a notion masquerading as an entity along with entelechies, mental faculties, and dormitive properties. "Dialectic" is at best a courtesy-noun; its most natural use (in English) is as an adjective, as in "dialectical process," "dialectical series," and the like. (On the other hand, there are no "dialectical laws," any more than there are "laws of dialectic.") At least to insist on this to some extent provides immunity against a century of modern usage in translated-from-the-German contexts in which something called "The Dialectic" acts, moves, shapes, necessitates, determines, and in general *does* things.

Although Collingwood was a dialectical philosopher, and although the sense in which he was a dialectical philosopher belongs more to the Hegelian tradition than to any other, it is important at the outset to avoid connotations which belong not to the idea of dialectic but to its mythology and counter-mythology. In Collingwood's view, the idea of dialectic is a complex idea representing an elucidation of the concept of *development* and other concepts logically connected with it. It is applicable to processes and *only* to processes, and,

moreover, only to processes of change in human life. For Collingwood, there is nothing like a dialectic of nature, although there may
be a dialectical history of the *concept* of nature, that is, of the course
of human thought in which the concept of nature has functioned as
a leading idea itself subject to change. Beyond this simple description, the positive account of Collingwood's idea of dialectic must
await the following chapters, where it is in fact the leading theme.
But it may be useful to summarize at this point some of the things
that dialectic is *not;* for although each of these characteristics has at
some time been attributed to the idea of dialectic, and has even been
thought to belong to its definition, none of them can be found in its
richest and most important modern examples—in Hegel's *Phenomenology of Mind,* for example, or Kierkegaard's *The Concept of
Dread,* in Marx's *Economic-Philosophic Manuscripts of 1844,* or in
Royce's *The World and the Individual.*

1. Dialectical thinking does not claim to replace ordinary deductive or inductive logic. It does not say that one proposition does
not follow from another which in traditional logic is implied by
the latter, nor that one proposition is formally implied by another
which in traditional logic does not follow from it. Nor does it claim
that generalizations or hypotheses are confirmed or disconfirmed
by kinds of evidence which inductive logic would regard as irrelevant or inadequate. Moreover, it does not assert that contradictions
are "true" or "real." It does include, however, a characteristic view
of negation, one which differs from the logical operation sym-
bolized by "∼".

2. Dialectic is not a substitute for empirical science nor a theory
of any particular subject matter. There is no "dialectical" interpretation of thermodynamic phenomena nor of population shifts, although there may be a dialectical account of the development of
thermodynamic theories or of sociological thought.

3. Dialectic is not tied to any simple formula of "thesis-antithesis-
synthesis," terms which appear hardly at all in Hegel or Marx but
have been given currency in textbook simplifications and popular
refutations. Even if such terms are admitted, it does not claim that
from a given thesis its specific antithesis can be deduced or the nature of an eventual synthesis predicted.

4. Dialectic does not postulate any forces of nature or of history
unknown to non-dialectical thought, nor regard natural or historical
events as necessitated according to laws which are discoverable only

by "dialectical thought." Nor is it intrinsically connected with the idea of social science despite the fact that Marxism-Leninism has attempted so to construe it. It *is* intrinsically connected with the idea of history in some sense, but not necessarily or mainly in a sense in which there can be a history of the future.

It may well seem to those acquainted with the idea of dialectic and with dialectical philosophers only through the standard refutations of them that these denials leave nothing positive for dialectic to be. But Collingwood found a good deal, and to say what it is is to give an interpretation of his philosophical career. It may also help to explain why, although the idea of dialectic has been regarded with a kind of official loathing in recent English-speaking philosophy, it has nevertheless quietly survived, like sex among the Victorians.

The figure in the carpet, I hope to show, has both form and detail, and the present essay is accordingly divided into two main parts. The form is the idea of dialectic; the detail consists of Collingwood's theories: his logic of question and answer, his theory of absolute presuppositions, his theories of art as imagination and of history as the science of mind. Part I traces the idea of dialectic through three main stages of its development, from the dialectic of experience in *Speculum Mentis* through the dialectic of concepts in the *Essay on Philosophical Method* to the dialectic of mind in *The Principles of Art* and *The New Leviathan*. Part II attempts to show that this development can be applied to the interpretation of his particular theories, and that their details seem much different and less paradoxical when seen as parts of the pattern. The order of discussion reverses the order of "forms of experience" in *Speculum Mentis*: Chapter 5 deals with philosophy, Chapter 6 with history, and Chapter 7 with art. In Part I, I have undertaken to give a good deal of exposition, as the only way of illustrating an idea of dialectic which in many ways is unfamiliar to contemporary habits of thought for precisely the same reasons as it calls those habits into question. In Part II, however, I have not tried to give synopses of books or outlines of theories. They can be read in their own right, if only they are read correctly.

PART I

THE IDEA OF

DIALECTIC

CHAPTER 2

The Dialectic of Experience

1 · Collingwood's Pentateuch of Forms of Experience:

A Summary

THROUGHOUT HIS LIFE COLLINGWOOD OCCUPIED HIMSELF WITH the relations and differences among art, religion, science, history, and philosophy, regarded sometimes as ways of life, sometimes as types of experience, and sometimes as modes of knowledge. At least one of his books is devoted to each of these, as their titles indicate: *Religion and Philosophy* (1916); *Outlines of a Philosophy of Art* (1925) and *Principles of Art* (1938); *The Idea of Nature* (1945); *The Idea of History* (1946); and, of course all of these, but also the *Essay on Philosophical Method* (1933), the *Autobiography* (1939), and the *Essay on Metaphysics* (1940) occupy themselves specifically with philosophy. Only *The New Leviathan* (1942) does not discuss explicitly and at length these special forms of experience and knowledge.

Again and again he returned to the task of drawing up constitutions for the kingdom of knowledge, and although he never argued that his Pentateuch of Art, Religion, Science, History, and Philosophy is an exhaustive list (cf. SM, pp. 39, 57), in practice it remained canonical, although the importance of Religion as a separate category became attenuated after 1928, as he came to identify his categories less with "ways of life" and more with types and methods of knowledge.[1] In an important way this series of constitutions pro-

27

vides a reduced and brilliant image of the changes (or development) of his thought, which sometimes are matters of nuance or emphasis, sometimes more fundamental alterations.

But although he undertook repeatedly to distinguish history from science, or philosophy from religion (always in such a way as to describe their connections as well as their differences) it is only in *Speculum Mentis* that he drafted a complete constitution, with equal attention to each of the five areas.[2] While in his later books many of his ideas underwent modification and change, I am convinced (and it is consistent with his own later views about historical understanding) that it is only against the background of *Speculum Mentis* that his later views can be correctly interpreted.

Speculum Mentis deals not with a single problem but with an entire family of problems, all of which arise out of reflection on the entire range of experience. As stated in the Prologue, the progenitor of these problems is the disintegration in the modern world of the conception—or rather of the *possibility*, since the conception survives to plague us by its lack of exemplification—of a "complete and undivided life," of experience regarded as an integrated *whole*, which Collingwood took to be a characteristic virtue of the medieval outlook. This is an outlook which we could not recover if we would— an enterprise which the attempts of neo-medievalists have not made more attractive. Yet, lacking that integrity by which the diversity of human activity was hierarchically organized under the unifying principle of faith, the special problem of modern life is that an increasingly unsatisfied demand for beauty, faith, and knowledge coexists with unwanted overproduction of art, religion, and philosophy. Moreover, these are detached from each other, so that they are separately unsatisfying and collectively unrelated. One can dabble in each, but how to combine them in a single complex unity, a *life,* is not understood.

There do exist ways of life which are alien but fascinating in their single-minded exclusiveness, and which for this very reason provide rich themes for biography and fiction. It is the plunge into a single form of life which unites Thomas Merton and Gulley Jimson, but at the same time separates the religious life from the artist's life. To one who is curious about both forms of life but exemplifies neither, there are problems of understanding. What connection, if any, is there between aesthetic experience and religious experience? There are, of course, theories about this: the view that religious experience is a work of aesthetic imagination or the counter-view that art is a form of religious expression—even when demonic. Both views are, as answers to such questions tend to be, reductive. Similar questions, in their most general form too well known to require listing, arise about the relation of religion to science, science to art, history to philosophy, and so on; again, answers are most often reductive, and are notable more for their number than for their cogency.

In *Speculum Mentis,* Collingwood sets out unabashedly to adjudicate the rival claims of all the major kinds of experience or "forms of consciousness." Such an ambition might appear immodest, but it is in fact what philosophers have always attempted collectively and often individually. It is sanctioned by both traditional and contemporary views of the philosopher's job, and both views are represented in the division and classification which Collingwood makes of major kinds of experience. He has two criteria for recognizing an activity as a "form of consciousness": it must in fact be capable of being regarded (even though in the end this may not be consistently possible), as a "way of life," enlisting all of one's faculties and energies, and at the same time it must be a claim to knowledge about the world or to a method of achieving knowledge. The former criterion is the older meaning of "philosophy," the sense in which both slave and emperor could be Stoic philosophers. The latter is the modern meaning of philosophy as the critique of knowledge—the sense in which Hume could give up philosophy as a young man and Whitehead could take it up as an old one. That Collingwood unites the two indicates his belief that the elucidation of experience and the critical analysis of theory can and must be done together.

These two criteria also jointly limit the possible forms of consciousness. They rule out the political and the economic lives merely as such, because utilitarian activity does not make a claim to knowledge although it may be the practical side of a form of consciousness which does. The criteria do not admit the differences between social, monastic, and reclusive life as fundamental, nor do they distinguish between types of personality or between cosmic attitudes such as pessimism and optimism. In fact, Collingwood finds only five candidates: Art, Religion, Science, History, and Philosophy. It is well to capitalize the names, as he does, not as honorific designations nor in order subtly to reify them, but as a reminder that in *Speculum Mentis* they do not necessarily refer to the professional or institutional activities called by those names in common language and by Collingwood himself in his later books. One might think of them initially as what we comfortably, if not very clearly, refer to as the aesthetic attitude, the religious life, scientific inquiry, the historical consciousness, and the philosophical temper.[3]

Art. By "Art," Collingwood means the activity and the products of imagination suspended from all questions and claims about the reality of the objects of imagination. Art (or imagination) asserts nothing, or rather, it can suppose everything without considering the question of the coherence of different acts or products of imagination. Whether a portrait "looks like" its model is not a question for Art (although this may be difficult to explain to a sitter who has paid for a satisfactory likeness). Nor is it a flaw in Sophocles' *Antigone* that the officious Creon of that play cannot be recognized as the wise and patient Creon of *Oedipus Rex*. Hence a primary characteristic of imagination is what Collingwood calls the "monadism of art," the reference being not to Leibniz's principle that "each monad mirrors the universe" but to his description of monads as "windowless," unrelated to and unaffected by all other monads.

Now "art" here clearly means not the artifacts viewed in galleries and the compositions reproduced in concert halls, but imaginative *acts,* whether of artist or spectator. Aesthetic experience as such does not distinguish between a limited class of things called "works of art" and the rest of the world; it is a possible attitude which may be taken up toward anything. It may be illustrated by what Collingwood elsewhere called the "principle of the picture-frame," [4] referring to the conscious act of attention by which, imaginatively, a frame can be set around part of the extended visual or auditory fields and what lies within the frame perceived as pure spectacle. Such an experiment is not difficult, and its results can be extraordinary: a bleak industrial wasteland, grimy and depressing, can take on an entirely different visual character when a segment is "framed" and regarded, so to speak, two-dimensionally rather than three-dimensionally. (Learning to draw in perspective requires a similar cultivated act of attention; in Collingwood's view it is quite right to regard this as already an imaginative act rather than a technical skill in the service of imagination.) Looked at from this standpoint, it is possible to see (although the example is not Collingwood's) the sense in which photography can be one of the *beaux-arts.* Many would deny photography the name of art on the grounds that a technical apparatus performs all of the functions usually associated with artistic creation.

And so it does; but selecting a point of vantage, composing the picture within the frame, and changing the frame in the process of developing the prints are nevertheless all imaginative acts, in Collingwood's sense.

The implications of identifying art with imagination rather than with a class of artifacts, with complex human activity rather than with physical objects, were not fully worked out by Collingwood until *The Principles of Art*. But the problem at hand is a different one: the claim of Art to be a possible way of life and a form of knowledge. One might think, regarding with a disenchanted eye the excesses of a century and a half of Romanticism, that neither claim has been made good or is likely to be. But it remains to understand why this should be so. In Collingwood's view, it is because the aesthetic life is inherently unstable and the aesthetic claim to immediate and intuitive knowledge is inherently inconsistent. The instability of a life of pure imagination might be thought due to the fact that a world of physical necessities exacts ultimate penalties from anyone who tries to convert it into pure spectacle. Standing in the middle of a busy road, one might manage to regard the approaching vehicles with disinterested imagination, but not for long. And imaginatively framing a bowl of slowly rotting fruit as model for a still-life will hardly protect a painter from the pangs or the effects of hunger. But although such considerations are obvious, Collingwood's point is that the world of fact does not merely constrain the aesthetic imagination but is necessary to it; and therefore in regarding itself as rejecting the world of fact the aesthetic consciousness is deceiving itself. But imagination, as such, is incapable of reflecting on itself, and therefore cannot recognize that it is necessarily dependent on what as a form of consciousness it excludes.

The instability of the "aesthetic life," in fact, is a consequence of the impossibility of maintaining the attitude of imagination without *assertion*. This attitude is like—and in Collingwood's view it *is*—an attitude of questioning or supposing which anticipates no answer or resulting assertion. But questioning, he argues, presupposes assertions which make the questions important or relevant; and it implies the possibility of an answer. Otherwise there would be no way of distinguishing one supposal from another.

This may seem a strained and over-intellectual analogy when applied to art. It is not without relevance to representational art, the epic and the novel, drama, and narrative dance; but in what sense are absolute music and non-objective art "supposals" or "questions"? They are, of course, suspensions of assertion; but a painting by Kandinsky would seem to be a suspension of assertion in a sense quite different from Dante's *Inferno*. The latter, despite its topographical detail, does not *assert* that one will find the entrance to Hell or the Mount of Purgatory if one explores the actual surface of the world we walk. There seems a lacuna here. In part, it was recognized and developed by Collingwood in *The Principles of Art,* where by careful argument he identified imagination with expression (an identification which, he remarked in *Speculum Mentis* [74], Croce had unsuccessfully attempted). But even so, it would be a mistake to suppose that the attitude of "questioning" means that a work of art asks a specific question or set of questions which could be given alternative verbal formulation. It refers rather to the act of imagination in general, not to this or that act of imagination; and in this sense, an imaginative act may be considered a general supposal that its object can be isolated from all other experience—without regard to what this other experience may be.

The instability of imagination as a claim to knowledge results from the fact that this claim cannot even be made without abandoning the standpoint of the immediacy of intuition. This may seem obvious, but there is also a special argument for it which is essential to Collingwood's project of relating Art to other forms of experience. The inadequacy of any general theory of intuitive knowledge is simply that no *theory* itself is intuitive. A claim to knowledge must at least be defended by an argument whose cogency as an argument is not incompatible with the truth of its conclusions. But this is just what occurs when the deliverances of intuitive immediacy are extended to include all possible knowledge: the possibility of an *argument* for this conclusion is ruled out together with all other arguments. It is not *prima facie* self-contradictory to believe that in art truths are revealed which are not accessible in other ways, and indeed this has been widely believed. But in any case one cannot defend this view without appealing to other standards of knowledge beyond the revelations of art. In his well-known study of Beethoven, Mr. J. W. N. Sullivan claimed that Beethoven had reached heights of understanding not available to more earth-bound spirits, and had expressed these insights in his late quartets and sonatas. But how could Sullivan discover this? If by the same process, presumably we should have another quartet—by Sullivan—rather than a book. But if by some other means, then Beethoven's late works, if they do in fact show forth a kind of knowledge, are checks for large amounts on a bank which is never open for business.

Collingwood's special argument for rejecting the claims of intuition both rests on and reveals his fundamental conception of experience, a conception whose most notable feature is the rejection of all dualisms: the dualism of sensation and thought (here he departs from Kant), the dualism of data and interpretation (here he departs from empiricism), and the dualism of emotion and intellect (here he departs from rationalism in both its exigent and mitigated forms). In this case the dualism rejected is that of intuition— whether sensation or imagination—and thought. *All* experience, from the perception of a color to the logical analysis of abstract argument, Collingwood regards as both intuitive *and* conceptual; "it is all intuitive and all conceptual" (SM, 95). The merits of this thesis may be debated later; at the moment it is its consequences that we are after. And the immediate consequence is that Art as a claim to knowledge is a claim to be merely intuitive, whereas it is at the same time implicitly conceptual although it represses its dim awareness of this fact and cannot in fact make it explicit without ceasing to be Art as such.

But to say that Art as a form of life is implicitly conceptual does not mean (as it did for Schopenhauer) that a *work of art* fleshes out a concept in vivid and particular illustration, as if every narrative must have a moral and every bit of music a "meaning." Collingwood uses the vocabulary of Hegel: intuition is "immediate," conceptual thought "mediates." But what is meant is not difficult to see: the immediacy of intuition (which still refers to imagination, regarded as a kind of knowledge) refers to the surface qualities of experience as such: the blueness of a blue patch, the pitch and timbre of a note or the legato or staccato quality of a melody. It also refers to the ease and fluency of a logical inference or to the frustrating puzzlement of a paradox; many years later, Collingwood pointed out in *The Principles of Art* that as emotion is never independent of reason, so reason is never independent of emotion, and there are "emotions of reason" (PA, 292–99). "Mediation" is simply experience reflected on and become self-conscious. In Art such reflection might seem to result in the acceptance of "standards," such as correct perspective in drawing, or the Unities in drama; the aesthetics of classicism was such an attempt to subordinate imagination to abstract and even mathematical formulae. Collingwood's point is that, entirely apart from this, any conscious *control* of imagination has already imposed some standard, however implicit. So the dramatist introduces a character, the painter thumbs out a line ("A little more? There, that's it.") because the work in progress seems to demand it. It is useless to ask him why, or to try to explain why, in any theory of general application. But some standard of relevance, fittingness, or appropriateness is at work here. It is not *applied to* experience, because it is *part of* experience itself; but it is not part of intuition itself. There survives here the ancient Platonic doctrine that recognition and comparison are implicitly conceptual; but Collingwood denies that a purely intellectual concept is being applied to a purely sensuous experience. "This blue is brighter than that" is both intuitive (so far as the blues are concerned) *and* conceptual (so far as the relation "brighter than" is concerned), and neither can be isolated from the other. Without the relation, there are not two blues; and without the blues there is no relation. Intuition and conceptual thought are not two different kinds of experience or functions of mind. Rather, intuition is that aspect of any experience which is immediate and unreflective; thought is that aspect of any experience which reflects upon itself or is capable of doing so. The form of experience called Art is precisely that aesthetic attitude which claims to be wholly intuitive; in fact, however, it is implicitly conceptual. To articulate its structure through self-reflection does not destroy the immediacy of imagination but supersedes its tacit claim to stability and exclusiveness.

Religion. The life of Art, therefore, is an error when it claims to be an exclusive possibility. But this failure is felt before it can be understood. It is felt as the failure of the imagination to assert a world of fact which it necessarily presupposes, to commit itself to a claim which it suggests in failing to make it. Art imagines but does not assert, even though imagining is a kind of supposal and supposal is a transient stage in the process leading to assertion. What carries this process to its end Collingwood calls "Religion." Religion is imagination which believes in the reality of its own products.

This definition of religion is not novel; it resembles Feuerbach's and is subject to the criticisms which have been brought against Feuerbach. It is easy to object that the definition seems designed to apply only to religions with an elaborated mythology and rules out purely ethical religions such as Confucianism. Yet no definition of religion can be made as a satisfactory inductive generalization which will simultaneously satisfy the demand of including everything ever referred to by the term and yet avoid the sterility of utter vagueness. The utility of definitions in such cases is to call attention to certain features commonly overlooked or underestimated; and in Collingwood's case it is intended to find a way of relating some, if not all, important features of religion to some, if not all, important features of art and science. From this standpoint, the relation, if arguable, is clear and memorable: Religion is Art asserting and worshipping its own object. But since this object is asserted as real, many consequences follow: where Art is monadic, hence pluralistic and tolerant, Religion claims its assertions to be *true,* hence all incompatible assertions to be false. Where the products of Art are not related at all to each other (although *we* may compare them), Religion is *cosmological,* and for the first time conceives the world as a single ordered whole; hence it is also *social,* both in the sense that it defines a community of believers and in the sense that this community must have *some* attitude toward unbelievers, for example, that "all those who are not for us are against us." Finally, it is credal, its creed preserving, defining and encouraging the central imaginative act.

But Religion, too, is subject to an inner development of the sort which revealed the instability of Art both as a way of life and as a claim to knowledge. This comes about, again, because Religion, although a legitimate and necessary kind of experience, cannot preserve its characteristics unaltered *once it becomes conscious of them.* The special problem of religion is that the direct objects of religious consciousness are symbolic, pointing to meanings which they do not contain. Yet their efficacy as symbols depends on the fact that religious consciousness ignores this distinction, which, in Collingwood's language, is only "implicit." Hence the literal acceptance of ritual and creed is natural and inevitable, but unstable. In one of his apter metaphors, Collingwood says that Religion is "thought growing up in the husk of language, and as yet unconscious that language and thought are different things. The distinction between what we say and what we mean, between a symbol or word and its meaning, is a distinction in the light of which alone it is possible to understand religion; but it is a distinction hidden from religion itself" (SM, 125).

Now this observation is in principle the legacy of the nineteenth century study of comparative religion and of the development of the "higher criticism" of the Old and New Testaments, which ended forever the literalist interpretation of Biblical mythology and chronicle except for sectarian groups determined to remain in a state of intellectual arrest. But Collingwood puts uncritical Religion in a novel framework in showing its development out of Art and its issue in Science. The conflict between "science and religion" can be seen in a new light: its basis is no longer a conflict between the superstitious literalism of religion and an enlightened scientific method, but a conflict between religion not yet conscious and religion become conscious of the distinction which defines it. (The historical implication is that the intellectual method of the sciences was itself a product of this religious instability; and in fact Collingwood maintained this historical thesis in *The Idea of Nature,* the *Essay on Metaphysics,* and finally in *The New Leviathan.*) Once the religious attitude has become aware that what it *says* is not what it *means,* it is a legitimate object for rational criticism, but the enlightened rationalism which points out that the concrete imagery of religion is neither historically true nor scientifically possible is using a weapon which has been forged and put into its hands by the development of Religion itself. And yet there is no return; as criticism owes its possibility to Religion itself, so in turn it produces a theology which reinterprets religious assertions to accommodate the meanings which have been uncovered. But as Collingwood observes, this reinterpretation is not a defense of Religion, but its negation. Theology cannot recover the lost innocence of the encompassing religious life, because it has recognized distinctions and accepted critical standards the *unawareness* of which is an essential characteristic of what it purports to defend. It has, in being explicitly a mode of thinking, forfeited its chance to return to the innocence of implicit thought.

The transition from immediacy to self-consciousness within Religion is a revolution sharper than the transition from Art to Religion. That replaced supposal by assertion, this replaces language by thought, or rather by a fusion of thought and language in which the two cannot be sharply distinguished. For the first time, therefore, a logic of propositions is possible, the proposition being the meaning expressed in a statement—e.g., the meaning, unstatable in itself, of equivalent sentences. Religion, like Art, therefore, turns out to be a "philosophical error": not as worship, which is the natural state of the religious consciousness, but as theology, which introduces standards of explication of meaning and criticism of inference which are alien to the primary religious consciousness. In fact, "theology is a manifestation not of the religious spirit but of the scientific spirit" (SM, 152), and therefore it is not a mode of experience but a transition to a different mode of experience.

Science. By "Religion" Collingwood obviously means something more limited than the extended contemporary senses of this term. On the other hand, by "Science" he means something much broader than the contemporary restriction of the term to the natural sciences. In neither case is he attempting a general description of all the things which happen to be called by a single name, but rather is identifying something like an ideal type to which a variety of instances more or less closely approximate. The first characteristic of "Science" is that it is a kind of thinking aware of itself as such or "explicit"; in both Art and Religion, thought is present, but only as "implicit." The primary objects of this self-conscious kind of thinking are not concrete objects of imagination, as in both Art and Religion, but concepts, or abstract universals. "Object of imagination" is itself, for example, a concept, as is "object of thought." And so are all the terms—"imagination," "relation," "supposal," "assertion"— in which Art and Religion are *described,* but which do not appear in their own vocabularies. "Classification is the key-note of the scientific spirit; but classification is nothing but the abstractness of the scientific concept" (SM, 162).

Collingwood's discussion of Science yields nothing in abstractness to Science itself. He is not generous with examples, but it is clear that his paradigm of science is not experimental inquiry but mathematics; it is not Faraday whom he has in mind but Plato and the Platonic insistence on the unintelligibility of phenomena, like triangles scratched in the sand, apart from the intelligibility of concepts, like the concept of triangle. In effect, he imputes Platonism to science (and not unreasonably so) when he describes Science as the "affirmation of the abstract or classificatory concept as real." (Art, it will be recalled, makes no assertions at all; Religion asserts the reality of an object, but one which is imaginative rather than conceptual.) Such a description resembles Whitehead's "fallacy of misplaced concreteness" (which it antedated by a year), but it is easier to bring out Collingwood's point if one remembers that he was not, like Whitehead, referring directly to contemporary physics. Otherwise some of Collingwood's statements seem simply perverse: "Sensuous experience is . . . unnecessary to the scientist, and all he has to do is to think." This is true of a mathematician if of anyone; and Collingwood emphasizes that mathematics is an exact or a priori science, the only one which is an unalloyed instance of his description. He claims, however, that the description has other applications, because it accounts for the mechanism (determinism) and materialism of empirical natural science: mechanism because physical events are regarded as indifferently comparable instances of abstractly formulated laws, materialism because the abstract universal is "indifferent to its own particulars" (SM, 167). This is, I think, exactly the meaning of "materialism" which Russell had in mind when he said that "matter is whatever satisfies the equations of physics"; and in this sense Collingwood is quite right in saying that "mathematics, mechanism, and materialism are the three marks of all science" (SM, 167); but the description is less interesting than it seems because "mechanism" and "materialism" are so broadly conceived that they include what ordinarily have been regarded as alternatives to them (e.g., vitalism, since the concept of "entelechy" has the same indifference to its manifestations as an abstract universal to its instances).

Collingwood knows perfectly well that modern natural science is empirical and that scientific hypotheses are related in complex ways to statements of experimental and observational evidence. He recognizes the heuristic necessity of factual experience in *suggesting* hypotheses, even in mathematics; but, strangely, he does not discuss what contemporary philosophy of science has so exhaustively explored, the confirmation and disconfirmation of hypotheses by the facts of the case. In part, this omission is dictated by his scheme: he wishes to reserve the "realm of fact" as the proper object of "historical" rather than of "scientific" thinking. But it is not merely gratuitous, if one distinguishes between an abstract and concrete sense of "fact": what *counts* as a fact in science is nothing more than the givenness, the datum-character of properties relevant to a hypothesis: "Scientific fact is a fact purged of its crude and scientifically scandalous concreteness, isolated from its historical setting and reduced to the status of a mere instance of a rule" (SM, 186). And, of course, it goes without saying that "concrete" fact is not just an aggregate or congeries of abstract "facts."

What Collingwood is aiming at here should now be clear: he wishes to show that what he chooses to call History emerges from Science as its development and fulfillment, as Science in its turn emerged from Religion and Religion emerged from Art. He thinks that the history of science since the Renaissance suggests this because of the introduction into sciences such as astronomy, geology, and biology of the temporal dimension: astronomy becomes the history of the universe, biology the history of species, and so on. This can hardly be taken seriously as more than an academic pun, because "history" in this case means no more than "change over time," and has nothing significant in common with what Collingwood himself means by "History." But he adverts to a second argument for the necessary passage from Science to History, namely that the framing and exploration of hypotheses itself *presupposes* the possession of an ordered body of facts, and "these facts, as actually ascertained by observation and experiment, are matter of history" (SM, 186). That this argument is not lightly advanced is indicated by the fact that Collingwood restated it without significant change, years afterward, in the conclusion to *The Idea of Nature* (IN, 174–77).

Now this argument inverts the commonly accepted opinion that the mere observation and recording of facts belongs to an elementary "natural history" stage of science and is to a more advanced theoretical stage as butterfly-collecting, say, is to genetics. In the accepted view, it is the ordinary activities of historians which are proto-scientific, rather than the ordinary activities of scientists which are proto-historical. Collingwood surely cannot mean that what we know as science will, as it becomes more sophisticated, look more and more like what we know as history. (It has been widely held, and one can at least imagine the possibility, that future historiography will be more like present natural science—like a science of society, that is—whenever it is not merely chronology or antiquarianism. None of this has anything to do, of course, with the use of scientific methods, like chemical analysis or carbon-14 dating of artifacts, by historians.)

Yet Collingwood is not just playing Paris to History's Aphrodite. The clue to his apparent inversion of the order of thought from the unintelligible aggregation of particular facts to the intelligible unity of an explanatory theory lies, I think, in the notion, as yet not clarified, of *self-consciousness*. Science as science need not be consciously aware of what it presupposes; yet once it has become so aware, it has reached a coign of vantage beyond itself. The analogy here is not to what has earlier been said of the relation between Art and Religion but to the different relation between Religion and theology: theology (which is implicit Science) is Religion become critical of its own meanings and claims. And something like this occurs when Science becomes aware of its own activity and *simultaneously aware* that, insofar as it attempts to describe, explain, or justify itself, *this* activity is not itself scientific inquiry, but something else.

Now when Science reaches the stage of recognizing this, Collingwood claims, it is able to see how much it has taken for granted. Beginning *in medias res,* as it were, it frames hypotheses about whole classes of events which exist for it as *data,* although the events belong to the past and as such are objects of *historical* knowledge (even though this may be individual memory). Perhaps this can be accepted as a truism; but it does not seem to justify the startling conclusion that "natural science as a form of thought exists and always has existed in a context of history, and depends on historical thought for its existence" (IN, 177). For one thing, the form of thought which we call specifically history "did not exist before the eighteenth century" (SM, 203). What Collingwood himself refers to in *The Idea of Nature* as science is at least as old as the Renaissance; how can it "depend for its existence on a form of thought" which it antedates by centuries?

Misunderstanding, at this crucial point, of the relation of Science and History is easy and almost inevitable, and Collingwood himself does not avoid misstating his point or obscuring it by special pleading. His argument in summary seems to be: Science as abstract, theoretical, and hypothetical presupposes a world of concrete facts to which its statements refer but which they do not exhaust. What does deal with them, at least in principle, is History. So Science as a form of thought is less adequate than and is fulfilled in History.

But as Collingwood sometimes fails to distinguish between nature and science, so here he fails to distinguish between history and the theory of history. Hence the shimmering ambiguity of a statement like this: "I venture to infer that no one can understand natural science unless he understands history: and that no one can answer the question what nature is unless he knows what history is" (IN, 177). The word "history," in the most natural reading of this, should mean "historical thought" in the first statement and "historical reality" in the second. Yet if we interchange these, we get two entirely different statements, namely that one can understand natural science only in terms of its own (real) history, and nature itself only as the object of a science historically understood.

To bring out the same point in a different way: one should not interpret Collingwood (despite his own encouragement) to mean merely that scientists use records of past observations, and so on, and therefore in order to be complete scientists should be better historians. Rather he means: if one *reflects on* the process of scientific inquiry (and a scientist may well not do so) he becomes aware that scientific facts are classes of occasions on which certain observations have been made, and these observations are, for us, historical facts. The problem is not, except in rare cases, whether they are indeed facts; it lies in the *concept* of historical fact, and this is a matter of the theory of historical knowledge. Thus it is not that a particular piece of scientific research leads on to a specific problem of historical research, but that the scientific attitude becomes aware of itself as an historical phenomenon and raises questions which call for a *theory* of history. Why, for example, has organized science been a phenomenon of Western civilization, and cumulative science as we know it today a phenomenon of the post-Renaissance period? Can one give a satisfactory account of what natural science is without taking these questions into consideration? It is not surprising that when Collingwood came to write that part of his systematic philosophy which would deal with Science, he produced not a philosophy of science but a history of the idea of nature, and found that different concepts of nature have been the presuppositions of different (Greek, medieval, modern) ideals of scientific inquiry.

History. As Science is the assertion of abstractions (concepts, theories), History is the affirmation of fact. As a form of thought, its object is the past and the present, but it is only incidentally the "study of the past," and that because there are no future facts (SM, 217). But, in any case, History is not the affirmation of facts as a disjunct plurality but of the "world of fact" as a concrete unity; the former is the province of Science, because its "facts" are abstractions from the latter. It is the concreteness of fact, not its pastness, which distinguishes it as the object of History. And the emphasis on "concreteness" rather than on pastness is underlined by Collingwood when he takes *perception* to be the origin and a specific instance of historical thought.[5] There is a faint echo in this somewhat odd use of the term "history" of Locke's "historical, plain method," a nontemporal meaning which otherwise survives today only in the term "natural history." It is clearly not Collingwood's intention merely to insist on a niggling etymological propriety; yet what is historical consciousness, apart from the fact that it is not Science, and what is the "concrete" apart from the fact that it is not the abstract?

As usual, Collingwood is less than helpful in his habit of conflating several different meanings in a single term. In this case there seem to be two main ones: with respect to knowledge, the concrete is the complete rather than the partial; with respect to the objects of knowledge, it is the independence of those objects from our ways of understanding them. Moreover, for Collingwood, Science deals only with *particulars,* artificially marked off or abstracted from the web of relations in which they actually stand; only History can deal with *individuality,* for "individuality is concreteness" (SM, 218). (And like Spinoza and Hegel, Collingwood's final judgment is that there can be only *one* true "individual," that which appears to the incomplete perspective of History as *"the* world of fact.")

To call History "concrete" thus refers at least to our inescapable sense of the expanding web of real relations in the environing world; it is the feeling of "More!" demanded by the real world of our every attempt to capture it in description or explanation, or rather it is this feeling elevated to conscious recognition. But "concrete" may also refer to the world of fact itself, standing resolutely over against any claim to knowledge of it. Collingwood is unlikely to have committed the simple fallacy of confusing knowledge *of* something concrete with knowledge as itself concrete, even though he does often verge on the philosopher's bad habit of letting nature solve his problems for him. (Speaking of "dialectical opposites" at one point, he says, "Hold up a stick and distinguish its top and bottom; there you have a concrete synthesis of opposites in an individual whole" [SM, 197]. But one cannot *explain* how "opposites" are "synthesized" by pointing to a natural object, as if to say, "It has solved the problem, so surely *we* can." Sticks do not have problems, nor syntheses either.) He not only recognizes the difference between historical knowledge and its object, but attributes to this difference the "breakdown of history" (SM, 231 ff.). The *object* of history is the infinite world of facts, an indefinitely complex totality of events and relationships; historical knowledge, on the other hand, is inescapably fragmentary and specialized. Hence its "superiority" to Science lies not in its practice but in its ideal conception of itself. The theoretical concepts of Science do not exhaust the world, but scientific thought can encompass them because they are its own constructions. The ideal object of History is the concrete world itself; it explains an event not by exhibiting it as an instance of a theoretical law but by tracing out in detail its real connections with the web of real events—it seeks the genealogy of events, as it were, rather than their genetics. But this means that every piece of history is necessarily regarded as part of a universal history of which there is no historian. Collingwood's point might be put this way: Science's concept of reality is attenuated but its performance is excellent; History's concept of reality is adequate but its performance is correspondingly unsatisfactory. Science dips a wide-meshed net which brings up a fraction of the ocean's teeming life; History dips a narrow-meshed net which brings up more than anyone can enumerate and describe; it faces the terrifying plenitude of *was eigentlich gewesen ist.*

So the sense of the concrete is in jarring conflict with the limitations of inquiry: "History is an unstable attitude which leads either back into science or forward into philosophy, according as the intellectual vigour of the historian is exhausted or stimulated by his attempt to get rid of the abstractions of science" (SM, 230). It is natural, of course, for professional historians (whose own form of experience may well be that of Science) to attempt to justify the specialization of historical inquiry by convincing themselves that historical events and processes can be isolated from one another as particular objects of inquiry; this is exemplified, for example, in periodization, although every historian will allow that there are no cut-off dates, the events earlier or later than which are of no relevance to, say, the Renaissance historian. But specialization cuts the Gordian knot only by relapsing into a pre-historical mode of experience: either it atomizes history into events which can be classified and regarded as instances of general laws, or it decomposes history into wholly unique and individual histories (e.g., biographies). The former is the atomism of Science, the latter the "Monadism" of imagination, or Art. So the historical consciousness is as unstable in its own way as the modes of experience which have preceded it. It is, in fact, the *"reductio ad absurdum* of all knowledge considered as knowledge of an objective reality independent of the knowing mind" (SM, 238). History, as it were, makes explicit an insoluble problem which was already implicit in the religious consciousness: it is the assertion of a completely objective and independent reality which in the end turns out to permit no knowledge of such a reality sufficient even to support the initial affirmation.

Probably no one would deny that this problem—or puzzle, or impasse—is the armature on which the history of philosophy has bit by bit sculpted its own body. Such a metaphor, if a bit strained, is a not inapt reference to Collingwood's view of *mind,* however, which he regards as having, like the history of philosophy itself, continuously recreated itself out of its own substance. So the Gordian knot of History's inability to realize its own ideal can be untied only by achieving the self-conscious recognition that the problem is one *of its own creation;* but in attaining this recognition it passes over into Philosophy. In technical terms, Collingwood regards History as taking for granted an epistemological distinction between subject (the activity of knowing) and object (the object of knowledge). But this distinction is itself an abstraction, a survival, as it were, of Science in the mode of History. How could it be avoided? By recognizing that "the world of fact which is explicitly studied in history is . . . implicitly nothing but the knowing mind as such" (SM, 245).

This may seem like solving a puzzle with a paradox; and Collingwood barely pauses to justify the identification of subject and object by the a priori argument that a mind's error about its own nature distorts its activity in a way appropriate to the error, from which it follows that no object of mental activity can be independent of the way in which it is known.

It would, I think, be a mistake to try to distill from *Speculum Mentis* alone what Collingwood might have meant by his cavalier identification of the historical *object* as the "knowing mind." The record of his succeeding books, especially *The Idea of History* and the *Essay on Metaphysics* is, as we shall see, clearly the history of his continuing attempt to explain it to himself. In *Speculum Mentis* he was bemused by the use to which he could put the formula without fully elucidating or justifying it: he could use it to good effect in bringing about the transition to Philosophy as the "self-consciousness of mind" which History achieves, at the expense of ceasing to be History once recognition is achieved; and, more importantly, he could use it as a stick with which to beat the contemporary philosophy of epistemological realism which in his *Autobiography,* with bitterness unsoftened by time, he described as a "futile parlour game" for "minute philosophers" (A, Chs. III, VI). But in exploiting the latter use he defeated the former purpose. It is not at the level of History but at the level of Philosophy that the self-knowledge of mind is relevant to the *issue* of realism; and he might better have left History at the stage of recognizing that it itself belongs to the world of fact which is its object, so that there is a history of histories, not as another field of specialization, like the history of plumbing, but as a constitutive element in the historical consciousness as such. For Gibbon the history of the Roman Empire was a series of purely Roman events. But the history of the Roman Empire now includes Gibbon and others, at least in the sense that a contemporary historian is aware that his concept of history is ingredient in his work and itself is *part* of the history of histories of the Roman Empire.[6] The logic of the concept of history, it is evident, is very intricate. For Collingwood it is enough to show that History passes through phases leading to an awareness of itself as part of its own object. The elucidation of this state is then no longer History but Philosophy.

Philosophy. In the series beginning with Art and continuing through Religion, Science, and History, each stage has proved to be the explicit formulation of something implicit in the earlier stage; each is an achievement but at the same time an error regarded from the standpoint of the next stage. But the error of each is not like that of a self-sealing delusory system but rather like the unstable error of self-inconsistency, which itself throws up the criterion of consistency by which it may criticize and transcend itself. At each stage, the activity of *thought* (which is a generic term comprising imagination, conceptualization, affirmation and denial, etc.) assumes itself to be distinct from its object. Thought which reaches the stage of explicit self-consciousness and has itself as its own object is Philosophy. And its object is not merely itself as a diaphanous activity, of course, but itself together with its objects. To choose an example which is not Collingwood's, it is a debatable question (at least for mathematical intuitionists, such as Brouwer and Heyting), whether the kind of inference involved in *reductio ad absurdum* proofs is a satisfactory proof, indeed whether the Principle of Excluded Middle holds at all. Now this and similar arguments about the foundations of mathematics are arguments about mathematics rather than mathematical arguments; insofar as they are about the standards of mathematical reasoning, they are also about its objects: no one ignorant of mathematics could think about mathematical thinking. So the philosophy of mathematics is not a branch of mathematics, like abstract algebra, but meta-mathematics (it will be remembered that mathematics is an instance of Science, in Collingwood's terms); and similarly historical thinking, conscious and critical of itself, becomes metahistory or Philosophy.

Each *direct* form of consciousness gives rise to its *reflective* form, and this reflective form may either pass over into the next form of consciousness or remain (no doubt by what C. S. Peirce called the "method of tenacity") in the dogged and repetitive affirmation of itself. As the latter, each form generates an erroneous and dogmatic philosophy. Dogmatism, in fact, is "simply the resistance which a given form of experience presents to its own destruction by an inner dialectic" (SM, 259). Aesthetic philosophy (Collingwood obviously has Bergson in mind although he does not mention him by name) exalts feeling and "intuition" as a substitute for intellect. Religious philosophy, whether as theism or atheism, interprets the metaphorical statements of religion as literal, and undertakes to prove or disprove what the religious consciousness itself is unable even to define.[7] Scientific philosophy is the justification, in logic and metaphysics, of the description of the world in abstract concepts. Finally, Historical philosophy is represented by epistemological realism, the view that knowledge makes no difference to its objects.

If each of these is an "error," philosophy as such (or "Philosophical philosophy") must be the vantage point from which this can be recognized and argued. But what is this vantage point? Insofar as each is or claims to be a kind of knowledge, it would be nothing more than special pleading to claim that "Philosophy" somehow knows *as they are* the *objects* which are in some distorted way grasped by Art, Religion, and the rest. Yet in some sense this is nevertheless the case, although only in the sense that "object" has for Philosophy alone a *critical* meaning. Collingwood does not mean that Philosophy is like an experimental psychologist's comparing with what he *sees* to be a circle the reports that it is elliptical by subjects wearing distorting goggles. Rather it is like a psychologist who knows that what he himself sees as elliptical is to be accounted for by the particular circumstances under which he himself sees it. Philosophy does not have a "truer" account of nature than does Science; but it has the explicit recognition, which is not essentially part of Science itself, that the idea of nature itself is partly constituted by the characteristics of Scientific thought. Nor does Philosophy have privileged access to the world of concrete fact which is the unattainable object of History. It is rather the self-consciousness of the genuinely historical attitude which recognizes that it is itself a determining part of the object of inquiry. There is no implication that Philosophy is free from error, but at least it is free from the *necessary* errors consequent for each of the other forms of experience on its failure to recognize the extent to which it has determined what it supposes itself to have found.

Such a failure of self-consciousness is what Collingwood refers to in distinguishing the "concrete thinking" of Philosophy from the error of "abstraction" which is imputed to all the other modes of experience; and it is, I think, all that he means. In the vocabulary of Hegel, from whom the terms have been borrowed, "abstract" means "partial" and "concrete" means "whole." For Hegel no theory is entirely false and no theory is entirely true, *except* that theory which shows the relation to each other within a single ("concrete") system of each partial or "abstract" theory. Collingwood has borrowed the terms but not all of their meanings or implications; he rejects, for instance, as "mere mythology" Hegel's notion of a "world-spirit" whose development appears in the evolution of human institutions and of nature itself. For Collingwood, the common characteristic of all forms of "abstract thinking" is the gratuitous assumption of a distinction between subject and object in which the latter is taken to be wholly different from and other than the former. "Concrete thinking" is the recognition that subject and object "can only be distinctions which fall within one and the same whole, and . . . this whole can only be the infinite fact which is the absolute mind" (SM, 310). And what holds for the subject-object distinction holds *mutatis mutandis* for other distinctions as well: condition and conditioned, ground and consequence, particular and universal (SM, 310), individual and society (SM, 304), determinism and indeterminism, "and in general every form of the two complementary abstractions one of which denies the whole to assert the part, while the other denies the part to assert the whole" (SM, 300).

It would be too mild to say that philosophers today are suspicious of references to "absolutes" (not to mention those who equally suspect references to "minds"). And it cannot be denied that Collingwood is more prophetic than analytical in his section on Philosophy. But if the language is Hegel's, the voice sounds strangely like the accents of Locke; and if Collingwood permits himself a poetic license which in his later work he did not disavow and even undertook to defend,[8] he clearly does not intend by "absolute mind" any frivolous hypostatization. Nor is it merely an "ideal concept," i.e., what mind could be if it were not so unfortunately what it is, nor yet is it a set of characteristics shared by all minds (such a description would obviously betray the abstractness of Science playing the psychologist). Collingwood never abandoned the view that mind "is what it does" (SM, 241); and "absolute mind" is therefore the historical record, with all its richness of difference, of human activity into which thought enters in any of its forms. So the record of "absolute mind" does not include knee-jerks, breathing, belches, and blinks (although it may include blushes and winks); but it does include, as for Hegel, works of art, religions, sciences, political and legal institutions, systems of philosophy, and so forth, and it is only through the construction of such external worlds that "mind can possibly come to that self-knowledge which is its end" (SM, 315). It is in the history of these human worlds that mind discovers the *speculum mentis,* the mirror of the mind. "The absolute mind is an historical whole of which mind is a part" (SM, 299), but a part, it is emphasized, which at the level of self-consciousness becomes a *different* part and therefore alters to a corresponding degree the whole itself.

2 · The Doctrine of the "Concrete Universal," and Its Consequences

Yet, "the absolute mind is not one stupendous whole! It lives in its entirety in every individual and every act of every individual, yet not indifferently, as triangularity is indifferently present in every triangle, but expressing itself in every individual uniquely and irreplaceably" (SM, 299). This comes near to being an Orphic saying, yet its meaning is not open to arbitrary interpretation and can, I think, be illustrated from a major aspect, omitted in the summary so far, of the five forms of experience.

Several times Collingwood describes the object of History or Philosophy (but not of Science) as a whole whose parts repeat in their structure the plan of the whole.[9] This is, in fact, a summary description of the difference between Science, History, and Philosophy: the objects of Science, which are abstract universals, are *not* wholes of which their instances are parts, nor do they stand to their instances as something whose structure is repeated in the instances. Presumably Collingwood means by this the well-known fact that the *concept* of circle (or the class of circles) is not circular—as the concept of man does not have a backbone. But whereas the object of Science is the abstract universal, the object of History is said to be the *concrete* universal, which is by definition a kind of whole whose essential characteristics are also characteristics of its parts. The difference between History and Philosophy, in brief, is that History cannot grasp this object and Philosophy can, because History does not recognize, and Philosophy does, that nothing can meet this specification except mind itself, embodied in or projected into its activities.

Now the objection to Collingwood at this point will be either that the notion of a concrete universal is too unclear to admit of reasonable dispute, or that it is clear enough but refers to nothing real. As we shall see, there is something to be said for the first objection; and after *Speculum Mentis* Collingwood dropped the Hegelian terminology of "organic whole" and "concrete universal." But he did not drop the nucleus of ideas which he was trying to express with this borrowed terminology, and they reappear in the *Essay on Philosophical Method* as the "overlap of classes" and the "scale of forms" and the principles associated with these ideas. One should at least not suppose that by "concrete universal" Collingwood (or anyone else) ever meant the abstract universal *plus* some conceptually undefinable and empirically unobservable added entity. "Abstract" and "concrete" are not two species of the common genus "universal," although the assumption that they are has vitiated almost all discussion of the issue and no doubt accounts for the fact that the issue has fallen into desuetude. But Collingwood never made this mistake. *Speculum Mentis* shows that he was aware from the beginning that the "concrete universal" is not a program for a new logic but is the leading idea of the *historical consciousness;* and as such it is the most important single strand which connects his earliest and last work. And it does so as one instance of its own meaning.

In *Religion and Philosophy,* Collingwood discussed and applied the idea of a whole whose structure is reduplicated in its parts, an idea which he regarded as identical with the so-called doctrine of "internal relations," i.e., the view that at least some entities are constituted entirely by their relations to other entities, as contrasted with the doctrine of "external relations" which holds that entities have some characteristics essentially, and independently of all other entities and their characteristics. So one finds Collingwood saying, "Every characteristic of the thing turns out to consist in a relation in which it stands to something else" (RP, 112), and in a whole consisting of three parts, *x, y,* and *z,* "the inner nature of the part, *x,* then is entirely constituted by its relations to *y* and *z*" (Ibid.). Therefore, in such a whole, a part is simply one perspective of the whole: "the part is not added to other parts in order to make the whole, it is already in itself the whole, and the whole has other parts only in the sense that it can be looked at from other points of view, seen in other aspects. But in each aspect the whole is entirely present" (Ibid.). A number of examples are adduced to support this apparently paradoxical view: a musical duet, which is not (conceivably) the *addition* of two independent parts but a single entity constituted by the relation between the parts; or a dramatic scene as the interplay of two or more characters; or the identity of a single personality throughout its thoughts and acts.

Now duets and dramas—aesthetic objects in general—are often adduced as examples of complex wholes which cannot be successfully analyzed as aggregates of independent parts. And Collingwood seems to have confused this kind of whole with the more special kind of whole (for which duets and dramas do not serve as examples) whose plan is reduplicated in each of its proper parts. It is significant that there is no mention anywhere in *Religion and Philosophy* of the "concrete universal," nor any mention of the latter after *Speculum Mentis.* Collingwood's route of thinking, I suggest, must have been something like the following: in *Religion and Philosophy* he regarded himself as an adversary of a contemporary philosophy of science which claimed the merits of science as its own. This philosophy of science was mechanistic and materialistic and its consequence was the denial to the human being of any authentic freedom or independent self-existence. In the course of defending these characteristics of human personality, Collingwood found himself distinguishing between the notion of *abstract identity* (e.g., the sense in which we say that all men are equal before the law) and that of *concrete unity* (e.g., the sense in which men may form a *Gemeinschaft* in virtue of having common although not identical interests).[10] There can be a concrete unity of two things which are part of the same whole, but ordinarily one would not say that such parts are identical with each other. Yet by a priori argument Collingwood concluded that if a whole is to be "strictly" knowable, its parts must be not simply added to one another but interconnected in such a way that "each part is the whole" (RP, 108). Hence in any "genuine" whole unity and identity are the same thing. And this is stated as a general doctrine or philosophical principle, although in fact it seems to be true only of the specific case of personality. Formally, it is an ad hoc argument; yet it is not unilluminating. What we mean by "personality" is clearly not some indwelling entity but a *pattern of behavior* such that no matter how we analyze or divide human behavior—whether into simple responses as on psychological tests or into complex events such as the carrying through of an expedition or a business venture—there are distinguishable characteristics (e.g., aggressiveness, caution, imaginativeness, reflectiveness) which describe not only momentary responses but complex actions over time and in fact the *person* himself.[11] It is still no doubt much too strong to say that "each part *is* the whole," but at the same time it clearly will not do to regard a personality as merely the aggregate or average of a person's responses over time. There *is* an identifiable patterning, and to say that each part is the whole is a mildly misleading way of calling attention to the fact that there is no *natural* way of dividing human action into units or further unanalyzable parts. No matter how we divide a human career, we must divide it into parts which have the characteristics observable in the whole or in other parts. And it is not then too strange to say that "each part [is] also in a sense the others" (RP, 108), remembering what that sense is.

But by the time he found himself adapting this argument to his purposes in *Speculum Mentis,* Collingwood had found a new way of generalizing it. The idea of a whole whose parts are "identical" with it and with each other now appears, not as a logical or metaphysical principle, generalized to refer to "any really organic whole" (RP, 113), but as the special object of *historical* consciousness.

It is as if, in the interim, Collingwood had read Kant's "Idea of a Universal History" and had adapted to his own use Kant's notion of a "universal history" which would "connect into something like *systematic* unity the great abstract of human actions that else seem a chaotic and incoherent *aggregate.*" [12] The idea of a whole "identical" with its proper parts is reasonably applicable to the unity of personality simply because the unity of personality is an historical unity. So by the time of *Speculum Mentis* Collingwood could, as it were, provide a gloss to Kant's reference to the "systematic unity" of history by suggesting that what makes it systematic is not anything like the logical relations of a mathematical or conceptual system nor the theoretical relations of natural science but the dialectical relation, already explored, of whole and part.

To call the relation "dialectical" does not, of course, either explain or justify it. Negatively, it is an indication that it is not to be understood either by analogy to mechanical models, which Collingwood never accepted, or by analogy to the biological model of "organic unity," which in *Religion and Philosophy* he did accept. The conception of the self in *Speculum Mentis* is not (as a mechanist would interpret it) that it is stratified like the many Troys, each layer built upon the one below but isolated from it so that the activities of each city are supported by the rubble and shards of forgotten pasts. Nor is it (as an organicist would interpret it) a set of functions mutually related as ends and means, illustrated by the way in which the circulatory system returns to the digestive system in usable form the energy which the latter has converted. Rather the self is a *reflexive process* which takes into itself and retains, while it transforms, its own past experiences and activities. If a metaphor is wanted, its appropriate field is neither archaeology nor physiology but history, and its modality is not space but time. But the dialectic of experience is not really to be understood by metaphors, since metaphors are themselves extensions of its own meaning. It is not like anything more fundamental than itself; other things, less fundamental, are like it. The identification of *any* change as a *process* rather than as a sequence of states reflects the awareness by the self of itself as a process which incapsulates and transmutes its past in a way quite unlike an organism assimilating food or an avalanche taking into itself the objects in its path.

Whatever one thinks of the merits of the dialectic of whole and part, there can be no doubt that it comes very close to being the central idea the elucidation of which is the strand of continuity in the record of Collingwood's philosophical career. We shall see how, in its various disguises, it solved some problems and started others. But since so far it has been stated very summarily and generally, it may not be out of place to observe that the application to history has an initial richness and plausibility which the generalized metaphysical version lacks. We cannot today think about history without some sort of essential, rather than merely chronological periodization. "Renaissance," "Enlightenment," "Feudalism," "Capitalism," even "Baroque," "Romantic," and other such designations are as indispensable as they are impossible to define precisely or to date sharply. An historical period is clearly neither merely the sum of its parts nor an entity which can be identified apart from them. It is, like national character or style in art, a partly but not completely analyzable pattern of complex form discernible in each of a wide range of instances. To say that "each part is the whole" means only that each *represents* the whole (cf. SM, 220), that the Renaissance style is not Renaissance architecture plus Renaissance politics, and so on, but is wholly represented in any one of these (although we can see what is relevant in one only by comparing it with others), as all the elements of an artist's style can be identified in a single composition or painting (but only with other instances in mind).

3 · *The Dialectic of Ethical Systems*

Now the little system of *Speculum Mentis* is itself self-exemplifying in this way. We have summarized Collingwood's discussion of Art, Religion, Science, History, and Philosophy as claims to knowledge or types of cognitive experience. But this is only part of what Collingwood means by "forms of consciousness"; they are also modes of action, or at least of the normative principles of action. So a practical ethics corresponds to each form of experience, and the connection between, say, Science as a mode of thought and Science as a mode of action is that each of these is a "part" in which the "whole" is fully exemplified. Thus they can be distinguished but not separated. And as each mode of thought is unstable and gives way to the next, or is true with respect to the mode it succeeds but is an error from the standpoint of its successor, so the corresponding systems of ethics go through a corresponding dialectical development.

To review this development from the beginning: Art is pure imagination, which makes no distinction between real and unreal and raises no questions about any relations among its self-contained objects. Now what sort of activity is analogous to this? It is hardly a guess: play, insofar as play is understood to be activity without ulterior ends and one which cannot be described as expedient or inexpedient, right or wrong. The question, of course, is not one of tactics or of rules. A move in chess may be expedient or inexpedient as a step toward checkmate, or legal or illegal according to the rules. But it is the activity of playing the game, *including* winning or losing, which is engaged in for its own sake. Chess as a livelihood, or as a way of making acquaintances, and so on, is of course not play at all. Nor should it now be any more difficult to identify the practical morality associated with Religion, remembering that this refers to the assertiveness of religious consciousness wholly without self-criticism: it could be nothing other than conventional morality, performances of all sorts which are chosen or avoided solely because they are or are not "done." Such a morality of propriety is, like the play of Art, capricious: it neither has nor claims justification. But it is a development from play, as assertion is from supposal, and differs from it by being *social;* conventional morality is to individual caprice as the creeds of Religion are to the free imagination of Art. Collingwood wisely remarks that even though conventional morality can only assert and not defend itself, mere rebellion against it is not an advance but a lapse into individual capriciousness.

What does represent the development beyond conventional morality (and is in fact the step taken by conventional moralists when conventions deteriorate and must be shored up by argument, viz., "Honesty is the best policy") is the utilitarian ethics appropriate to Science, which abstracts from the class of intentional actions their common element of purposiveness and calls it "utility." [13] That utility is an abstraction can be seen if one remembers that the notion of a calculus is essential to utilitarianism; John Stuart Mill effectively abandoned utilitarianism in his defense of it by introducing the notion of qualitative, or incommensurable, differences among pleasures.

In general, as Science abstracts from the untidy concreteness of physical objects the measurable properties of mass, velocity, etc., so in the consideration of action it abstracts the concept of an action as such as well as the measurable properties of the effects of actions. This point is best brought out by the contrast between the abstract ethics of utility and the concrete ethics of duty appropriate to History; the latter ethics regards action not as a purely instrumental means to an end, with no value other than that derivative from the value of the end, but as something required in a specific situation, and needing no inherited justification from anything lying outside itself. But Collingwood argues that this account, like the others, will not suffice. An action is regarded as obligatory because it is demanded by the facts of the situation. Action may, however, alter the facts; and insofar as it does so, it is no answer to the question of how they *should* be altered that they are indeed thus and so. So the ethics of duty ("Historical ethics") is ambivalent; it says on the one hand that the will is autonomous, and on the other that the world of concrete fact lays upon it an obligation which is its duty. Hence the peculiarity of *law,* which is the embodiment of concrete ethics. Law achieves, unlike utilitarian ethics, the notion of responsibility, but enforces it from without; one obeys the law not because it is the law but because disobedience has predictable and painful consequences, and this attitude, needless to say, is a relapse into utilitarianism. Or again, the instability of "concrete ethics" is signified by the inescapable conflict between the claim of law and the claim of individual conscience. But this again (Collingwood claims) reveals a distinction between individual and society, which as an abstraction indicates that History has not yet fully emancipated itself from Science.

So as History is fulfilled only in Philosophy, the ethics of duty is fulfilled only in "absolute ethics," in which the distinction between individual and society disappears, and "the agent acts with full responsibility," the sense of compulsion by external law having disappeared. At this point Collingwood is at best programmatic and at worst filling out his a priori scheme. (The section on "Absolute Ethics" is the shortest in *Speculum Mentis,* less than two pages long.) He returned again and again to his classification of types of ethical theories, but in every later recapitulation the scheme culminates not with "Absolute Ethics" but with Duty. One must assume that in *Speculum Mentis* Collingwood felt that Hegel had spoken the last word; later he decided that Hegel had had one word too many.

4 · *The Unresolved Problem of* Speculum Mentis

The eloquence of Collingwood's eulogies to "absolute mind" and "absolute ethics" cannot conceal the fact that the stage of Philosophy, far from being the developed and comprehensive fulfillment of Art, Religion, Science, and History, seems, unlike these others, to have no positive content of its own; the great climax of the drama of development turns out to be nothing but the playwright stepping in front of the closed curtain to remind the audience of what it has already seen. But no transformation scene was advertised, and it is just Collingwood's point that Philosophy stands apart in having no special object or method of its own. It is in fact part of his objection to "aesthetic philosophy," "religious philosophy," "scientific philosophy," and "historical philosophy" that they commit the "error of conceiving philosophy as one specialized form of experience, instead of realizing that it is merely the self-consciousness of experience in general" (SM, 256).

The record of the development from Art through History is itself the dialectical growth in thought's consciousness of itself; so one might say that it is Philosophy which fills up all the interstices of the series—or, since it is a dynamic series, Philosophy is the uneasiness with which each moment of thought backs into the next with its eye fixed unwaveringly on the last. *Speculum Mentis,* that is to say, is a philosophical book, and as such it must *exemplify* throughout what it may or may not illuminatingly describe in the final section as its own procedure. And this procedure, all things considered, is clearer and more cogent than the concluding description of Philosophy as the last term of the five-part series. It cannot be correct to say that Philosophy has no object: the whole of *Speculum Mentis* is a demonstration that the forms of consciousness, *including Philosophy itself,* and their relations to each other constitute the object of Philosophy. Nor can it be correct to say that Philosophy has no method: how are the features of a mode of experience identified and analyzed, for example, or the relation between one mode of experience and another discerned? The method of Philosophy at least must be the kind of thinking exemplified in the recapitulation of the series of modes of experience. Collingwood began *Speculum Mentis* with the "suspicion that a philosophy of this kind . . . is the only philosophy that can exist and that all other philosophies are included in it" (SM, 9). But by the end of the argument there is generated an uneasy and unresolved tension between two different ways of viewing philosophy: one is that philosophy has its own province, which includes those of other forms of consciousness but is distinguishable from them, and the other is that philosophy is only the reflective self-awareness of any mode of experience, the bringing to explicit (i.e., *self-*) consciousness of principles, criteria or presuppositions normally implicit in the thought and action of that mode of experience.

Now if one recognizes this unsolved problem as the major issue of *Speculum Mentis,* it helps to account for many of the otherwise extraordinary passages in that book. They are neither uncontrolled flights of speculative imagination nor unabashed special pleading for the philosophical party of absolute idealism but attempts to elucidate the peculiar logic of a theory which is an instance of itself, to achieve a systematic comprehension of philosophy as it is described and philosophy as it is exemplified. But, more significantly, the whole series of Collingwood's books then falls into place as a continuing attempt to answer the unresolved question of *Speculum Mentis.*

To put this development in the briefest way, the *Essay on Philosophical Method* ignores the other forms of experience to elucidate a method claimed to be the special province of philosophy; it fulfills, or attempts to fulfill, what in *Speculum Mentis* is left as programmatic, and provides a conceptual analysis of the concept of philosophy which in the earlier book is poetically expressed. The succeeding books, *The Idea of Nature, The Idea of History,* and *The Principles of Art,* are analyses of other forms of experience from the standpoint of philosophical reflection on them. In the *Essay on Philosophical Method,* Collingwood discusses philosophy but does not permit himself to think about the way in which his own discussion exemplifies it; in the later applications, he exemplifies it but does not directly discuss it. Yet while attacking either half of the problem, the awareness of the other half persists. It was not until the *Essay on Metaphysics* that Collingwood attempted a synthesis which would illustrate that *coincidentia oppositorum* which, according to *Speculum Mentis,* is the living nature of thought itself.

The uneasy tension in *Speculum Mentis* between the claim of philosophy to be an independent (and the highest) form of experience and the conception of philosophy as the reflective self-consciousness of other forms of experience is itself a dialectical tension. The development of the former in abstraction from the latter results in the dialectic of concepts which is the subject of the *Essay on Philosophical Method;* the development of the latter in abstraction from the former results in the dialectic of mind which Collingwood had partially worked out even before the *Essay on Philosophical Method* but did not publish in explicit form (in *The New Leviathan*) until shortly before his death. The clue to understanding each is to see that it replicates the other, just as, in Collingwood's view, the "concrete universal" is a whole whose parts replicate the form of the whole and of each other; the later developments are intelligible only when they are seen to have a common dialectical form. The rather traditional defense in *Speculum Mentis* of the "concrete universal" is transformed by Collingwood into his theory of concepts as comprising a scale of forms (Chapter 3, below) and into his theory of mind as constituted by levels of consciousness related to each other like the basic types of experience and concepts on a scale of forms (Chapter 4, below). Collingwood's ultimate dialectic of mind grows out of the dialectic of concepts, as that grows out of the dialectic of experience.

CHAPTER 3

The Dialectic of Concepts

1 · From the Dialectic of Experience to the Dialectic of Concepts

IN THE DECADE WHICH SEPARATED *Speculum Mentis* FROM the *Essay on Philosophical Method,* Collingwood wrote a number of articles and reviews which mark out for discussion details from the panorama of *Speculum Mentis,* primarily on art, religion and history as modes of experience and of knowledge. None of these extend or develop the programmatic description of philosophy with which *Speculum Mentis* concludes, although he cannot have been content with it. Perhaps while thinking about the problem he avoided educating himself in public; in any case, he discussed the problem of philosophical method, during this period, in his introduction to the lectures on moral philosophy which he gave annually at Oxford, and in expanded form this introduction appeared in 1933 as the *Essay on Philosophical Method,* which Collingwood later called "the only [book] I ever had the time to finish as well as I knew how" (A, 118).[1]

The unresolved problem of *Speculum Mentis* is that the book itself does not exemplify the description of philosophy as "absolute" with which it concludes. In describing philosophy as a "form of experience" toward which other forms of experience tend to develop because of their inherent instability, it has some success in describing "aesthetic philosophy," "religious philosophy," "scientific philosophy," and "historical philosophy" as types of conceptual dogmatism which arise as the reflective justification of their associated forms of experience. "Dogmatism is simply the resistance which a given form of experience presents to its own destruction by an inner dialectic" (SM, 259). How these incomplete and dogmatic forms of philosophy are to be superseded is the problem. Collingwood is clear that they must be passed through in thought and recognized as the necessary conditions of their own supersession (SM, 289). But what then? To draw up a history of errors does not afford guidance for the next step beyond, since even though the direction of this step is implicit in the identification of errors as such, it must still be brought to explicit recognition. And this is the task of a method.

It is evident from all of his work that Collingwood was an unusually self-conscious philosopher, preoccupied to an extraordinary degree with the problem of analyzing his own thought in the way in which he had learned to interpret the thought of classical philosophers. This habit, moreover, was not just a personal characteristic but a necessary consequence of a view of philosophy which remained fundamental throughout his lifetime. The philosophy of history, for example, consists for Collingwood of the analysis of the intellectual principles implicit in the process of raising and solving historical problems. To be a philosopher of history, you must first have the experience of historical thinking; then, as philosopher of history, you make explicit by analysis those principles which you reflectively discover to have been implicit in your own successful historical thinking. Now it follows from this conception that there will be a philosophy of every distinguishable mode of thinking, and, since philosophy itself is a mode of thinking, there must be a philosophy of philosophy. (There must also, of course, be a philosophy of philosophy of philosophy, etc.; Collingwood was aware of this regress, as we shall see in discussing his "dialectic of mind" in Chapter 4, and his solution was both ingenious and original.) It is from the standpoint of philosophy of philosophy that the continuity between *Speculum Mentis* and the *Essay on Philosophical Method* is most evident. The latter attempts to make explicit the principles of thinking which the former exemplifies. Reflecting on the philosophical thinking which *Speculum Mentis* exemplified, rather than pursuing the "absolute philosophy" which it envisioned, Collingwood moved from a dialectic of experience to a dialectic of concepts.

2 · *Formal Logic and Collingwood's "Logic"*

Speculum Mentis is the outline of a dialectical system. It orders modes of experience into a series such that later stages of the series are developments out of earlier stages; the latter make explicit the principles and possibilities which were only implicit in the earlier stages; they are related to earlier stages not as mutually exclusive alternatives but as more inclusive extensions (hence a later stage appears to an earlier stage as a contradiction of itself, but not vice versa); in short, "one tries to be what the other is, one implies what the other expresses, one questions where the other answers, one overlooks what the other recognizes; and . . . the more primitive is absorbed without residue in the more advanced" (SM, 200).

But although *Speculum Mentis* describes a dialectical system, its description of the philosophy which *should* be the full and final self-consciousness of the series of modes of experience remains, as we have seen, a promissory note of uncertain amount and indefinite date. The *Essay on Philosophical Method* is one payment on that note: it is the logic of dialectical method. And it must be recognized as such, I believe, not in spite of but because of the fact that the term "dialectic" nowhere appears in the book. Collingwood could only have been deliberate in his avoidance of the term in what is in fact a detailed analysis of dialectical logic, a study of the formal features of what in *Speculum Mentis* was indistinctly celebrated as "concrete thought." The *Essay on Philosophical Method* stands to *Speculum Mentis* exactly as Hegel's *Logic* stands to his *Phenomenology of Mind;* but there is nothing to indicate that Collingwood was deliberately constructing this resemblance or even that he would have been gratified by its discovery.

The argument of the *Essay on Philosophical Method* is organized according to the traditional division of logic under the rubrics of *terms* (Chapters III–IV), *judgments or propositions* (Chapters V–VI), and *inference* (Chapter VIII). In connection with the first, Collingwood discusses classification and division, definition and description, but not predication or the denotation and connotation of terms. In connection with the second, he discusses the quantity and quality of judgments (i.e., as universal and particular, affirmative and negative), but has nothing to say about the distribution of terms, the distinction between categorical, hypothetical and disjunctive propositions, or the distinction between analytic and synthetic propositions. In connection with the theory of inference, he mentions deduction and induction, but he has nothing to correspond with the analysis of either syllogistic inference (in traditional logic) or of axiomatic systems and propositional calculi (in modern logic). It is evident that the *Essay* is not intended to be a complete logical theory or even a philosophical commentary on traditional Aristotelian logic or modern mathematical logic; rather it is, as it claims to be, an analysis of a particular kind of thinking—philosophical thinking—and not of thinking in general, although it touches on the latter just at those points where distinctions are necessary. But this is not merely to say that logic, as it is usually understood, is an analysis of or is applicable to thinking in its most general aspects only, while Collingwood is interested in the specific characteristics of a particular kind of thinking; the course of his argument implies that formal logic as it has been usually understood is itself the theory of *scientific* concepts;[2] and this in turn suggests (consistent with his general thesis and with the interpretation of the *Essay* as the formal analysis of the kind of thinking represented in *Speculum Mentis*) that Collingwood was prepared to deny—or committed to deny—the possibility of a completely formal logic perfectly indifferent to the content of statements and inferences. This consequence he later acknowledged and defended (A, 33–35).

At the same time, there is no impediment to recognizing a completely formal logic as the legitimate product of reflection on the principles of scientific thinking: logic as the theory of scientific concepts is not false but partial. It is partial because it does not apply to philosophical thinking (as exemplified in *Speculum Mentis*); reflection on *that* sort of enterprise results in a theory of philosophical concepts, not of scientific concepts nor, a fortiori, of conceptual thinking in general.

3 · Philosophical Method and the "Overlap of Classes"

The two related notions which distinguish Collingwood's theory of philosophical concepts are those of the "overlap of classes" and of the "scale of forms." In the discussion of each, his constant point of reference is the logic of scientific method (including both mathematics and empirical science), and his single purpose is to distinguish philosophical method from scientific method in all those points which are essential to the latter. As we shall see, it is not only the exposition of his argument, which abounds in tangential discussions and in avowedly provisional conclusions abandoned or revised much later in the book, which makes the *Essay* deceptively difficult. If it is interpreted, as it usually has been, as a theory of formal logic, his argument seems direct but untenable; interpreted, however, as a theory of philosophical method, his argument is oblique but more characteristic of the continuity of his thought, and intrinsically much more defensible.

Read directly, and for the moment without criticism, Collingwood's elaborate distinction between scientific and philosophical method seems to be as follows:

Types of inquiry may be regarded as differing not merely in subject-matter, that is, by reason of the fact that the concepts they employ refer to different kinds of things, as molecules differ from revolutions and chromosomes from social classes, but also in the logical characteristics of the concepts appropriate to a particular kind of inquiry. In general, a concept denotes a class of entities which share the characteristic or set of characteristics referred to by the concept. Such a class may be further divided into sub-classes, and this further division may or may not be a specification of the class-characteristic itself. When it is not, it may be quite arbitrary, like dividing the class of men into orphans and non-orphans or into bearded and beardless. When it is, the concept determines a genus, of which the sub-classes are species, as red, orange, and yellow are species of the genus color, or equilateral, isosceles, and scalene are species of the genus triangle. So far there is no difference between "scientific" and "philosophical" classification.

Traditionally in logic and effectively in scientific classification, the species of a genus must be mutually exclusive and exhaustive: every instance of the genus must also be an instance of at least one and not more than one of its species. Species, in turn, may serve as genera with respect to their own division into further specifically differentiated classes; so a generic concept, articulated into its specific differentiations, determines a classificatory scheme. In empirical science, borderline and paradoxical cases may arise (such as the platypus), but they affect not the logical criteria of classificatory schemes but their empirical adequacy.

In the case of philosophical concepts, however, the specific classes of a genus do not exclude each other but "overlap," in the sense that an instance of the genus will be an instance of more than one and possibly all of its species. To take a self-reflexive example, traditional logic distinguishes within the genus thought two species, judgment and inference. But an inference may also be a judgment, as "It is raining because I can hear it" is both.[3] Similarly, judgments are either affirmative or negative, but there are no *purely* affirmative or negative judgments. A negative judgment affirms something; and an affirmative judgment denies at least its opposite. The singular judgment combines universality and particularity; the disjunctive judgment is both categorical and hypothetical; and so on. In ethics, goods are divided into the pleasant, the expedient, and the right; but these again are not mutually exclusive, because the pleasant may be both expedient and right; no one (not even Kant) would hold that the rightness of an action excludes the possibility of its being also pleasant or expedient. Similarly, actions may be performed from motives of desire, self-interest, or duty, but a single act may fall into two or even all three of these classes.

And so it will turn out, Collingwood claims, for all "philosophical concepts"; presumably any concept not specified into overlapping classes is thereby disqualified as a philosophical concept. But the distinction would not be trivial even so: it would be enough to show that *some* concepts determine overlapping classes without the necessity of showing that all concepts do so which anyone for any reason would wish to call philosophical concepts. Moreover, some concepts may have what Collingwood calls a "dual significance," or philosophical and non-philosophical phases (EPM, 35), just as "matter," "mind," "evolution," or "art" may apply either to a limited class of objects and events or to an aspect of phenomena extending indefinitely beyond what would ordinarily be accepted as the denotation of the term. Presumably, when employed non-philosophically, "evolution" denotes only a specific bio-genetic process, and "art" denotes only a specific class of artifacts. But when these concepts are used philosophically, "evolution" may refer, say, to cosmic or social processes, and "art" to such non-artifacts as the totality of an individual human life, the sense in which the phrase "life as art" is intelligible. Philosophers may not agree on the question whether such concepts have any *proper* "philosophical" meaning; but it cannot be denied that since Thales said that everything is water, philosophers have in point of fact used both ordinary and extraordinary concepts in such a way that the intended denotation of the concepts, in Collingwood's phrase, "leaks or escapes" out of the limited classes to which others have attempted to restrict them.[4] The simplest way of accounting for this feature of philosophical concepts is to regard it as resulting from unjustifiable intrusions of poetic metaphors into a rational discipline. Why should anyone attempt, as Collingwood does, to *justify* avoidable vagueness as a *logical* characteristic of concepts?

On such a "direct" reading of Collingwood, his view is clearly open to serious criticisms. In saying that the species into which a "scientific" genus is differentiated are exclusive, it might be said, he is describing not science but a traditional logic which is of dubious adequacy as an account of scientific method. Even in "exact science" (i.e., mathematics), his account does not hold, and so is a fortiori inapplicable to empirical science. On the other hand, his own examples do not justify the conclusion that the species of a philosophical genus "overlap." To take the latter point first: even granting, for example, that goods can be classified as the pleasant, the expedient, and the right, and that actions may exemplify more than one of these, we could still devise mutually exhaustive and exclusive classes:

a. pleasant and expedient and right
b. pleasant, but not expedient nor right
c. pleasant and expedient, but not right
d. pleasant and right, but not expedient
e. expedient, but not pleasant nor right
f. expedient and right, but not pleasant
g. right, but not pleasant nor expedient

These seven sub-classes clearly exhaust the genus "good," on the original assumption, and they do not overlap. But as this exhaustive and exclusive set of species of the genus "good" is a more exact statement of the division of that genus into three "overlapping" species, so conversely one could reverse the procedure in the case of scientific concepts to produce apparently overlapping classes. Collingwood himself observes that such a figure as a semicircle does not form an overlap of rectilinear and curvilinear figures, but a "third class." But no criterion is suggested, and none readily comes to mind, for deciding whether or not a semicircle belongs to an overlap or a third class. One suspects that it is purely a matter of stipulation, just as it is stipulative whether "isosceles" is defined as having at least two sides equal or as having at least and at most two sides equal. In the former case, equilateral and isosceles would overlap as species of the genus triangle; in the latter case they would not. One could hardly accept the conclusion that the difference between a philosophical and a non-philosophical concept, or between a philosophical and a non-philosophical employment of a concept, is a matter of stipulative definition. Collingwood might reply that when "isosceles" is defined in such a way that equilateral triangles are isosceles, "equilateral" and "isosceles" are not true species. But this would be special pleading—the use against the counter-example of precisely the same objection which critics can bring against Collingwood's examples of "philosophical" species.

The trouble is that the direct reading of Collingwood's argument makes it seem wrong in such an elementary way that either generosity or caution or a bit of both should inspire second thoughts. Even partisan critics should be suspicious of interpretations which make their opponents appear to be fools. It may be remembered that our working hypothesis is that Collingwood was trying to work out the formal features of a dialectical logic; and if this were so, it might be expected that oddities would appear to anyone regarding it as simply a modification or misstatement of traditional formal logic. But to adjudicate this question, it is necessary to turn to Collingwood's notion of a "scale of forms," which complements that of "overlapping classes."

4 · The Scale of Forms

Overlapping classes (if there are any) are species of a genus denoted by a philosophical concept. But if they overlap, in what sense are they *different* species? (This question does not arise in the case of non-philosophical concepts; the *differentiae* which distinguish species of a genus also guarantee their mutual exclusiveness.) They cannot differ merely in degree—as in the classification of motors by horsepower or of men by age in years—for in that case they would not overlap. Nor can they differ merely in kind—as in the classifica-

tion of sensations by the sensory modalities of vision, hearing, etc.—
for the same reason. But there are, according to Collingwood, cases
in which a generic concept is specified in such a way that difference
in kind is associated with difference in degree. An example is Plato's
classification of four kinds of knowledge in Book VI of the *Republic*.

In such cases, each of the species of the genus "not only embodies the generic essence in a specific manner, but also embodies
some variable attribute in a specific degree" (EPM, 57). Moreover,
the increase or decrease of this variable attribute is not smoothly continuous, but is subject to critical points at which one specific form is
replaced by another; Collingwood suggests breaking-points, freezing-
points and minimum taxable income as examples. It is any such system which he calls a "scale of forms." The examples just mentioned
are obviously not philosophical; but neither, in these examples, is the
variable attribute (e.g., temperature) intrinsically connected with
the generic essence (e.g., the chemical formula of the substance). In
a *philosophical* scale of forms, Collingwood claims, the variable is
identical with the generic essence; e.g., in Plato's four kinds of
knowledge (and the same could be said of Locke's "degrees" of
knowledge, or of Spinoza's or Kant's) each lower form is an inadequate specification of the same essence more adequately represented
in higher types.

The focus of attention here is the way in which the different
terms in a scale of forms resemble each other—or, rather, on the explanation of their resemblance as a consequence of their embodying
the same generic essence. But how do they differ from each other? It
is not enough merely to say, "They differ in the adequacy with
which they incorporate the generic essence"; it is this itself which requires explanation. It is characteristic of Collingwood's examples
and it follows from the principle of critical points of transformation
in the series that its terms are differentiated; but what sort of differentiation is this? Two things may be differentiated as *distinct* from
each other or as *opposite* to each other. Opposition "is a relation sub-
sisting between a positive term and its own mere negation or absence" (EPM, 75); distinction is, apparently, any relation of difference between two positive terms which differ in meaning. Collingwood adduces physical heat and physical cold (i.e., the absence of
heat) as an example of opposition, felt heat and felt cold as an example of combined opposition and distinction. The difference between,

say, sensed red and felt heat would be an example of distinction without opposition.

The upshot is that the *fusion* of opposition and distinction is characteristic of the relation of philosophical terms on a scale of forms, although not peculiar to philosophical terms, as the example of felt heat and felt cold shows. (These differ in degree but not in kind. Properly philosophical terms on a scale of forms differ in both respects.) "Good and bad, truth and error, beauty and ugliness" indicate such a fusion. One formal consequence is that on such scales there is no zero degree. The minimal degree is still a realization of the "generic essence" so far as it belongs to the scale at all; as a limiting case it is an opposite relative to the rest of the scale, but in any case it is never the pure absence of the generic essence which determines the scale.[5] On the other hand, Collingwood does not directly discuss the question whether such a scale has a maximum, although later in the *Essay* (EPM, 191, 195) he suggests that it does not. This is a point of the utmost importance in understanding the development of his concept of dialectic; for, as we shall see in Chapter 4, it was by historicizing the scale of forms that Collingwood, in the manner of Hegel, brought together logic and history so as to account for the retrospective rationality of the development of ideas without implying that there are laws of development which determine the future as well as illuminating the past.

The "fusion" of opposition and distinction by itself does not seem to characterize philosophical concepts exclusively; in fact, it merely defines what is meant by a "scale," insofar as the latter means a graduated series of terms, individually identifiable and arranged according to the possession in greater or less degree of a variable quality. A "scale of forms," Collingwood concludes, is defined by a logical relation which synthesizes the four kinds of relation discussed: difference of degree, difference of kind, relation of distinction, and relation of opposition (EPM, 88). And such a scale of forms uniquely embodies the overlap of philosophical concepts: "The overlap consists in this, that the lower is contained in the higher, the higher transcending the lower and adding to it something new, whereas the lower partially coincides with the higher, but differs from it in rejecting this increment" (EPM, 91).

"Higher" and "lower" are not merely metaphors; a scale of forms is unidirectional in a way in which, say, the color spectrum (qualitatively) is not, or even in which quantitative scales, as of frequencies, are not. The visible spectrum of frequencies is "higher" than the audible spectrum in no other sense than that in which the numbers associated with the former frequencies are larger. Blue, or the frequency of blue, does not *contain* red or the frequency of red. In a philosophical scale of forms, however, the higher levels include the lower as constituents. Consequently, they are higher in the sense that they are more inclusive and therefore more extensive and more complex. The passage from a lower to a higher specific concept is nevertheless unlike the passage from a narrower to a broader generalization or that from a class to a more inclusive class. In such cases, the denotation is merely extended to include more objects. In a scale of forms, however, the passage from lower to higher does not necessarily or ordinarily involve an increased extension; rather it involves taking account of more characteristics of the objects. It follows that the doctrines of traditional logic, that a genus (whose species are not null classes) has greater extension and smaller intension than its individual species, and that intension and extension vary inversely, do not hold of philosophical concepts.

Given the sort of examples Collingwood has in mind, these implications are not so odd as they appear at first glance. It does seem characteristic of philosophical concepts and theories that they apply to an unspecified range of objects. (This is in fact the root of almost all criticisms of philosophy, whether they are vulgar or learned.) So, one might say, logic applies to all propositions and inferences, ethics to all actions; philosophy of history, if it is a theory of historical process, applies to all historical events, and, if it is a philosophy of historical knowledge, to the entire activity of historical inquiry. Aesthetics applies not just to a predetermined class of artifacts but to an indefinite range of experience; no one, therefore, should be surprised by the fact that aesthetic concepts (such as "elegance") turn up in mathematics or that moral categories (such as "intention") turn up in aesthetics. Some concepts have always been recognized as logically peculiar and peculiarly philosophical: the *unum, verum, bonum* which were called by the scholastics "transcendental concepts" because they are predicable of anything whatsoever, for instance, or the concepts of identity and difference, which Plato showed in the *Sophist* to be predicable of everything including each other, or of being and non-being, which Hegel claimed were indistinguishable from each other. Philosophy has often been regarded, by those who had such concepts in mind, as a science which studies certain types of entities or employs certain concepts different from those studied or used in any other science. But this is not Collingwood's theory at all, as indicated by his emphasis on concepts which have a "philosophical" and a "non-philosophical" phase. It is the use of a concept, not its "meaning," which determines whether it is philosophical; and the pertinent question about its use is whether, regarded as a species of a genus, it applies to the same range of objects as the other species of the same genus. Collingwood specifically rejects the commonly accepted principle that "when a generic concept is divided into its species there is a corresponding division of its instances into mutually exclusive classes" (EPM, 49). This principle may be "true in exact and empirical science, [but] is false in philosophy" (Ibid.). The overlap of classes is an overlap of the intension of concepts, not of their extension (EPM, 91; cf. 63 ff.). Hence it would be useless to search for counter-examples to Collingwood's view; the issue turns entirely on the *interpretation* of such examples. A scale of forms guarantees, in fact, that every lower stage of the scale will generate counter-examples against a higher stage; otherwise there would be no "relation of opposition." But what appears to be (and therefore *is*) opposition from the standpoint of the lower stage is *inclusion* from the standpoint of the higher stage.

Now it follows, although he does not explicitly point out the consequence, that whenever a generic concept (such as "good") is divided into species (such as "productive of pleasure," "conforming to a rule," or "according to duty"), each of which has an extension in principle coincident with the genus and with each other, theories can be elaborated each of which *identifies* the genus with one of its species, and these theories will contend with each other, each claiming the sole right to make such an identification. Moreover, it follows that no one of these theories can make out its case against the others by pointing to any instance or set of instances which it but not they can account for; for any instance of the genus can be regarded as an instance of any of the species. Now if this were so, it would go far to explain the peculiar inconclusiveness of the strife of philosophical theories (which, as has often been observed, are not refuted but abandoned), and the absence in philosophy of anything like an *experimentum crucis*. It would explain, or partially explain, why moral philosophers disagree so seldom on whether an action is right (i.e., whether it belongs to the genus) and so often on why it is right (i.e., whether it belongs to this or that species). To order such disputes on a scale of forms simultaneously accounts for their occurrence and avoids the relativistic conclusion that the choice among theories is arbitrary: the question is not one of the extension of concepts but of their intension, which is to say of the relation of theories as higher or lower on the same scale of forms.

But even apart from these consequences, Collingwood is certainly right that it is characteristic of philosophical theories to emphasize aspects of all experience rather than to investigate the properties of a specific class of experiences. If this is so, then it should not be surprising that philosophical thought proceeds neither by inductive generalization nor by ever more precise analysis of classification and sub-classification—nor that philosophical propositions have not often seemed confirmed or refuted by empirical evidence. A proposition about the color of swans is not a philosophical proposition; but on the other hand a question like Hume's whether one could imagine (as an "idea") a color which one had never seen (as an "impression") is not a question to be settled by "experiment" (unless the *interpretation* of the experiment simply begged the question at issue).

One might say that this is Collingwood's point: ethical questions, for example, are not to be settled by studying the phenomena of human behavior. We already experience and interpret ethical behavior with the help of a variety of concepts: pleasure, expediency, rightness, obligatoriness, and the like. Each of these provides a way of classifying actions, but none affords a *fundamentum divisionis.* The major questions of ethics turn on the relation of these concepts to each other, not as the relation of a pleasurable action to an expedient one (since the same act may be both, and it might even be held that any act which has one characteristic has the other as well), but as the relation of pleasure to expediency with respect to any given act. Collingwood's proposal is to resolve the debate among philosophical theories of ethics as coordinate (i.e., non-overlapping) and exclusive alternatives by regarding one as a special and limited case of another, the higher incorporating the truth of the lower and going beyond it in ways impossible for and unintelligible to the latter.

But "higher" and "lower" are also indefeasibly normative terms. On the face of it the usage is suspicious. It is not unknown in the history of philosophy and on its borders for appeals to be made to "higher truth," "higher wisdom," and the like, in lieu of arguments. But it is clear that Collingwood is appealing to no mysterious or privileged faculty, which awards itself the prize in every contest. If his notion of a scale of forms is granted at all, "higher" and "lower" are natural and appropriate terms. Significantly, all of the illustrations (e.g., from logic and ethics) are intrinsically normative. Given his understanding of philosophy as "criteriological," that is, that characteristically philosophical positions are both descriptive and normative (EM, 107–111; PA, 171 n.), this is only what one would expect. But at the same time, he is not merely begging the question whether philosophy is criteriological by admitting only normative propositions as examples. Since he holds philosophy to be not only criteriological but systematic, every philosophical doctrine will be at least implicitly normative in virtue of its systematic connection with other doctrines which are explicitly so. On the other hand, the theory of the philosophical scale of forms is calculated to antagonize many—all those, in fact, who find their own views relegated to a "lower" level. Collingwood makes few such relegations, but it is clear enough that the effect of his view is to transform philosophical argument. Utilitarians, for example, could no longer defend their theory as an *alternative* to, say, Kantian ethics. In Collingwood's rewriting of the rules, an ethics of duty absorbs, replaces, and goes beyond an ethics of utility; it is adequate to everything to which the latter is adequate, and to more. If Utilitarians regard this as condescending, they can hardly be blamed. Yet utilitarianism itself has tried very much the same tactic, as for instance in Mill's theory of sanctions, which in effect was a proposal to absorb the concept of duty without remainder into utilitarian theory.

The sketch which Collingwood gives of the scale of forms, one should remember, is a formal one. It tries merely to characterize philosophical concepts as determining an overlapping scale with the properties of opposition and distinction of degree and of kind. This formal characterization can be distinguished from the ordering of specific concepts on such a scale. Collingwood had his own views as to which is higher and which is lower, and his own ethics is based on a scale (from lower to higher) of utility-right-duty. But one could accept the theory of a scale of forms without being committed to a particular scale. The former is the logic of dialectic; the latter (like the argument of *Speculum Mentis*) is dialectical philosophy. The logic of dialectic does not entail specific propositions of metaphysics, ethics, aesthetics, etc. It *does* imply that all such propositions can be assigned to a locus in a scale of forms which clarifies their relation to other propositions; it does not of itself assign such a locus to any proposition. In this respect it is like the logic of scientific method, which specifies how a scientific hypothesis is to be confirmed but does not prescribe which will and will not be.

5 · *The Change in Collingwood's Idea of Dialectic*

The *Essay on Philosophical Method* is, throughout, an ex post facto justification of the dialectical system of *Speculum Mentis,* but it is also implicitly a criticism of that system. It describes the formal properties of a scale of forms which exactly corresponds to the hierarchical series of Art, Religion, Science, History, and Philosophy. It is thus an exemplification of its own principle that reflection upon the experience of philosophical thinking is a part of philosophical thinking (EPM, 1). In *Speculum Mentis* Collingwood was thinking dialectically about the relation to each other of generic forms of experience; in the *Essay* he is attempting to state explicitly as principles of method the formal characteristics of that dialectical thinking. Thus the theory of a scale of forms sets out the logical form of a conceptual scheme of which *Speculum Mentis* is one (although, of course, not the only) realization:

> Each term . . . has a double relation to its neighbors: in comparison with the one below, it is what that professes to be; in comparison with the one above, it professes to be what that is.
>
> This relation may be described by the metaphor of promising and performing; or it may be described by saying that the higher is the reality of which the lower is an approximation, or the truth of which the lower is a perversion. These are not so much metaphors as descriptions of something simpler and therefore more truly intelligible in terms of something more complex and, to us, more familiar. . . . [The former] is a purely logical relation, . . . a synthesis of the four relations which it has been the task of this chapter to discuss: difference of degree, difference of kind, relation of distinction, and relation of opposition [EPM, 87–88; cf. SM, 206–207].

Now this account does not describe aesthetic experience, religious experience, etc., but Collingwood's *concepts* of these forms of experience and their relations. But this serves to emphasize the difference between a particular dialectical philosophy and the general form of a dialectical philosophy; *Speculum Mentis is* the former, and *exem-*

plifies the latter. (Kierkegaard's famous account of three stages of the aesthetic, the ethical, and the religious is a different dialectical philosophy but exemplifies the same general form. It is even somewhat closer to Collingwood than it appears to be, since the essential element of Kierkegaard's "ethical stage" is the activity of abstraction and of the attribution of objective reality to the results of abstraction, i.e., what Collingwood calls "Science.")

The theory of a scale of forms, however, has a double relevance to *Speculum Mentis*. It is the structure not only of the concepts implicit in forms of experience but of the philosophical theories which consist of the dogmatic application of those concepts. The series of the forms of experience, it will be remembered, replicates itself at the level of Philosophy, so that corresponding to each form there is a reasoned vindication of it in the form of a philosophical theory. The "aesthetic philosophy" which corresponds to Art as a form of experience, for example, reduces all philosophical problems to terms of imagination or intuition. However, Collingwood took pains to say, in *Speculum Mentis,* that "there is no dialectical transition from aesthetic philosophy to religious philosophy and so forth" (SM, 263). His reason was that such theories are types of dogmatism, and dogmatism is not part of the process of experience but the *resistance* of any form of experience "to its own destruction by an inner dialectic" (SM, 259). Hence they appear as epiphenomena on the surface of the process of experience but are not subject to the changes which experience itself undergoes.

In the *Essay on Philosophical Method,* however, this doctrine is abandoned. It is not difficult to see why. For one thing, Collingwood must have seen on reflection that the philosophical argument of *Speculum Mentis* is not itself an exemplification of *any* of the characterizations of philosophy given there. It is beyond any of the "dogmatic" philosophies, since it describes and explains them, but it is not and does not claim to be that "philosophical Philosophy" which is the "concrete life of philosophy" or "philosophy as absolute knowledge"; if such were possible, one would not look for it in a book of 317 pages, provided with a Preface and an Index.

That *Speculum Mentis* itself exemplifies neither any of the philosophical errors which it analyzes nor the absolute knowledge which it eulogizes reflects the unresolved tension, which we noted at the end of the last chapter, between regarding philosophy as a separate form of experience (in the scale of forms) and regarding it as the reflection—an activity, so to speak, without content of its own—on every form of experience. The latter conception reflects the survival in Collingwood's thought of the opinion which he had stated in *Religion and Philosophy,* that while the sciences are distinguished by differences in their problems and methods, philosophy has no methods of its own at all (RP, 16).

The very title of the *Essay on Philosophical Method* announces the renunciation of this view. But it is not a complete renunciation: it is not a contradiction but a dialectical shift to another view of which the former is only a partial realization. Early in the *Essay on Philosophical Method* Collingwood assesses Plato's contribution to the theory of philosophical method as "the conception of philosophy as the one sphere in which thought moves with perfect freedom, bound by no limitations except those which it imposes upon itself for the duration of a single argument" (EPM, 15). Plato's statement of this view he finds in the discussion of "dialectic" in the *Republic* (509D ff.), and an application of it in the dialectical examination of hypotheses in the main body of the *Parmenides.* In the former passage, Plato has Socrates say that, while, in the several sciences, thinking provides deductive demonstration of conclusions from hypotheses which are regarded as given (although not self-evident), in "dialectic," thinking regards these postulates of the sciences as problematic and "goes from hypotheses to a non-hypothetical principle."

Clearly Collingwood has attributed to Plato his own earlier view of Philosophy as independent of methodological principles derived from the methods of mathematics and empirical science. His criticism of Plato is therefore in effect a criticism of his own difficulties in *Speculum Mentis:* to say what philosophy is not does not make clear what it is. Philosophy is left as something distinct from science but not opposed to it, differing from science in degree but not in specific kind. The *Essay* therefore undertakes to give a theory of what philosophy is as well as of what it is not, and in so doing it provides what was missing in *Speculum Mentis:* a theory of philosophy of which the argument of *Speculum Mentis* can itself be regarded as an example.

The scheme of *Speculum Mentis,* regarded now from the standpoint of the *Essay on Philosophical Method,* has the structure of a scale of forms: Art, Religion, Science, History (and Philosophy, in intent) differ both in kind and degree, and are both opposed to and distinct from each other. But the series of dogmatic philosophies, which make explicit the conceptual structures implicit in forms of experience, are now *also* regarded as exemplifying a scale of forms. The question then arises, which in the *Essay* is only obliquely recognized: Does a scale of forms have a highest level? In *Speculum Mentis,* Collingwood's answer was in the affirmative; Philosophy was clearly terminal. It was conceived as "absolute mind," or thought liberated from the abstraction and incompleteness of other forms of experience. Now in *Speculum Mentis* Collingwood had held the view that concepts are implicit in all experience, are made explicit as abstractions only at the level of Science (and this is why theology is the transition from Religion to Science), and are reunited in the "concrete universal" at the level of Philosophy. The *Essay on Philosophical Method,* we may assume, set out to clarify the dialectical order of the forms of experience by giving the formal properties of the concepts implicit in them. But Collingwood came to realize that the scale of forms applies not only to forms of experience as he had conceived them, and not only to philosophical as distinct from "scientific" concepts, but also to philosophical theories and the *history* of their development. And in regarding the history of philosophical thought as a series of stages, each of which "promises" what the next "performs," it becomes evident that there is no highest or *last* term in the series, but only a *latest.* In the history of thought so conceived, "all the philosophies of the past are telescoped into the present, and constitute a scale of forms, *never beginning and never ending* (EPM, 195; italics added). Thus, "what is permanent or essential is not this or that system, for every particular system is nothing but an interim report . . . " (EPM, 198).

In effect, the idea of a scale of forms determines two types of dialectical order. One is the dialectic of concepts within a particular philosophical theory (for example, the series of the concepts of utility, right and duty as species of "good" in Collingwood's own ethics). The other is the dialectic of philosophical theories seen as an historical development from the standpoint of a particular philosophical theory (for example, the histories of the idea of nature and of the idea of history in which Collingwood later applied his principles of philosophical method). Such a theory represents other theories as belonging to a scale of forms in which it makes explicit what is progressively less implicit in them, completes what has become less partial through them, and solves the problems whose formulation has become clarified through them. But at the same time it is aware that its summation of the scale up to its own position *will* from the standpoint of the next summation have modified it, and that from *that* more inclusive standpoint what is implicit, partial, and unsolved in it will be corrected (cf. EPM, 194–98).

Collingwood's original reason for holding that "philosophy has no methods of its own" was that the adoption of a method, like the adoption of a technical vocabulary (EPM, 201–208; PA, 174), imposes on experience a conceptual scheme which determines a priori at least the general features of what will then be "found" there. One would like to make no assumptions at all, to experience the world with innocent receptiveness. And Collingwood for a while shared the Platonic and neo-Platonic conception of philosophy as a learned innocence which leaves behind the partial and abstract perspectives of the special sciences to achieve a comprehensive vision of reality just as it is. But in the years between *Speculum Mentis* and the *Essay on Philosophical Method* his debates with his "realist" colleagues gave him more and more arguments against the doctrine that knowing can be a simple and immediate intuiting of an independent "reality" (cf. A, 25). He may well have recognized that the logic of the realist doctrine of perception is the same as the logic of the Platonic doctrine of "philosophical" knowledge. His objections to realism became increasingly clearer and more urgent: in sum they were that the realist theory of knowledge as simple apprehension cannot account for *historical* inquiry and, moreover, has resulted in "grotesquely irrelevant" misinterpretations of the history of philosophy itself (A, 26–28). But as historical inquiry and historical interpretation became for him paradigmatic examples of knowledge, they corroded not only epistemological realism but his own conception of philosophy as "the attempt to conceive reality not in any particular way, but just to conceive it."

The solution of the *Essay* is that philosophical thinking must have a method but one which is self-conscious and self-corrective. No particular stage of philosophical thinking escapes the consequences of its own assumptions; but the *process* of philosophy, dialectically conceived, escapes determination by any a priori conceptual scheme because it progressively calls into question as objects of criticism the assumptions on which prior theories on the scale of forms proceeded. That philosophy reflects on itself is true not of this or that doctrine or argument but of the *history* of doctrines and arguments as stages of a scale of forms. Hence in philosophy "the whole body of knowledge must be remade from the foundations at every step in advance" (EPM, 180). This is the appearance in philosophy of the historical maxim that "every present has its own past." It is sometimes said that the British neo-Hegelians (for example F. H. Bradley, in *Appearance and Reality*) went "to the Absolute like a shot out of a pistol"; that is, they retained Hegel's Absolute but avoided his dialectic of concepts. Collingwood has now set the stage for the opposite movement: he has retained dialectic and abandoned the Absolute.

CHAPTER 4

The Dialectic of Mind

1 · Collingwood's Moral Philosophy

THREE THEMES CONSTANTLY RECUR THROUGHOUT COLLING-wood's work and serve as landmarks by which to measure the continuity of his thought: the idea of philosophy as self-reflecting, the idea of a dialectical series, and the idea of the continuity of thought and action. The connection of any two of these can be understood only in terms of the third.

The first of these ideas was relatively dominant in *Speculum Mentis* (as the title itself indicates) and the second in the *Essay on Philosophical Method*. The third is not in the focus of attention in either; and when in his *Autobiography* Collingwood wrote that all his life he had been working at a rapprochement between theory and practice (A, 147), few readers remembered that the first sentence of *Speculum Mentis* is "All thought exists for the sake of action," and most dismissed the final chapter of the *Autobiography* as an unfortunate attempt to find scapegoats for the agonies and confusions of a Europe on the brink of war.

But the continuity of thought and action was not just an *obiter dictum* of Collingwood's. He had a firm grasp of its detailed elaboration as the continuity of a dialectical series and one which exhibits the self-reflective character of philosophical thought; this theory was the substance of his moral philosophy, which expanded from the initial sketches of the ethical chapters of *Speculum Mentis* to the final form outlined, after a lapse of years, in the first part of *The*

New Leviathan. It was in fact to moral philosophy that the method expounded in the *Essay on Philosophical Method* was first applied in his unpublished lectures.[1] The latter, as we can see from their partial use in *The New Leviathan,* contained his attempts to give content to the otherwise formal stages of a dialectic abstractly conceived; at the same time they contribute half of his dialectical theory of mind of which the other half is contained (mostly) in *The Principles of Art* and (partly) in *The Idea of History.*

One might say that in his lectures on moral philosophy Collingwood was discovering the link between the dialectic of forms of experience, in *Speculum Mentis,* and the dialectic of concepts, in the *Essay on Philosophical Method.* The former was, so to speak, too rich to be comprehended (as experience itself is), and the latter too thin and formal to substitute for its exemplifications (as concepts themselves are). The middle ground between the dialectic of experience and the dialectic of concepts, Collingwood found, is the dialectic of mind. This completes the overall figure in the carpet; and its importance for the understanding of Collingwood is enhanced by the fact that his complete theory of mind does not appear in any one of his books but is distributed among them according to the specific topics they take up. In this regard I think it true to say that one cannot understand *The Idea of History* apart from *The Principles of Art,* nor *The Principles of Art* apart from *The New Leviathan.* Each contains arabesques and variations of the figure which is discernible in all but contained in none.

When Collingwood wrote *The New Leviathan,* he consciously modeled the organization of the book on the predecessor whose title he adopted. It has four main parts, "Man," "Society," "Civilization," and "Barbarism," corresponding to Hobbes's sections, "Of Man," "Of Common-wealth," "Of a Christian Common-wealth," and "Of the Kingdome of Darknesse." It contains "Three Laws of Politics" corresponding to Hobbes's "laws of nature." Most importantly, the order of chapters and of the argument itself in Part I roughly corresponds to that in Hobbes: both begin (strikingly enough for books on political theory) with studies of the human faculties of sensation and thought, of passion and desire; both devote an early chapter to the connection of language and reason and both advance a theory of language as "naming"; and both show the emergence of moral terms such as "good" and "evil" as the names of the objects of men's desires and aversions (*Leviathan,* I, 15; NL, 11.5 ff.).

One cannot read *The New Leviathan* without regarding it as a series of reflections on Hobbes, an attempt to bring the *Leviathan* up to date, as Collingwood says (NL, iv). And yet, at least where the important Part I is concerned, this impression is undoubtedly specious. Hobbes provides the literary form and a *point d'appui*. But the *Leviathan* is actually an occasion for Collingwood's reflection, not the object of it. The real object is the sketch of an ethical system in *Speculum Mentis,* as Collingwood had extended and revised it over many years in his lectures on moral philosophy. Part I of *The New Leviathan* contains little that Collingwood had not worked out more elaborately many years before. In both the order and content of argument it repeats his lectures on moral philosophy, which applied to ethics the characteristics of philosophical argument discussed in the *Essay on Philosophical Method.* It is an analysis of "orders" of consciousness or mind whose formal properties are those of the "scale of forms" in which, according to the latter book, philosophical concepts are ordered.

In Hobbes's *Leviathan,* the order of topics discussed is: sense, imagination, speech, the passions, the virtues. In *The New Leviathan,* the order is: feeling (which includes sensation), language, appetite and desire (together corresponding to Hobbes's "passions"), choice, and will. Why did Collingwood omit "imagination"? Because he had said all that he had to say on that subject in *The Principles of Art* and because, while imagination is obviously part of a philosophical psychology systematically developed, it is not specifically relevant to answering the questions directly raised in *The New Leviathan.* Consistent with his own Logic of Question and Answer, Collingwood never undertook to state a *complete* theory of anything, one which would anticipate all possible non-factual questions about its subject-matter. Rather he developed only so much of theory as necessary to answer the questions specifically posed. No doubt this is the only effective way to prosecute one's own inquiries; yet it puts on one's interpreter—in the course of pursuing *his* inquiries—the burden of reconstructing the connections or lack of them between the fragments here and there revealed. The important fact is that in Collingwood's case this can be done with fair completeness and precision.

The two sections which follow attempt to outline in some detail Collingwood's dialectical theory of mind, divided into "levels" of practical consciousness (section 2) and "levels" of cognitive consciousness (section 3). The former section is mainly an account of the moral philosophy finally recorded in Part I of *The New*

Leviathan; the latter section draws mainly on *The Idea of History* and *The Principles of Art.* Sections 4 and 5 extend the interpretation and assessment of the integral theory, and section 6 shows its formal correspondence with the dialectic of experience in *Speculum Mentis.* This chapter is exclusively concerned with what might be called the "vertical" series of levels of consciousness. In the following chapter I shall try to show that Collingwood's famous "theory of absolute presuppositions" introduces a "horizontal" dimension of change over time into the fourth or highest level of consciousness in the vertical series. The diagram on page 117 may be convenient for reference, since it sums up the complicated dimensions and relations of the theory of mind, but it is of course barely intelligible apart from the specific discussions which it represents. Visual models are at best not very suitable for representing dialectical relations. They are neatly adapted to the discussion of extensional logic (for example, to the representation of a class divided into mutually exclusive and exhaustive sub-classes); but how could one represent in spatial properties that relation of concepts which "fuses difference of degree and difference of kind, relation of distinction and relation of opposition"?

In the sketch of Collingwood's theory of mind which follows there is some criticism and modification; the difference is clear, I hope, between what Collingwood said and what I believe him to have intended, between what he meant and what, for critical reasons, I believe he ought to have said. But the purpose of the following sections is not primarily to assess the merits of the theory but to show that it exhibits the same structure which we have seen evidenced in the dialectic of experience and the dialectic of concepts. For if this interpretation is correct, the question of assessment is greatly altered, and most of the criticisms which have been lodged against Collingwood by other philosophers prove to have been very wide of the mark indeed.

2 · *Collingwood's Theory of Mind: The Levels of Practical Consciousness*

The moral philosophy which Collingwood developed systematically after the initial sketches of *Speculum Mentis* has two main divisions, an analysis and criticism of ethical theories and a philosophical psychology. The connection between these two parts of moral philosophy is very intimate: the philosophical psychology is not just a preface to ethics but was developed point by point in parallel with the latter. The ethics consists of an analysis of three types of ethical theory: utilitarianism, which regards actions as means to ends; the ethics of right, which regards actions as conforming to rules; and the ethics of duty, which regards actions as inseparable from the "concrete" responsibility of human agents. The philosophical psychology has as its main descriptive categories, or levels of consciousness, appetite, desire, and will. The preference for triads of categories has no especial significance; Collingwood neither mentions nor covertly relies on the textbook dialectic of "thesis-antithesis-synthesis." Nevertheless, the relation among the three ethical theories and that among the three psychic functions is that of a dialectical series.

In both cases there is an order of "higher" and "lower" levels: the ethics of duty is the highest of the types of ethical theory, and will is the highest of the psychic functions. Each lower level is a necessary condition of, although it does not necessitate the emergence of, the next higher level. It cannot give rise to anything other than the next higher level, but it may not, in any specific case, give rise to anything at all. Moreover, each lower level survives in the next and, in fact, in all higher levels; and each higher level makes explicit or actual what in the lower level is only implicit or potential. Ethical theories deal with intentional action, which is possible only at the level of will; thus Collingwood is not naively regarding the three ethical theories as simply coordinated with and expressions of the three levels of consciousness respectively. Yet the kinds of action with which the ethical theories deal replicate, at the level of will, the same dialectical order as the levels of consciousness themselves.

Collingwood's view of the psyche can be compared (recognizing that no spatial metaphor adequately represents a dialectical series, whose stages do not have "simple location") to the concentric layers of an onion or to the ancient models of the planetary system as a set of nesting spheres. At the core are the organic processes of the body, those physical and biological processes which go on in independence of any level of consciousness. These are in a sense outside the psyche, since as purely organic processes they are never direct objects of consciousness, although they are the necessary condition of all consciousness; but they are "outside" only in the sense in which the convex shape of a curve is outside its concave shape, not in the sense in which, for example, a cause is outside its effect. The first level of consciousness, which Collingwood calls *feeling,* is not an effect or concomitant of processes in the sensory-motor, physico-chemical, metabolic, and other systems of the functioning organism, it *is* those processes as they are felt rather than observed. Feeling is the completely transient, momentary, unlocalized and undifferentiated awareness of the organic states and changes of the body. Enough traces of pure feeling, even though fleeting ones, survive in higher consciousness for us to identify and evoke this most rudimentary level: it is exemplified in the vague sense of well-being, irritation, or unease, or in the feeling that something is wrong without identifying it as internal or external or even being able to raise that question (since the distinction between "internal" and "external" itself emerges only at a higher level). Even the awareness of the continuity of feeling, i.e., the awareness that one *has* the feeling (an awareness which requires a rudimentary sense of the difference between self and environment) emerges only at the second level, that of *appetite.* Undifferentiated awareness of organic lack or need is feeling; appetite is the awareness that *I* want something, don't have it, but cannot say what it might be. The well-being and unease of pure feeling now are specified as satisfaction and dissatisfaction, as the *consciousness* of well-being or unease. The moment one is able to identify an object or state which seems to be the object of appetite, one has moved to the third level of *desire.* At the level of appetite I want something; at the level of desire I am conscious of wanting something; and at this level one can for the first time identify something specific as possibly satisfying desire, and therefore for the first time question whether it really will do so. The level of desire is thus the level of questioning, or the lowest level of *explicit* thought, capable of recognizing alternatives: "Which do I really desire: this or that?"

Now as appetite is the consciousness of feeling, and desire is the consciousness of appetite, so to take one more step to the consciousness of desire is to move to the fourth level of *will,* the characteristically human level. At the level of desire there is already rudimentary or implicit choice, but it is awareness of *having* an option (like Buridan's ass, say) not yet consciousness of oneself as *making* a choice. Desire becomes action as one thing is chosen in preference to another. Furthermore, only at the level of will does the notion of value become explicit, and this alone makes possible the criticism and modification of desire; so at the level of will, or explicit choice, the objects of choice are not things but *actions*. (Buridan's ass cannot decide, as a third-level choice, between exactly equal piles of hay as objects of desire, and since it cannot move to the level of will, it cannot choose, as a fourth-level action, between eating something and eating nothing.)

In this series of mental functions, the level of will is the highest order of consciousness; but it also contains sub-levels within itself. Choice, at the level of will, may be either "capricious" or "rational." In either case, a course of action is chosen as the most valuable alternative. Capricious choice, however (and while caprice is not fully rational, in Collingwood's special sense, it is not irrational), consists of acting in this way or that in the conviction that it is *good* but without reasons for that conviction. Rational choice, on the other hand, is acting in this way or that *because* of a reason for thinking it good. It represents the highest possible level of consciousness, presumably because the recognition of oneself as acting because of reasons for choosing that action could be superseded only by further acts of the same level, e.g., by justifying, explaining, modifying, or even perhaps abandoning the relevant reasons by reference to *other* reasons. In capricious choice I may act *as if* I had a reason; I may even, as in the case of habitual actions, have a reason in the sense that I am always capable of producing a reason *if the question is raised*. To produce a reason is of course to move from capricious to rational choice. But in capricious choice the reason remains implicit, and the action does not proceed, as it does in the case of rational choice, from the *awareness* of the reason as my reason.

The dialectic of consciousness is thus an example of a scale of forms leading from the lowest level of pure undifferentiated feeling to the most complicated level of rational deliberation by a series of stages in which the conscious acts of each level above the first transform lower level acts by making them objects of consciousness. But what we have considered so far is only the armature of this series of levels; appended to it are other and corresponding series, most notably the series of emotions, more complex at each level but similarly derivative from the emotional states of lower levels, and the series of intrinsic values, that is, of goals of action or ideal states of being.

Pure feeling itself, although undifferentiated with respect to locus, object, or type, has both sensuous and emotional aspects. At the second level of consciousness, or appetite, sensation and emotion are distinguishable from each other and each supports its own distinctions: within sensation there are differences among different sense-data and types of sense-data (Collingwood discusses this only in *The Principles of Art*); within emotion there is a difference between the two primary emotions, hunger and love, corresponding to the organic processes of nutrition and reproduction. Hunger is the active element in any appetite which seeks the restoration of vital energy. It is directed entirely to a state of the self, although it is not itself capable of distinguishing self from not-self. Love, which is not a form of hunger but could not exist except as an active element in appetite which also included the element of hunger, seeks attachment to or possession of something other than present wants or needs; it is, Collingwood says, the appetite for a self not yet realized.[2] Both hunger and love are subject to frustration, and, as they themselves are activities, the forms of their frustration are *passions*. The sense of hunger thwarted is fear; as hunger is the appetite for self-restoration, fear results in the impulse to self-protection. The sense of love thwarted is anger; like love, anger is directed outward and seeking an object, but expresses itself as an impulse to destroy that object rather than to possess it.

FIGURE I

The Levels of Practical Consciousness

Levels of Consciousness:	1st	2nd	3rd	4th
Psychic Functions: Active Emotions: Passive Emotions:	PURE FEELING Hunger, Love Fear, Anger	→APPETITE —— [Repeated and transformed at all higher levels]	→ DESIRE	→ WILL Capricious Ration... Choice → Cho... ↓ Utili... ↓ Rig... ↓ Du...
Forms of Value:	Pleasure and Pain	Satisfaction and Dissatisfaction	Happiness and Unhappiness	Good and Evil

Hunger and love, fear and anger, also reappear at the higher level of desire but they now have identifiable objects, as "hunger for X" and "love of X"; and in fact these activities and passions survive also at the level of will, although they are transformed at the higher levels not per se but in the complexity and relations of their objects. There is not a fourth-level hunger, but the appetitive activity of hunger survives in the moral convictions and deliberations at the fourth level, which have, however, objects unknown to appetite itself.

To each level, also, there corresponds a form of intrinsic value and disvalue: to the level of feeling, pleasure and pain; to the level of appetite, satisfaction and dissatisfaction; to the level of desire, happiness and unhappiness; and to the level of will, good and evil. Feeling, appetite, and the rest are activities or acts; pleasure, satisfaction, and the rest are qualities of the states in which activity, at least temporarily, terminates, and pain, dissatisfaction, and the rest are qualities of the activities insofar as they are felt as incomplete. But these forms of value and disvalue also are points of transition from one level to the next—that is, they make the transition possible although they do not compel it. Satisfaction, for example, implies the presence of dissatisfaction being overcome. (In this it is unlike pleasure, which does not imply the overcoming of pain. There can be pleasant surprises, but not satisfying surprises.) Hence appetite, unlike feeling, necessarily contains both positive and negative elements; dissatisfaction is a condition of satisfaction. Pleasures and pains, like feeling tones, are momentary and "here-and-now"; satisfaction and dissatisfaction cannot exist without continuity and as elements of a process containing both. In this they reflect the characteristics of appetite; but they are also the characteristics which make possible the transition from appetite to desire. Appetite itself is a drive toward a goal, although it is not aware of itself as this; to become so aware is already to have been converted into desire. But such awareness comes about only when satisfaction is singled out from appetite as something absent compared with something present. Presumably animals are incapable of this; also, at the level of appetite satisfaction as well as dissatisfaction must be felt at every stage. An animal hunts not only because as hungry it is dissatisfied but also because it enjoys hunting, and finds satisfaction in the activity itself. The step from appetite to desire comes with the consciousness of the *absent* satisfaction, for only with such consciousness of the absent can satisfactions be postponed, expedited, compared, and criticized.

As the bridge between appetite and desire is the transition from satisfaction as a state to satisfaction as a goal, so the transition from desire to will crosses the bridge of happiness and unhappiness. With happiness emerges the notion of *worth*. Any satisfaction of an appetite has value; for happiness, however, some satisfactions are worth having and some are not. Collingwood approved of John Stuart Mill's apostasy from "utilitarianism" in his doctrine that pleasures are comparable qualitatively as well as quantitatively (cf. EPM, 79). In Collingwood's terms, one might say that Bentham's form of utilitarianism reproduces at the level of thought the characteristics of the level of appetite ("push-pin is as good as poetry"). Mill's distinction of qualities of "pleasure" is a move to the level of desire, with its proper value of happiness ("better to be Socrates dissatisfied than a fool satisfied"). For Collingwood, the ethics corresponding to this level is an ethics of rule or principle; and the relevance of his categories may be confirmed by the fact that Mill verged on such an ethics in his attempt, quite foreign to Bentham, to give a "utilitarian" defense of moral principles as having no practical exceptions.

What satisfaction is to appetite and happiness is to desire, the *good* is to will. Collingwood stresses that the activity of choice does not presuppose but is identical with the judgment of value. One does not judge something to be good and then choose it for that reason; "it is in choosing it that [one] comes to think of it as good. The act of choice and the judgment of value are the same thing." "Good" is not properly a predicate of things or of states but of actions (as only actions are the proper objects of choice, whether capricious or rational). An action is called good to the extent that it is part of a larger whole of activity for the sake of which it is done. One might ask: but then what is the value of the "larger whole"? This question conceals a fatal objection to the attempt to define good relationally; but so far from being an objection to Collingwood's provisional statement, it actually precipitates a dialectic of the idea of good which itself recapitulates the dialectical order of appetite, desire, and will—or of satisfaction, happiness, and good. There is, so to speak, not only second-level satisfaction and third-level *consciousness* of satisfaction (whose own value is happiness), but a fourth-level *theory* of satisfaction.

Such a theory is possible and even inevitable once the fourth level is reached, but it is nevertheless unstable. Its principle is the principle of utility: the attempt to define "good" as the instrumental value of means to ends. It is unstable because the "ends" are found to recede and turn out themselves to be only instrumental rather than consummatory; and as ends recede, the derivative value of means evanesces.

In this logical predicament, one might try to pin down and justify particular ends by references to sources of value outside the process of thought and action. (As the Tablets of the Law shatter into shards, hopeful empiricists tell us that biology and psychology will discover the *natural* good for man if we will just wait a little longer.) Collingwood does not dignify such fantasies even by noticing them. In his view, the natural logic of thought, once the principle of utility has proved unstable, is to move from the relation of incomplete and completed acts to the relation between a particular act and the schema or abstract idea which it exemplifies. By this move the principle of utility is transformed into the principle of right; goodness then is seen as belonging derivatively to particular acts in virtue of their conformity to general commands or rules. But "the good itself escapes once more," because neither the act nor the rule is good per se. The act is good only derivatively as conforming to the rule; the rule, on the other hand, is abstract and cannot be willed in itself: it is as impossible to will a law without willing instances of it as it is to will an end without willing the means.

Thought therefore is impelled to a "third form of goodness." [3] This is Collingwood's own ethics, as obscure as it is interesting and for the same reason: it has few affinities with recent (that is, in the last half-century or so) discussions of ethics, almost all of which deal with problems arising at the two prior levels. The nerve of argument in the discussion of the "third form of goodness" however, is plain. Collingwood has argued that means and ends, acts and rules, both undergo upon analysis a kind of diremption; in neither case can one identify a *concrete* whole which can be called good in such a way that the value of the whole is replicated in each of its parts (like the vital energy of an organism) rather than vanishing when the whole is analyzed into its parts (like the shape of a physical object). Suppose, Collingwood suggests, that in a particular action we could be aware of ourselves not as *doing* A and *intending* to do B when the completion of A has made it possible (and this is how we ordinarily think of a series of actions), but as already completely engaged in doing the whole act A—B. Then the relevance of the distinction between means and end would disappear; A would be good not as a means to B but as already sharing all the value of A—B. Suppose again that in obeying a rule we could think of ourselves as not only obeying it but making it (this is Kantian), and that making the rule and applying it to an individual case could be conceived as one and the same act so that the rule is no abstraction but "the presence of the whole in each of its parts" (but this is not Kantian). The coincidence of these two suppositions is the third form of goodness.

The key terms in these "suppositions" are, I think, not the terminology of whole and part, but those from the vocabulary of consciousness: suppose that we "could be aware . . . ," "could think of ourselves," that a rule "could be conceived." At bottom, Collingwood's thesis is that the moral characteristics of action are inseparable from the way in which the agent thinks of the action and from the extent to which the action is what it is as part of intentional activity which goes beyond—possibly far beyond—it. The third form of goodness therefore includes the other two forms: it combines the means-ends analysis of a situation with the act-rule analysis of a situation but it transforms both from the standpoint of a consciousness for which the logical disparateness of means from end and act from rule has disappeared. From such a standpoint, Collingwood indicated in his *Autobiography,* action is "extemporized" or "improvised" (A, 102, 105) without recourse to any "ready-made rules at all," although it is possible "only for people of experience and intelligence, and even then occurs only when they take a situation very seriously" (A, 105). Within such an action, one might say, it is possible to distinguish rule from act, or means from end, *only in retrospect.* The action itself goes beyond counsels of prudence or rules of morality in attempting to respond to features of a concrete situation which escape codification by "ready-made rules"—even though it may well provide the experience from which, on reflection, more subtle codifications may emerge. The third form of goodness is itself an historical enactment.

Strictly speaking, the principle of utility and the principle of right were not for Collingwood moral principles at all. Utilitarianism is the conceptual theory of economic activity, regularianism the conceptual theory of political activity. Both are useful and necessary; the former is the rationale of choice in the satisfaction of wants, the latter the rationale of choice in the ordering of social life under institutions of law. Either can be (as both have been) transformed into ethical theory; and even as such neither the ethics of utility nor the ethics of right is wrong in what it affirms. Like any member of a scale of forms, each is in principle wrong only in its own self-limitation and in denying what can be affirmed only at a higher level.

What morality, as the third form of goodness, affirms is that intentional action is always at the same time a choice of oneself; one acts not merely because of what one is but also in order to become what one is not. Yet such a self-creative choice is not a kind of *fact* of which we may (or may not) become aware; it is a situation which comes into being and is constituted only as it is consciously affirmed. It is at this point that Collingwood comes closest to the view of human nature which has been given currency in modern existentialism, but with a difference. Collingwood is more radically dialectical than any existentialist in this respect. For an existentialist like Sartre, consciousness or *l'être-pour-soi* is completely cut off from the causal nexus of nature, although it evades the anxiety of total responsibility for its own self-creation by inventing pathological forms of inauthenticity in which it regards itself as a "thing," a determinate outcome of causal forces in its own past and in its contemporary world. For Sartre, the self is always absolutely free, self-creating, and responsible; but it also regards itself as conditioned, determined and excused. The forms of this pathology are many; but all depend on the dichotomy of *l'être-en-soi* (or physical nature including the body) and *l'être-pour-soi* (or human consciousness). These are mutually exclusive; but the latter may *masquerade* as the former so successfully as to deceive itself.

Collingwood's theory of mind admits no such dualism, nor any "single-level" view of human nature. Fourth-level consciousness is not an intrusion into the causal nexus of the natural world, "superfluous" and *de trop*. It emerges from that world, to which it remains forever attached through its bodily processes and activities, and the elements of all lower levels of consciousness survive at higher levels. But as consciousness at lower levels reflects the world, at higher levels it transforms and expands it. From the standpoint of lower levels, the human world contains only behavior, which can be adequately described as it appears to an observer; for the fourth level, the world contains also *action,* which is constituted as well as recognized only by rational consciousness; and action cannot be described merely as it appears to observers but requires essential reference to the way in which it is conceived by its agents (cf. A, 102).[4] The freedom of consciousness is not an "absolute" freedom; it is the freedom of men who are creatures of feeling, appetite, and desire as well as the creators of mind.

3 · Collingwood's Theory of Mind: The Levels of Cognitive Consciousness

So far we have sketched out Collingwood's system of levels of consciousness, almost entirely as it was developed by 1933, not so much for the purpose of defending or criticizing it as to show the extent to which its controlling ideas are dialectical and exhibit the complexity of consciousness itself as having the pattern of a "scale of forms." But even so the theory of mind is not complete and the evidence for the interpretation is not all in. Dealing with questions of moral philosophy, Collingwood worked out only those strands in the series of mental functions which relate forms of emotion, activity, and value at the different levels of consciousness. These are the strands involved in an analysis of action; but rather obviously the theory of levels of consciousness should also be relevant to an analysis of knowing; and indeed Collingwood worked out, in other contexts and in order to answer different questions, the connections of the levels of consciousness as stages of cognitive activity. Two discussions of these stages complete the theory which Collingwood never stated or outlined in a single place: one in *The New Leviathan,* the other in *The Principles of Art.*

In the final form of the theory as we may reconstruct it in toto, both practical activity and cognitive activity are distinguished into four levels of consciousness. At the first level they are not separated at all. At the second and third levels, they are connected but may be separately analyzed At the fourth level—and, as we shall see, this is one of Collingwood's most original and difficult doctrines—they are reunited. The second level has *imagination* as the cognitive activity corresponding to the practical activity of appetite; and the third level—although at this point Collingwood's scheme must be filled out inferentially—has *perception* as the cognitive activity corresponding to the practical activity of desire. Fourth-level cognitive activity, as one might expect, is *reason,* or intellect; it has a degree of identity with the practical activity of will—it is, so to speak, the obverse of will—which is impossible of attainment at the second and third levels.

In distinguishing the levels of practical consciousness, Collingwood throughout took pains to characterize the development from feeling to rational choice as a development of "thought," by which he meant the activity, at any level, of making distinctions within what, at a lower level, is an undifferentiated field, or of unifying elements which at a lower level are discrete, and of seeking not only to unify them but to "find in them or put into them some concretion." In general, Collingwood regarded "thought" as present in any conscious activity which is aware, however dimly, of a contrast between what is immediately present and what is not. Absent from the psychical level of pure feeling (which contains only an undifferentiated here-and-now), thought appears in its most rudimentary form at the level of appetite, in which consciousness is modified by an orientation toward an unrealized future, even though this future appears not as something imagined or conceived but as a "feeling-tone suffusing the present." Thought as the possibility of knowledge appears first at the level of desire, at which level there is both explicit recollection and imagination, and satisfaction regarded as a future state is the want which impels action. In discussing "desire" Collingwood once quoted Spinoza, "Cupiditas est appetitus cum cuisdem conscientia" (*Ethics* III, ix, *Schol.*), and he apparently regarded desire as the minimum level of characteristically human rationality, remarking that "the price of knowledge is to lose the consciousness of wanting to do just what we are doing and nothing else. . . . The sword of thought prevents us from returning to the paradise garden of the beasts." At the level of will, thought introduces a new complexity because of its capacity to criticize desire: desire, so to speak, knows what it wants but not what it does not want. The *comparison* between what is desired and what is not is an activity of the fourth level; moreover, it is a kind of thinking which may actually modify desire. The comparison between what is desired and what is not further makes it possible to recognize a distinction between what is apparently desired and what is *really* desired; desire, because it is a form of thought, can be mistaken. Finally, only at the level of rational choice does thought become fully explicit in its ordinary sense of inferential reasoning. This completes a cycle at the level of will which reproduces a similar cycle at the level of desire, a cycle which moves from opinion through reflection to conviction. At the level of desire, the first stage beyond appetite is an affirmation: "What I want is X"; reflection then introduces a negative element: "What I want is X, and not Y"; and this leads to the conviction, which is identical with "capricious choice," that "what I *really* want is X rather than Y." But the latter is equivalent to "X is good," an immediate judgment for which reflection can then produce a reason; and rational choice is the reaffirmaton of X as good *with* the reason for its being so. For Collingwood, knowledge, as Socrates says in the *Meno*, is "opinion fastened by a chain": at the level of desire opinion becomes conviction as a result of critical comparison, at the level of will as a result of inferential reasoning.[5]

In *The New Leviathan* appetite, desire, and will are explicitly identified with forms of *cognitive* consciousness, and consciousness in general is identified with thought. Second-level consciousness Collingwood calls "conceptual thinking"; third-level consciousness is called "propositional thinking"; and fourth-level consciousness is called "rational thinking." In general, the relations among these are the relations which have already been described as characterizing levels of consciousness themselves: in particular, each level is said to come into being in the form of acts which have as their objects activities of the next lower level.

"Conceptual thinking" is not in any way a process of inference, as its name may misleadingly suggest. Rather, it is identical with the act of *selective attention* by which discriminations are made within the undifferentiated here-and-now of sensuous-emotional feeling. Thus it is the same activity which in *The Principles of Art* is called "imagination," and it has the same double reference which that term has even in ordinary language: it refers both to the activity of practical consciousness and to the products of that activity, which are objects of contemplation to theoretical consciousness (NL, 4.6). But this is theoretical consciousness in its most embryonic form, and its objects are not categorically different from feeling but are *parts* of the mass of feeling, which become discriminable parts only as they are demarcated and selected by acts of attention. Collingwood even calls this process "abstraction," in the sense in which one abstracts a coin from a heap of coins rather than in the sense in which one abstracts the number five from sets of five objects. In general, the "concepts" of "conceptual thinking" are not the concepts which we would naturally adduce in illustration: *our* fourth-level minds naturally fasten in reflection on third-level concepts. Second-level concepts are not even, as we normally suppose concepts to be, general; an example of a second-level concept is not the concept of redness, but *this* particular red, separated by attention from an attendant flux of feeling (NL, 4.53–4.56; 7.31, 7.38). The justification for this extraordinary usage is that Collingwood is giving a *genetic* account of higher level functions; he is defining the concept of "concept" (and simultaneously exhibiting its connections with the definitions of other concepts, such as "thinking," "consciousness," "knowledge," and "abstraction") exactly as prescribed in the *Essay on Philosophical Method:*

> To define a philosophical concept, . . . it is necessary to think of that concept as specifying itself in a form so rudimentary that anything less would fail to embody the concept at all. This will be the minimum specification of the concept, the lower end of the scale; and the first phase of the definition will consist in stating this. Later phases will modify this minimum definition by adding new determinations, each implied in what went before, but each introducing into it qualitative chances as well as additions and complications . . . [EPM, 100–101].

Propositional thinking, as the activity of third-level consciousness, and rational thinking, as the activity of fourth-level consciousness, require less elucidation. Propositional thinking is explicitly identified with—as in the series of practical functions desire was illustrated by examples from—question-and-answer thinking. "A proposition is an answer to a question" (NL, 11.22): this repeats in the context of the dialectic of mind the doctrine of *Speculum Mentis,* "Assertions are only answers to questions" (SM, 77). The primary questions of propositional thinking are practical: "Which do I want, *a* or *b*?"; but the answers to such questions are statements of fact which may be true or false (NL, 11.32); hence on the theoretical side the *concepts* of truth and falsehood—like the concepts of good and evil on the practical side—emerge at the level of propositional thinking where they were absent from the level of rudimentary conceptual thinking. This illustrates the general point that each level generates new concepts as well as transforming concepts originating at a lower level. Similarly, although the third level *is* propositional and *has* the concept of truth, it follows from Collingwood's scheme that propositions *about* truth, like knowledge in its "eminent" sense (NL, 11.11, n. 1) belong to the fourth level.

Rational thinking, finally, results from reflection on propositional thinking; it too is question-and-answer thinking, but its questions are about the connections among propositions. Distinguishing between the "that" and the "why" as propositional thinking itself does not (NL, 14.2), it is the consciousness of thinking one thing (a proposition) because one thinks another which stands to the first as a reason or ground. There is no higher level of consciousness than this; but there is within it a sub-dialectic of the *kinds* of reasons which can be given in explanation and justification of actions, and this hierarchy we have already met with as the concepts of utility, right, and duty.

Now it may well seem that in his dialectic of consciousness Collingwood has produced the rabbit of reason from the hat of feeling. But it is worth reminding ourselves at this point what he has *not* done. He has not, like traditional rationalism and the rather extensive survival of rationalism in "common-sense," opposed reason to emotion as if one could distinguish between ways of acting which because they are rational are not emotional or which because they are emotional are not rational. He has connected the emotions and passions in such a way that each survives in higher levels but is transformed from being merely a way of being conscious of objects into being itself an object of a more inclusive level of consciousness. The fundamental fact of ethics is the possibility of consciousness of self, where the self is not something which is *there* to be disclosed but comes into being in the process by which it is converted from barely conscious activity to fully conscious action. Moreover, as a higher level gives form to a lower, so the lower gives content to the higher. Whether one moves from a lower to a higher level is always a contingent fact, but it is a necessary truth that the higher depends on and cannot exist apart from the lower. Thus each form of rational activity has its specific emotional aspect. The grain of the marble, so to speak, survives in the finished statue, not eliminated but literally "transformed" or exploited as in the sculptor's use of its definiteness and intractability for his own purposes.

The dialectical relation of emotion and reason, however, has two sides. One is the survival of emotion at higher levels of consciousness and in the more explicit and rational forms of thinking; the other is the presence of thought in more rudimentary and implicit ways at lower levels. Reason and emotion can in fact be distinguished *and* related only at higher levels, and related (dialectically) only at a higher level than that at which they are distinguished (first conceptually and then propositionally). In the earlier versions of his dialectic of mind, Collingwood was primarily concerned with what traditionally has been called *practical reason* rather than with *theoretical reason.* The distinction was not explicitly made until *The New Leviathan,* where he said of practical reason that it "comes into existence when a man forms an intention, reflects on it and asks himself whether he really means it" (NL, 14.32); theoretical reason, on the other hand, "comes into existence when a man first, by propositional thinking, makes up his mind that something is so; and then, seeking to confirm this piece of propositional thinking, looks for a reason why he should think so" (NL, 14.35). By this time, of course, the outline of the dialectic of mind was complete: the analysis of the genesis of practical reason had been supplemented by an analysis of the genesis of theoretical reason in the place where one might least expect it—*The Principles of Art.*

The Principles of Art begins with the problem of defining the term "art" and ends with a theory of aesthetic experience. The link between these is a theory of imagination which alone systematically connects the definition of art with its description. At the same time, Collingwood explicitly claims for his theory of imagination that it has wider relevance to our understanding of the "general structure of experience as a whole," and that it explains the relation of sensation and intellection. His terminology is not uniform with *The New Leviathan* (or for that matter with *The Idea of History,* although to my knowledge no one has yet sought to explain what he says in the latter book about the "historical imagination" by reference to his theory of imagination in *The Principles of Art*), but the relations of ideas, as will appear, reveal the same pattern.

Again Collingwood begins with a discussion of *feeling,* this time distinguishing within it aspects of *sensation* and *emotion.* (Imagine a baby experiencing a terrifying red color.) The two are not separable within feeling, but nevertheless sensation takes a kind of precedence (the baby experiences a terrifying red, not a red terror) in the sense that emotion is a "charge" on a sensum; and there are probably (but how would one tell?) no sensa without their emotional charges. The "sense-data" of empiricist philosophies since Locke are abstractions from the experience of first-level consciousness, not the most concrete constituents of it.

Feeling at this its most primitive psychical level is, as we have already seen, transient, momentary, and unlocalized. Ordinarily we pass from feeling uncomfortable to having an uncomfortable feeling, and thence to "I'm tired" or "It's hot." It is by an act of *attention* that we become aware of having feelings and of their continuity from one moment to another. This is the "primary form of thought"; and it corresponds to the process by which pure feeling is converted into appetite. By the act of attention the sensuous-emotional flux of feeling is converted on the cognitive side into the differentiation of sensations from each other and from their emotional "charges." This conversion is brought about, not by any arbitrary "interpretation" but by the activity of consciousness focusing on a part of the sensory-emotive field, and sharpening and giving definite form and outline to this part while leaving the rest of the field as a penumbra not so converted. This remainder—the "unconscious" part of pure feeling—*could* itself be made an object of attention, but only by an act of attention which differently divided the sensory field. Any given field of feeling can thus be divided in indefinitely many ways by selective attention. There is no normal or correct division, nor is attention causally determined in making one division rather than another, although there are (presumably) some effective determinants, those for instance of habit and of language, both of which are involved in recognition. An architect will *notice* details of a building which another person will not separate out from a more general impression; a painter will attend to contrasts of intensity between two colors where another person will attend only to differences of hue. Such illustrations, however, are partly misleading: they involve relations between sensa explicitly recognized, and the recognition of relations, for Collingwood, belongs to a higher level of consciousness than attention. Attention itself only focuses on a sensory field in such a way as to produce awareness of it; relations are implicit in this awareness, but they become explicit only upon higher-level reflection on the second-level activity of attention. The thought of relations has as its object not sensuous-emotional feeling itself, but the conscious attention to this primary level of consciousness.

Selective attention is directed upon sensuous-emotive feeling from the second level of consciousness; and Collingwood calls this level "imagination." As an activity, imagination (which, in *The Principles of Art,* Collingwood often calls "attention" and sometimes just "consciousness") performs a number of functions. It divides what otherwise is an undifferentiated "block of feeling," separating this into a ("conscious") focus and an ("unconscious") penumbra (PA, 204); it then divides the field of attention into differentiated sensa (NL, 4.54–4.6); it "sterilizes" sensa by separating them from their emotional charges (PA, 162–63; NL, 4.62); finally it converts the sensa so demarcated from transient "impressions" (in Hume's sense) into sensations of which we have become conscious ("ideas," in Hume's sense) and which therefore can be perpetuated beyond momentary experience, revived by thought and compared with other ideas independent of the flux of feeling at the moment (PA, 202, 209). Such comparison, however, does not belong to imagination but to a higher level of thought, which asserts relational patterns among the ideas which are supplied to it as a result of the conversion of impressions into ideas by the activity of imagination (PA, 215–16). Finally, imagination has a kind of bipolarity which is present in any activity of thought but absent from the psychical level of pure feeling. Imagination is not assertive, hence it makes no statements capable of being true or false. But at the same time it does *express,* although it does not assert, propositions about feeling. Collingwood somewhat misleadingly but not inconsistently says that "the kind of phrase which expresses what [consciousness at the level of imagination] thinks is something like 'This is how I feel'" (PA, 213, 216). (Properly, I think, the "kind of phrase" which *expresses* second-level consciousness is a poetic image or metaphor, understood from the viewpoint of a higher level as expressing what cannot be formulated at the second level itself.) The logic of "something like 'This is how I feel,'" Collingwood says, differs from the logic of statements (i.e., the logic of propositional thinking at the third level of consciousness): it does not involve the subsumption of experience under (third-level) concepts and therefore is not subject to that kind of error (e.g., "This is a book," when it is not a book but a trompe l'oeil cigarette box). Hence what "This is how I feel" expresses cannot be false. But it does have an opposite, although a pre-logical one; it may *fail* to express a feeling, in the sense that it fails to bring that feeling into consciousness, and such disowning of feeling or distraction from it Collingwood calls the "corruption" of consciousness (PA, 217). The distinction between truth and falsehood cannot be made at the second level, but there exists even at this level the rudimentary bipolarity, the "protoplasm" of untruth out of which the concepts of truth and falsehood develop (or, in the language of *The New Leviathan,* from which they are "abstractions"). Imagination can thus be untruthful but it cannot be aware of itself as untruthful; such an awareness can occur only at a higher level (PA, 219).

Brief as this summary is, it may serve to indicate that "imagination" is for Collingwood a versatile activity indeed. And it may serve also to suggest that the dialectical series of mental functions is not at all like a production line, in which each worker repeats the same job over and over as raw material enters the line at one end to emerge at the other as a complex product. Imagination does not just solder a connection as each bit of feeling passes by. As analogies go, imagination is more like a housewife, at various times selecting foodstuffs at the market, storing them for future use, arranging them in storage according to some pattern of use, and finally combining and transforming them into dishes for consumption. (This homely analogy may even bear the weight of saying that as a consumer of her own product a housewife is engaged in a third-level activity and as a judge of its culinary and nutritive merits she is engaged in a fourth-level activity). But the versatility of imagination is emphasized at a price: how, as a form of theoretical consciousness, it is related to the forms of practical consciousness finely detailed elsewhere by Collingwood is not easy to spell out.

This is not, I think, to Collingwood's discredit. It shows rather that in *The Principles of Art* he was asking and trying to answer questions about *art,* with the leading principles of his theory of mind as guides, rather than asking and answering questions about the formal structure of his theory, using art as a convenient source of illustrations. But it is not impossible to show how, with minor modifications, his theory of imagination can fit comfortably into the theory of mind. In the discussion of imagination as second-level cognitive consciousness, Collingwood means by "imagination" in some contexts the activity by which the second level is attained, in others, the results of that activity (i.e., the second level itself), and, in still others, the activities by which the second level is transcended and a higher level reached. (The same would be true of "appetite" as second-level practical consciousness.) This ambiguity is perhaps inescapable in expressing the fundamental character of the series of mental functions as stages in a continuous *process:* levels of consciousness are not separated from each other like the floors of a building but like the ontogenetic stages of childhood, adolescence, and maturity. In the case of "imagination," the range of the series which it is used to denote is rather broader and therefore somewhat more various.

All of the different functions of imagination fall into three main types. First, there is the differentiation of an otherwise undifferentiated flux of feeling at the psychical level; this is an activity of practical consciousness producing objects of cognitive consciousness (cf. NL, 4.6), which are *sensa,* or "impressions," differing from each other within a single experience with respect to position and order, separated from the emotional charge on feeling, and distinguished by modalities of the sensory order: seeing, hearing, etc. The result is sentience or *sensation,* a modification of pure feeling but not yet imagination proper. Second, we may become conscious of our sensation and its sensa; the act of sensation is not present to itself, but may be present, together with its objects, to the form of consciousness called attention (PA, 206); and this consciousness, which is the subject of almost all of the discussion in the theory of imagination in *The Principles of Art,* is the one which converts impressions into ideas, distinguishes between act and object, and therefore as theoretical consciousness first gives rise to the distinction between self and not-self corresponding to that distinction at the level of appetite as the second-level form of practical consciousness (cf. PA, 206, 222). The consciousness of feeling differentiated into sensation is imagination—the second level of consciousness in its theoretical form. But the object of imagination is still a "here-and-now." By attention it has transformed impressions into ideas, although as objects which it can merely retain beyond momentary impressions but not recollect, compare, or modify; and "the conceptions of past, future, the possible, the hypothetical are as meaningless for imagination as they are for feeling itself" (PA, 224).

Hume asked whether it is possible to have an idea of a shade of blue which one has in fact never seen (*Enquiry Concerning Human Understanding,* II, 16). This was an embarrassing but honest question, since he was inclined to admit that one could, although it followed from his own principle that all ideas correspond to prior impressions that one could not. For Collingwood it is also clear that the idea of a hypothetical sensum is as impossible as is an unsensed sensum. But the problem suggests that one must take one more step, to the consciousness whose object is imagination together with *its* objects. There is no name for this third-level cognitive consciousness, but the third main type of functions of imagination which he recognizes must belong to this level, or at least to the activity by which it is reached. Two of these are especially important: the "bi-polarity" of imagination and the capacity to compare present experience with past, anticipated, and possible experiences. Collingwood consistently insists that the *comparison* of ideas is a function of thought higher than imagination. But he did not clearly see that some bridge is necessary between the temporary perpetuation of sensa by fixing attention on them, and the availability to comparative thinking of a wide range of ideas, revived in memory and summoned up in what is ordinarily called "imagination," as well as merely salvaged temporarily by becoming conscious of impressions which otherwise would drift out of consciousness with the rest of feeling. And this bridge can be provided by imagination itself, with the proviso that as sensation is not present to itself but becomes an object for imagination, so imagination is not present to itself but becomes an object for third-level consciousness. Imagination revives and constructs ideas as well as converting impressions into ideas, but although it can hold together in a single experience present, remembered past, and anticipated future, it does not itself distinguish past, present, and future. It adds to the here-and-now of present experience a there-and-then of other experience, although it does not recognize the difference between them, and fuses them into a single imaginative experience, where what a higher level of consciousness will distinguish as *relations* between parts of the experience appear only as qualities of the total experience itself (PA, 253; cf. also PA, 237). This activity provides the transition from the second to the third level; it corresponds, on the side of theoretical consciousness, to the passions on the side of practical consciousness. Such an extension of imagination is clearly necessary if any credit is to be attached, for instance, to Collingwood's claim that the understanding of language depends on the hearer's ability to reconstruct by an act of imagination the ideas expressed by the words he hears (PA, 251). Here, "imagination" clearly extends beyond the conversion of present impressions into ideas.

The bipolarity of imagination also, as we have seen, belongs neither to the second nor to the third level, but to the transition from one to the other. In the series of forms of practical consciousness, appetite has no negative form (NL, 11.21) and desire has, as a form of propositional thinking which is subject to criteria of truth and falsity (NL, 11.3). The bipolarity of imagination, represented in the possibility of "disowning feeling," therefore, is also a step beyond the second level but one which has not yet reached the third level.

Yet the "third level" cannot itself be the level of "intellect"; like intellect, it can deal, as imagination cannot, with relations; but as one step removed from imagination whose object can only be a here-and-now, its obvious function is the *consciousness* of the here-and-now as *here* and *now,* which permits it to compare it with a there-and-then. Its characteristic statements are like, "It's warmer than it was," or "The colors in this reproduction are washed out." It requires *another* step beyond this to reach the level of abstract thought, clearly an example of intellect if not coextensive with it, which can compare its immediate objects not only with others remembered or imagined, but with others *not even imagined* but thought of as variables defined in a relational scheme (PA, 253–54); e.g., one decides whether a figure is a chiliagon not by comparing it with the remembered image of a chiliagon but by seeing whether it has the properties which any chiliagon must have. As Kant pointed out, the image of a 1000-sided figure does not *appear* different from that of a 999-sided figure; they are distinguished by counting the sides, which settles the question although it does not make the *images* any more precise or discriminable.

It seems therefore that we must interpolate a third level, some of whose characteristics Collingwood casually identified with the process *from* the second level by which it is reached, and others with the process *to* the fourth level of intellect to which it gives rise. This level corresponds appropriately to desire as the third level of *practical* consciousness: as desire is the appetite for a specific object with the consciousness of alternatives to it, so third-level cognitive consciousness is the apprehension of specific objects with the consciousness of their contrasts. Desire asks, "Which do I want, X or Y?" and answers "X *and not* Y." Third-level cognitive consciousness (interrogative, like all propositional thinking) asks, "Is that animal a small pony or a large dog?" and answers "Not a pony but a dog."

The proper name for this level, I presume, is "perception," the link between imagination and intellect as imagination is between sensation and itself. Now although Book II of *The Principles of Art* discusses many of the problems arising out of an analysis of perception, the term "perception" is so conspicuous by its absence that it must have required controlled effort to avoid it. No doubt this is in part because, as was said above, Collingwood was not undertaking to outline a complete theory of knowledge but to answer questions about art, and therefore ignored distinctions and problems not directly relevant to this purpose. But he had also written, in 1935, that the accounts of knowledge by English philosophers, "based as they seem to be primarily on the study of perception and of scientific thinking, not only ignore historical thinking but are actually inconsistent with there being such a thing" (IH, 233). The secret background of his avoidance of a theory of perception as such may well have been the sense that to pursue its special problems is to risk accepting the presuppositions in terms of which those problems are formulated, presuppositions which inhibit the possibility of attaining historical consciousness—as, say, a preoccupation with the theological problems of the idea of Providence can abort the scientific consciousness which seeks the natural causes of events rather than their divine purposes.

Nevertheless, that a third level of perceptual consciousness can be interpolated in the series of cognitive functions without strain, if also without Collingwood's explicit authority, shows that the dialectical schema of mind is open although not indeterminate. Collingwood's leading ideas are regulative ideas, not axioms of a deductive system. They are, at bottom, ways of thinking about something, not premises from which deductions are made. To adapt the neat image which Collingwood used in *The New Leviathan,* they are rules for determining the positions at which soundings are to be taken, and one cannot deduce or predict from such rules the depth of water that will be found (NL, 9.37–39). The reconstruction suggested above shows that the problem of fitting Collingwood's three-termed schema of cognitive consciousness to his four-termed schema of practical consciousness reveals no inconsistency in his doctrines but rather a remarkable consistency in his method.

The fourth level of cognitive consciousness, called "intellect" in *The Principles of Art* and "rational thinking" in *The New Leviathan,* is divided, like will, into two sub-levels; these forms of thought are called "primary" or empirical, and "secondary" or "thought about thought" (PA, 164–68, 221). The objects of the former are the data which second-level consciousness has organized out of amorphous feeling, together with the interrelations of those data recognized in third-level consciousness. Empirical thought—which in the form of scientific inquiry is a more elaborate and coherent version of common-sense experience—consists of detecting and constructing relations and networks of relations among the complex objects of third-level consciousness; relations subsist, so to speak, *in* perception but *for* empirical thought. "Thought about thought" (traditionally distinguished, Collingwood observes, from empirical thought as "reason" from "understanding" or as "philosophy" from "science" [PA, 167]) has as *its* objects the relations among acts of thinking. "To discover the distance of the earth from the sun is a task for thought of the first degree, in this case for astronomy; to discover what it is exactly that we are doing when we discover the distance of the earth from the sun is a task for thought of the second degree, in this instance for logic or the theory of science" (IH, 1).

Empirical thought, of course, is inferential, and as such is distinct from the (merely) "propositional thinking" or assertiveness of the third level. But as capricious choice is not accompanied by the explicit awareness of itself as choosing, so empirical thought is not accompanied by the explicit awareness of itself as reasoning. Such awareness is the function of thought about thought. Like rational choice, only this second degree of thought can affirm a proposition because it both has a reason (as indeed empirical thought may have) and is aware of having that reason.

It is thus only at this higher level of intellect that *principles* of inference can be formulated and reflected upon. The codification of "thought about thought" is logic, not only in the restricted sense of formal deductive logic but in the broader sense in which one can speak of the "logic of science" or the "logic of criticism," i.e., the examination of the processes of successful thinking often intimately tied to specific subject-matters. This level of thought, Collingwood insists, is both normative and descriptive: both at once and inseparably so. It is "criteriological" or concerned with the standards of inference which thought imposes on itself (PA, 171 n.); but these standards are attained only by reflecting on the *experience* of the activity of thinking. It follows that principles of inference are subject to change if and as the experience of thinking changes; and in fact Collingwood enacted this consequence in the practice of his own professional work. He not only held that the "principles of history" result from reflecting on the experience of historical thinking, but in *The Idea of History* he wrote a history of the idea of history, i.e., of the change of those principles over time. A similar task was attempted for the history of scientific thinking in *The Idea of Nature*. And in the next chapter we shall see how his theory of absolute presuppositions was the ultimate result of his thinking about thought about thought.

4 · *Abstraction and Freedom*

The general theory of levels of consciousness has as one of its most powerful consequences a methodological imperative: look for the connection among apparently unrelated mental functions as occurrences at different levels of consciousness of the same fundamental activity. It does not at all enable one to deduce what connections may be found or suggested, but it does entail that there will be some connections or other. Moreover, it is a program for analyzing many general concepts into species of the concept at different levels of consciousness. "Knowledge," for example, while it has a fourth-level definition (NL, 14.22), is the explicit reflection on the experience of third-level propositional thinking, which in turn has as its object the experience of second-level conceptual thinking. It is arbitrary, so long as one understands what one is doing, whether "knowledge" is restricted to its eminent sense as a fourth-level term and other terms are found for the issue of thinking at the second and third levels, or whether the same term, appropriately qualified, is used in reference to each level. The latter practice expresses the fact that what is called "knowledge" at the second level is an undeveloped form of a higher level activity from which it differs in degree; the former practice emphasizes the real differences among the levels which differ also in kind. In *The New Leviathan,* Collingwood called third-level or propositional thinking ("asking questions and answering them") "knowledge" (NL, 11.11), but he later retracted this use and reserved the term to fourth-level application (NL, 14.22, n. 1). In *The Principles of Art,* he called art (which, as imagination, is second-level consciousness) "knowledge of the individual" (PA, 289). These apparent discrepancies represent neither confusion nor any change of Collingwood's views. To anyone who has grasped his dialectical theory of mind, they merely indicate whether he is emphasizing the continuity of levels or their differences.

In principle, all concepts must for Collingwood have this structure: the structure of a scale of forms. Consider the difference, for example, between the concept of triangle at the second level, where it is exemplified in the ability of a pigeon to distinguish a scalene triangle from other rectilinear shapes when he has been trained by reward to respond to an equilateral triangle; the concept of triangle at the third level, where it is exemplified in the psychologist's description of the shapes he uses in his experiments with pigeons; and the concept of triangle at the fourth level, where it is exemplified not only in Euclidean theorems about "the triangle" but in the concept of triangle familiar to those who can illustrate it from non-Euclidean as well as from Euclidean geometry. But the concept of triangle, like most concepts, while it is specified in relatively more simple or more complex ways at different levels of consciousness, illustrates but is not itself part of a theory of consciousness or mind, and differs from the concepts which enter into such a theory because they are instances of themselves and it is not. A fourth-level definition of "triangle" is intelligible only to someone who has attained the fourth level through the lower levels, but it can be understood apart from explicit reference to those levels. A fourth-level definition of "knowledge," in Collingwood's view, cannot even be understood except as a development from its proto-forms at lower levels. This distinction between two kinds of concept reproduces within the dialectical theory of mind the distinction between "scientific" and "philosophical" concepts in the *Essay on Philosophical Method*.

One might say, therefore, that a *complete* theory of mind would include a dialectical account of every self-instancing concept and would also elucidate the relations among all such concepts as well as among the "levels" of each. Collingwood gave such an account only of a few concepts: mind, consciousness, thinking, value (i.e., the series pleasure $\rightarrow$ satisfaction $\rightarrow$ happiness $\rightarrow$ good), emotion, action, and freedom. Others are left incomplete or barely suggested. To illustrate the dialectical method, it may be useful to examine briefly one such example: *abstraction,* or rather that activity of consciousness of which this is the most common name.

Except from a point of view incompatible with Collingwood's one cannot *define* "abstraction" or any other of the activities and products of different levels of consciousness. The generic concept of such an activity and its products lives in the series of its exemplifications; the exposition of the relations of this series replaces what is usually called "definition" (cf. EPM, 100–101). Nevertheless, such a concept can be characterized, if it is understood that the characterizations themselves are differently exemplified at different levels. Now the characteristics of "abstraction" which Collingwood refers to in different places are three: selectivity, indeterminacy, and self-determination. As a process, abstraction is the activity of consciousness (also called "attention") directed on an object in such a way as to spotlight some features of the object and neglect others; these features are thus "abstracted" from the object, and they can be named and themselves made the objects of other and repeated acts of consciousness without the repeated presentation of the object. The only direct, or "first-order" objects of any act of consciousness are *activities* of a lower level, and these activities are in themselves, no matter what the level, as transient as feeling. I cannot repeat or revive the total perceptual consciousness of a moment, but by attending to some of its features I transform them into "second-order" objects which can later be summoned up and compared with other second-order objects, present and past. However, because second-order objects have been selectively abstracted from the totality of activity, they are *indeterminate* in all respects except those by which they have been constituted (PA, 254; NL, 7.56, 11.54). Finally (and this is the characterization which bears the burden of Collingwood's ethics and his aesthetics alike), the activity of consciousness in abstracting is a *free* activity, determined by nothing except (to speak tautologously) by itself in abstracting these features rather than those from its object. Since *naming* (in the extended sense in which Collingwood calls even a gesture a "name") is the way in which we express our becoming conscious of our own activities (NL, 6.21–28; 13.41–42), it might be said that the very existence of a verbal language determines the limits of abstraction: we can attend only to those distinguishable features of experience for which we *have* names. Collingwood could very well admit, and could hardly deny, that in the run of experience the language we speak very often determines what we consciously notice in experience; but clearly he would add that it does so only to the extent that we permit it to do so. The culprit is not the irresistible power of language but our own laziness. In his view, common language is a habit of consciousness and by no means a bad one insofar as it is the medium of social life. But habits are compulsory only when we are not conscious of them, and they can on suitable occasions be superseded to the extent that we are conscious of them. Even at the lowest level at which abstraction occurs, "attention is in no sense a response to stimulus. It takes no orders from sensation. Consciousness, master in its own house, dominates feeling" (PA, 207).

The process of abstraction is thus the originative power of consciousness at all levels. This is quite different, of course, from the ordinary sense of the term, according to which "concepts" are abstract but perceptions, say, are not, and one will not understand Collingwood if one thinks of abstract concepts as products of an intellectual process categorically different from non-rational activities of appetite and imagination, desire and perception. "Abstraction" is, so to speak, a fourth-level name. But the process which it names is continuous, although differing in degree of complexity and explicitness, through all the levels of consciousness.

The first and simplest product of abstraction is the division of a mass of feeling into a part attended to and a part not, and then the division of the former into differentiated sensa. Here it is called "attention" or "selective attention." Then, by further attending to sensation, it converts selected sensa from transient "impressions" into relatively enduring "ideas," and also divides the *experience* of sensation into activity and objects of activity—sensation and sensa. Here it is called "imagination." At the third and fourth levels it is called only "abstraction"; but in each case it attends to aspects of lower level activity and transforms these in the same way that imagination transforms impressions into ideas. The *concepts* of satisfaction and dissatisfaction, for example, are abstractions from second-level appetitive activity by third-level consciousness, which is aware (as appetite itself is not) that such activity tends *from* a state which impels it to activity to one which does not, and which abstracts from its awareness of initial and terminal points in appetite the concepts of dissatisfaction and satisfaction. Satisfaction *is* the form in which value appears at the second level; but although appetite can be satisfied, it is not *aware* of itself as satisfied (animals, so to speak, can take no satisfaction in being satisfied). It can be *recognized* as such only by an act of third-level consciousness. To complete the series: third-level consciousness has the concept of satisfaction, but is not *aware* of itself as having this or any concept. The concept *of* a concept is a fourth-level abstraction, and the description of third-level consciousness abstracting the concept of satisfaction from second-level appetitive activity is itself the result of fourth-level abstraction from third-level activity.

If all this seems formidably complicated, it is still not as complicated as human consciousness itself, and it should not be forgotten that the organization of "levels," much as it may satisfy our ordinal urges and our preference for the natural numbers, especially the smaller ones, is in many ways arbitrary. Collingwood did not "discover" that consciousness has four levels, as one might discover that a drawer has four compartments. The dialectic of mind is itself a way of schematizing certain general conceptions so as to make them applicable to details of experience and to forestall errors, or what from this point of view are errors. It calls for a genealogy of ideas, which, like the genealogy of man, reminds us that rational consciousness is neither an epiphenomenon of non-rational organic and psychic functions nor an entity which has inexplicably escaped from or supervened upon the nature which we share with our fellow animals. The dialectic of each concept carries its own cautions and reminders; and the particular reminder of the dialectic of abstraction is that although the highest achievement of abstraction is the construction of formal systems and models (the concept of a variable is the final step in the process of converting concrete experience which will sustain relational analysis into abstractions which can be thought of only as belonging to a relational system: the "thought of something indeterminate, which if it were determinate would occupy a certain position" [PA, 254]), the process by which this achievement is reached includes steps which are essentially arbitrary, acts of selective division of experience which could have been otherwise and would, had they been otherwise, have led to a different development of thought. Abstraction is the exercise of radical freedom. Its occurrence at each level is an achievement, but at the same time it is a development from its more primitive form. Thus freedom, for Collingwood as for Sartre and the existentialists, is an essential characteristic of consciousness and is possessed, willy-nilly, by everyone. But at the same time, the exercise of freedom at the higher levels of consciousness is guaranteed to no one, simply because the attainment or retention of those levels is not assured. It is worth noting, too, that for Collingwood, freedom belongs as much to theoretical as to practical activity, as much to cognition as to action. This is a consequence —one might say, an advantage—of the fact that freedom is an aspect of consciousness and that the theory of consciousness is general, subsuming and relating both thought and action.

5 · Beyond Realism and Idealism

Collingwood is an empiricist, but one who belongs to no identifiable school. Every stage of inquiry, in his view, yields results which are *about* experience, and about nothing else. But "experience" includes both knower and known, and is practical as well as theoretical—that is, in the process of inquiry the self creates itself as well as coming in increasingly complex ways to know a world; and these are not merely correlative but interdependent processes. Hence, although knowledge has both its source and objective reference in experience, it is experience which cannot be analyzed into hard data. Most empirical theories of knowledge *begin* with what for Collingwood is already the second or even the third level of consciousness, and they separate cognitive from practical consciousness so completely that they can be reunited, if at all, only at the level of ethical deliberation (the fourth level). In affirming that sensory "data" are already "facta" and that the distinction between practical and cognitive itself is an abstraction from levels of experience in which they are not actually separable, Collingwood is much closer to sophisticated pragmatism than to traditional empiricism. But while he differs from the latter in extending the *lower* levels of the forms of consciousness, he differs from the former in extending the *upper* levels, and recognizing that rational consciousness develops its own criteria and ends out of the matrix of the lowest levels of consciousness rather than constructing increasingly complex techniques of adaptation which remain, through all the variations of intelligence, inveterately biological. Thus he avoids, at least, the genetic fallacy which has plagued pragmatic philosophies, as well as the fallacy of non-genesis which has foreshortened the perspectives of empiricism. As an empiricist, Collingwood is a radical empiricist, but he is also a radical idealist, for whom the originative powers of thought are coeval with the most rudimentary forms of experience. This suggests, I think, that the traditional opposition of "empiricism" and "idealism" is not a fruitful subject for investigation or debate, and that all of the interesting problems cluster around what it means to be *radical*. The idea of dialectic is Collingwood's answer to that question.

Collingwood is often thought to have been deliberately indecisive or confusing. Certainly he left some lethal booby-traps for anyone who attempts to disentangle empiricist or "realist" from "idealist" strains in his thought. We noted above his view that thought seeks not only to unify elements which are discrete at a lower level but to "find in them or put in them some concretion." An exactly parallel refusal to choose appears in *The Principles of Art,* where Colling-wood says that "the work of intellect is to apprehend or construct relations" (PA, 216). These deliberate disjunctions show, I believe, that it is useless to ask whether Collingwood was, at least in inten-tion, a "realist" or an "idealist." They suggest that, as one would ex-pect from a dialectical viewpoint, he wished to avoid identification with either because he regarded both as partial views which could be taken into and corrected in a more comprehensive theory. It is not that thought *sometimes* "apprehends" and *sometimes* "constructs": this would be a weak compromise, not an illuminating synthesis. Rather thought *always* does both. The key to understanding this is the pattern of implicit-explicit in a dialectical series. The act of con-scious attention to lower-level experience as an object makes explicit distinctions and relations which *from the standpoint of the experi-ence itself* are implicit. To say that they are implicit does not mean that they are there but unrecognized, rather that something is there in a relatively amorphous way which is given form only in the act of being made an object of attention but which contains the ground or possibility of the forms which it can sustain. An example of this would be the inattentive experience of a visual field (especially to-ward the periphery of vision). In focusing attention on a specific area one cannot see what is not there to be seen, but at the same time it is clearly false that in inattentive vision one is seeing exactly what one becomes through attention aware of seeing. The objective side of inattentive experience is a mélange, relatively lacking in form, dis-tinction, and recognition; hence it is most natural to refer to it as a "field." Attention converts a field into a concatenation of individ-ually identifiable shapes, colors, etc.; but while the field-characteris-tics of inattentive experience will permit alternative identifications, they will not support just *any* set of identifications. Yet they are not (as many analyses of perception hold or suggest) those identifica-tions already but indistinctly made.

Collingwood does not want to decide whether thought "appre-hends" or "constructs," "finds" or "puts." In his view, it does both.

As the activity of converting implicit differences into explicit distinctions, it seems *to itself,* at any level, to be apprehending. But as an object of consciousness to a higher level, it seems to be constructing. Experience, one might say, is the realist, reflection on experience the idealist. Neither is false; what is false is the presumption that there is irreducible logical incompatibility between the theories expressive of each. In the dialectic of theories, realism states the viewpoint of any level of consciousness from its own standpoint, idealism the viewpoint of any level of consciousness in its reflection on a lower level. The theory of levels accounts for each by assigning to each a function which cannot be usurped by the other. Collingwood always denied that he was an "idealist," and complained in the *Autobiography* about the inability of his colleagues even to entertain the possibility of a position which was neither "realist" nor "idealist" (A, 56–57). That his own position was different from both is implicit in many of his *obiter dicta,* in all his writing after *Speculum Mentis:* in such a remark, for example, as that "philosophy is never concerned with thought by itself; it is always concerned with its relation to its object, and is therefore concerned with the object just as much as with the thought" (IH, 2). The vagueness of "thought," "relation," and "object" is mitigated once these terms are interpreted as referring to relative levels in the dialectical series of orders of consciousness. The false antithesis between "realism" and "idealism" is exposed and dismissed in Collingwood's transcendental deduction of the possibility of historical knowledge in the fourth Epilegomenon of *The Idea of History.* That argument, as I shall try to show in Chapter 6, presupposes throughout and is impossible to accept apart from the dialectical theory of mind which it barely serves to suggest.

6 · *From the Dialectic of Experience to the Dialectic of Mind*

Since Collingwood did not undertake to state in one place and very probably never himself reviewed at one time his dialectical theory of mind in all its aspects, its reconstruction must be a matter of interpretation and even of conjecture. But we can now see that in general outline it is fully continuous with the dialectic of experience in *Speculum Mentis*. Collingwood's end was in his beginning, although in the way and only in the way that this is true of any historical process.

The second level of consciousness is identical with the form of experience which in *Speculum Mentis* is called "Art," the third level with what was there called "Religion," and the fourth level with what there was called "Science." The "supposal" of art becomes the "conceptual thinking" of appetite and imagination, and the "monadism" of art becomes the immediacy of appetite and the indivisibility of imagination.[6] The practical form of "aesthetic consciousness," which in *Speculum Mentis* is called "play," also has the same unawareness of purposes, reasons, or specific objects as the forms of appetite in second-level consciousness.

Similarly, what in *Speculum Mentis* appears as the primary characteristic of "Religion"—namely, assertion—becomes the "propositional thinking" of third-level consciousness; and the bipolarity of Religion, which distinguishes, as Art does not, between real and unreal, true and false (SM, 112), corresponds to the distinction of real and apparent desires and of truth and falsity in general at the third level, just as propositional thinking, like "Religion," "claims truth but refuses to argue" (SM, 131). The practical aspect of religious experience, which is conventional morality "asserting as real an end which is still an imaginary or capricious end" (SM, 135) becomes the morality of the level of desire, and of choice as rudimentary will, which in undertaking action can recognize alternatives but does not deliberate among them because the sanctioned action presents itself immediately as "right."

The correspondence between the "Science" of *Speculum Mentis* and the fourth-level consciousness of the dialectic of mind also holds up in many details. As "the separation of knowledge from conduct is a result of scientific abstraction, and it is therefore under the heading of science that we first find a special doctrine of the will" (SM, 170), so fourth-level consciousness is divided into will and intellect and it is only *for* fourth-level consciousness that this distinction is explicit and can be, once attained, retroactively applied to analyzing the practical and theoretical forms of lower-level consciousness. Moreover, Science, like fourth-level consciousness, is the stage at which explicitly rational thought emerges, in the form of hypothetical argument; and both distinguish between a practical reason ("If you want A you must do B") and a theoretical reason ("if A is the case, then B is the case") (SM, 171, 182–83; NL, 14.32, 14.35). The fundamental ethical concept belonging to Science as the lowest form of rational thought in *Speculum Mentis* is the same as that attributed to the lowest form of fourth-level consciousness: the concept of utility.

Beyond this point, however, the correspondence is unclear. In *Speculum Mentis,* Science was followed by History, and finally Philosophy, both distinguished from Science as "concrete" from "abstract." To what stages in the dialectic of mind could these correspond? The answer, I think, is as follows: Collingwood had distinguished two forms of fourth-level practical consciousness, or will: capricious choice and rational choice. His main discussion of the forms of theoretical consciousness, in *The Principles of Art,* did not, as we have seen, distinguish in detail levels of consciousness above that of imagination, for the understandable reason that the theory of imagination alone was germane to the topic at hand: art. As a result, the higher levels were in almost every context conflated into one, which is called, variously, "intellect," "the secondary form of thought" (imagination being the "primary form"), or, even more vaguely, "the further development of thought" (beyond imagination). It will be remembered that in *Speculum Mentis* the most significant transition is from Religion to Science, which is the movement from implicit to explicit thought; although Science, History, and Philosophy are forms of explicit thought quite different from each other, they are alike in this categorical distinction from both Art and Religion. In *The Principles of Art,* therefore, Collingwood regarded only their common characteristics as relevant to his immediate purposes, and neglected their differences. The common characteristic which he refers to again and again as distinguishing "intellect" from "imagination" is that the latter has for its objects sensa but not their relations, while the former has for its objects relations and relational patterns.

Now this is very general indeed. One cannot complain that Collingwood did not provide answers to questions he was not asking, but it is obvious that there are different kinds of "relations," as there are different kinds of terms: for example, relations among sensa ("warmer than," "larger than," "earlier than") and relations among the acts of recognizing or affirming relations among sensa, i.e., among propositions ("x is larger than y *and* y is larger than z"). How do such differences fit into the dialectic of mind? Relations among mental acts should clearly be at a higher level than relations among sensa, since the former depend on consciousness *of* the latter. Are the latter in the province of "Science" and the former in that of "Philosophy"?

At one point in *The Principles of Art,* Collingwood suggests that he had this correspondence in mind. "All the propositions which express the results of our thought [i.e., "intellect"] belong to one of two types: they are either statements about [imagination], in which case they are called empirical, or statements about the procedure of thought itself, in which case they are called *a priori*" (PA, 221). Now a statement about imagination itself belongs to a higher level of consciousness, and therefore, if we were correct in extending "imagination" to the third level, it belongs to the fourth level; and as there are two levels of will—capricious and rational choice—so there are two stages of intellect—reflection on perceptual experience (corresponding to "Science") and reflection on the activity of empirical or scientific thinking (corresponding to "Philosophy"). And this is exactly the distinction made in *The Principles of Art* and in the Introductions of both *The Idea of Nature* and *The Idea of History.*

The correspondence between the levels of practical consciousness and the levels of theoretical consciousness becomes virtually complete when the primary types of rational choice are identified by Collingwood with the epochs of Western science as having a common conceptual structure: Utility (i.e., means-end deliberation) is associated with Greco-Medieval Science (i.e., teleological explanation), and Right (i.e., rule-act deliberation) with modern science (i.e., explanation by law) (NL, 18.51). And this identification formally reunites practical and cognitive consciousness and completes the pattern suggested in the otherwise cryptic comment in *The Principles of Art,* that the step from simple consciousness to second-level consciousness "is thus a step forward both in theory and in practice, although it is one step only and not two; as a progress along a railway-line towards a certain junction is a progress towards both the regions served by the two lines which divide at that junction. For that matter, it is also a progress towards the region in which, *later, these two lines reunite*" (PA, 292; italics added).

But what, in this reconstruction, has happened to History? The development which we have so laboriously traced from *Speculum Mentis* to *The New Leviathan,* from the dialectic of experience to

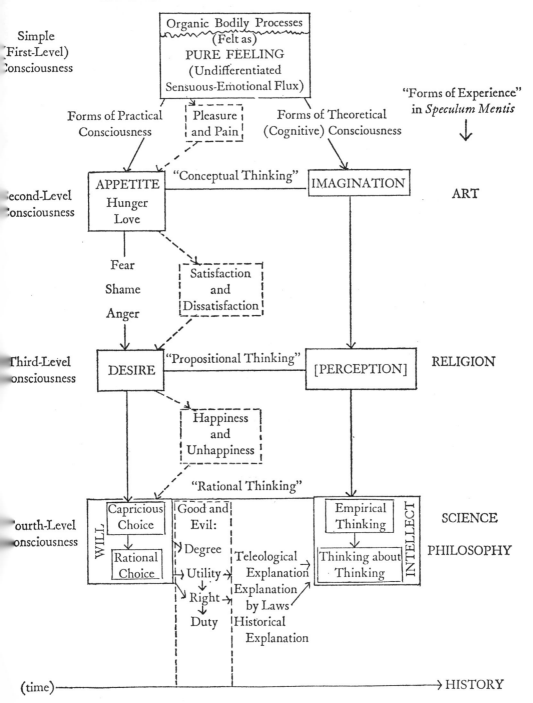

FIGURE 2

The Dialectic of Mind as a Scale of Forms

Simple
(First-Level)
Consciousness

Organic Bodily Processes
(Felt as)
PURE FEELING
(Undifferentiated
Sensuous-Emotional Flux)

"Forms of Experience"
in *Speculum Mentis*
↓

Forms of Practical
Consciousness

Pleasure
and Pain

Forms of Theoretical
(Cognitive) Consciousness

Second-Level
Consciousness

APPETITE
Hunger
Love

"Conceptual Thinking"

IMAGINATION

ART

Fear

Shame

Anger

Satisfaction
and
Dissatisfaction

Third-Level
Consciousness

DESIRE

"Propositional Thinking"

[PERCEPTION]

RELIGION

Happiness
and
Unhappiness

"Rational Thinking"

Fourth-Level
Consciousness

WILL

Capricious
Choice

↓

Rational
Choice

Good and
Evil:

Degree

Utility →

Right →

Duty

Teleological
Explanation →

Explanation
by Laws

Historical
Explanation

Empirical
Thinking

↓

Thinking about
Thinking

INTELLECT

SCIENCE

PHILOSOPHY

(time) ————————————————————————→ HISTORY

the dialectic of mind, has been like a game of musical chairs in which the five forms of experience have finally settled (panting slightly) into four levels of mind; and History is odd man out. Yet at the same time what we have called "Philosophy" has come to look very much like History. As Knox has remarked, Collingwood was inclined to identify philosophy with whatever he happened to be studying most intensively at the time (IH, xv); and to the extent that he regarded philosophy as "thought about thought," this is only natural. But in the *Essay on Metaphysics* and the *Autobiography,* he announced his discovery that metaphysics is the asking and answering of *historical* questions about the presuppositions which people do make or have made in the course of "scientific" thought. Whether this innovation assimilated "philosophy" to "history" or "history" to "philosophy" is a disputable question and not a very profitable one insofar as those names are rather arbitrarily applied to specific kinds of inquiry. But the theory of presuppositions—with its propaedeutic, the logic of question and answer—is nevertheless the final step in the dialectic of mind, and one which Collingwood could not have taken unless his conception of mind was already dialectical. The relevance of this step should not be difficult to see. Why should the fourth level of consciousness be a terminus? Could there be a further level, which is to "rational thought" as "rational thought" is to "propositional thought" and "propositional thought" to "conceptual thought"? If not, why not? If so, what would it be like? Collingwood's theory of absolute presuppositions provides the answer to these questions. The answer seems to be a paradox: the dialectic of mind has no terminal point, and yet there is no level higher than the fourth. To give sense to this answer is the aim of the next chapter.

PART II

THE

DIALECTIC

OF IDEAS

CHAPTER 5

The Logic of Thought

1 · Why Collingwood's "Logic" Is Not Logic, and His "Metaphysics" Is Not Metaphysics

ALTHOUGH THERE IS NO "SCHOOL OF COLLINGWOOD," A NOT inconsiderable number of articles and sections of books have been devoted to discussing—and, almost invariably, to refuting—doctrines which he is supposed to have held. The vast majority of these criticisms, unfortunately, are subject to the same comment which Collingwood made on the critical methods of his "realist" colleagues at Oxford: their only method, he said, "was to analyse the position criticized into various propositions, and detect contradictions between these. Following as they did the rules of propositional logic, it never occurred to them that these contradictions might be the fruit of their own historical errors as to the questions which their victims had been trying to answer" (A, 42). To anyone who reviews the critical literature on Collingwood, it is astonishing to see how widely divergent are the descriptions of the views attributed to him. His "theory of absolute presuppositions," for example, has been criticized both for treating absolute presuppositions as propositions and for *not* acknowledging them as propositions. His account of historical knowledge has been criticized *both* for claiming that historical statements can be incorrigible and for holding that they are undecidable.

If the sketch given in the preceding chapters of the development of Collingwood's idea of dialectic is to be credited at all, we can see in a general way why such remarkable differences in the interpretation of Collingwood should occur. For it is of the essence in his method that the crucial terms of argument and explanation do not occur in a univocal way. The same term may refer to different levels of experience, of concepts, or of mental functions located on a "scale of forms," and for anyone who does not have and keep this possibility in mind, difficulties are certain to arise analogous to the widely known confusions of "use" and "mention." Paradox is a feature of Collingwood's style, but not of his thought; *le style n'est pas toujours l'homme même.* It only *appears* contradictory to say at one time that imagination is a form of thought (that is, the most rudimentary level of attention, "abstraction," and self-consciousness), and at another that imagination is not thought (that is, not characterized by the higher level activities of propositional and rational thinking). Yet paradox is also an indispensable feature of such a style, for it reminds one that it is sometimes the continuities and at other times the differences of conceptual transformation which are relevant. Different answers should suggest that there are different questions.

In this chapter and the two following I propose to review some of Collingwood's better known doctrines, in an attempt to show that when they are understood from the standpoint of the dialectic of conceptual process they are very much more coherent and defensible than they have seemed to most of their critics; for when so understood they are simply not the "doctrines" which have been criticized. Of course this is not to say that they are not open to other objections, and at a number of points emendations are suggested and uncertainties acknowledged. But in the end, I believe, the edgy provocativeness which leads one from page to page in Collingwood gives way to a reasonably solid coherence which connects book with book.

The chapters to follow deal respectively with Collingwood's account of historical understanding and description of history as the "science of human nature," and with his theory of imagination and account of artistic creation. The present chapter will take up his "logic of question and answer" and its sequel, his theory of "absolute presuppositions." In effect, we shall move backward through the levels of mental functions, and such a description already previsions the kind of interpretation for which the present chapter argues. The difficulties which have been engendered by his discussions of "question and answer" and of "absolute presuppositions" have for the most part resulted from reading those discussions *one level lower* than Collingwood intended. Thus, as will emerge, the logic of question and answer is not a substitute for propositional logic but rather a theory of the process of inquiry; its locus is, so to speak, not logic but reflection on logic. Similarly, the "reform of metaphysics" to which the theory of absolute presuppositions is intended to contribute, does not result in the elimination of metaphysics, but to its reinterpretation. It seeks neither to answer nor to dismiss metaphysical questions but to raise the quite different question, "How is it possible for metaphysics to have a history?" And the answer to this question, I believe, is identical with the answer to the question whether there can be a "level of consciousness" higher than the fourth level of the dialectic of mind. On this interpretation, the theory of absolute presuppositions completes and cannot be fully understood apart from the dialectic of mind, even though there is no place where Collingwood discusses them together. But to reach the theory of absolute presuppositions one begins with the logic of question and answer.

2 · The "Logic of Question and Answer," and Some Criticisms of It

In his *Autobiography,* Collingwood claimed to have developed, as early as 1917, a "logic of question and answer" which he regarded as replacing practically the whole of the traditional theory of deductive logic. He wrote in that year—not a good year for treatises on logic—a book called *Truth and Contradiction,* which was refused publication. The only manuscript was destroyed by Collingwood after he had written the *Autobiography;* so all that survives of his "new logic" is his brief summary in Chapter V of that book and in Chapter IV ("On Presupposing") of the *Essay on Metaphysics.* Apart from a short section in *Speculum Mentis* (SM, 76–80), there is no specific mention of a logic of question and answer earlier than the *Autobiography,* and the absence of such a discussion is especially notable in the *Essay on Philosophical Method,* the main part of which is arranged according to the traditional classification, in logical treatises, of concept, judgment, and inference.

Yet what Collingwood says of the "logic of question and answer" is provocative, and it is logically involved in his more extended theory of presuppositions. It has therefore been thought unfortunate that he left his "new logic" in the wax, with only tantalizing pages to suggest what it was or might have been. But this opinion could be held only by someone who thought that such a "logic" would have been a formal logic in the traditional sense. If one abandons this expectation, it appears that Collingwood did in fact say everything he had to say on the subject, and that what he had in mind was not a propositional logic at all, or a substitute for one, but a *theory of inquiry*. He was interested not at all in the theory of *proof*, which is the subject of formal logic, but in the theory of *discovery*, which formal logic does not even claim to deal with. His complaints against "propositional" or formal logic can be understood, therefore, as a special case of the distinction developed in the *Essay on Philosophical Method* between scientific and philosophical thinking. Formal logic, as the theory of the former, is not dismissed but assigned a locus of restricted universality; it is inapplicable, most notably, to the interpretation and assessment of propositions which involve concepts belonging to a scale of forms. What Collingwood opposes is the claim made for formal logic of unrestricted applicability, a claim precisely identical with what in *Speculum Mentis* he called "scientific philosophy" as a form of dogmatism. Or, in terms of the dialectic of mind, one could say that Collingwood opposes the claim of formal logic to range over all the levels of mental functions without regard to their differences and oblivious to the fact that it represents the principles of thinking at only one of those levels and not the highest level at that.

The briefest glance at the history of logic is enough to show that there has always been something like an inverse law holding between the rigor and the applicability of logical systems: to the extent that logic is rigorous, that is, it is not very successful in throwing light on any form of argument except mathematical reasoning, and to the extent that it has provided norms of actual arguments in law, theology, criticism, history, philosophy, and even natural science, it has evaded canons of strict rigor. This dilemma is partly, although not entirely, associated with the difference between deductive logic, rigorous but empty, and inductive logic, rich but lacking in demonstrative certainty. At the very least it is clear that all sorts of people whose business it is to convince others by argument have had little use for the logic purveyed in textbooks; legal argument, for example, can seldom be strictly formalized. Like the descendants of Aaron, formal logicians have formed a closed priesthood, respected as guardians of the holy but not often consulted on the affairs of life. This may well be due to the frivolous human tendency to evade the demands of reason; but it is also possible that reason is more concrete and dense than the structures of abstract form. This was Collingwood's view in any event; he expressed it repeatedly from his first book to his last, and it is the background of the Logic of Question and Answer.

Collingwood sums up the "principle" of his "Logic of Question and Answer" as follows: ". . . A body of knowledge consists not of 'propositions,' 'statements,' 'judgements,' or whatever name logicians use to designate assertive acts of thought (or what in those acts is asserted: for 'knowledge' means both the activity of knowing and what is known); but of these together with the questions they are meant to answer; and . . . a logic in which the answers are attended to and the questions neglected is a false logic" (A, 30–31). Elsewhere this is put more shortly: "Every statement that anybody ever makes is made in answer to a question" (EM, 23). This does not mean that in making a statement one is necessarily aware of the question to which the statement is an answer; Collingwood significantly says that in the desultory and casual thinking of our "unscientific consciousness, . . . we hardly know that the thoughts we fish up out of our minds are answers to questions at all, let alone what questions these are" (EM, 24). It is by retrospection rather than by introspection that ordinary thought can be so analyzed into question and answer. (Such an analysis, therefore, is partly logical and partly historical; Collingwood's later extension of the scope of historical knowledge is already implicit.)

Moreover, in Collingwood's view, the asking of a question, whether explicit or "desultory," logically involves the presupposition of one and only one proposition, from which the question "arises"; and one, again, may not be aware that one is making a specific presupposition but must recover it analytically; therefore, so can someone else. The capacity of a supposition to cause a question to arise Collingwood calls its "logical efficacy"; and this efficacy depends neither on its being true nor on its being believed to be true but only on its being supposed or entertained (EM, 28); the importance of this qualification is that it accounts for those cases, such as those in theoretical thinking in science, in which the entertaining of an hypothesis gives rise to questions about ways in which it could be confirmed or disproved.

A number of corollaries are drawn by Collingwood from the simple statement of the Logic of Question and Answer. The most important of these constitute his theory of absolute presuppositions—presuppositions, that is, which are presupposed by questions but are not themselves answers to any question whatever—but we shall return to this theory in the latter part of this chapter. Since the theory of absolute presuppositions itself presupposes the Logic of Question and Answer, the present question is whether the latter can withstand criticism sufficiently to provide a foundation for anything.

The first direct corollary is that question and answer are correlative in the sense that a precise statement can be elicited only by a precise question, and conversely a precise question will admit only a precise statement as an answer. Collingwood had little sympathy for "big problems," or rather he believed that the way to deal with such problems is to break them down into a series of questions each of which can be formulated in such a way that an answer clearly leads to the next question. In *The New Leviathan* this corollary is restated as the "principle of the limited objective," which Collingwood sees as the most fundamental difference between modern science and the sciences of antiquity. Ancient science regarded inquiry as ending in real definition, or the statement of the essence of something in such a way that its properties can be deduced. Hence the Greek question was of the form "What is *x?*" And this, when one substitutes, say, "Nature" for the variable, suggests sciences with unlimited objectives; "when they asked that question the Greeks were asking a question too vague to be precisely answered" (NL, 31.67). Now the correlativity of question and answer is a useful principle even though it results in no *method* for asking the right questions after one has learned not to ask the wrong ones. But it is logically independent of the more controversial parts of the Logic of Question and Answer, and therefore does nothing to support them. It is not even *prima facie,* as they are, based on a rejection of "propositional logic."

A second corollary, however, clearly does make such a rejection. This is Collingwood's inference that two propositions do not contradict each other unless they are answers to the same question. This principle depends upon, although it does not strictly follow from, the principle that the meaning of a statement is a function of *the* question to which it is an answer. That Collingwood draws the corollary makes it clear that he is committed to the extraordinary position that there are *no* logical relations among statements unless they are answers to the same question; for if statements cannot contradict each other, neither can they imply each other. It is significant that Collingwood never even mentions *implication;* the "logical efficacy" of presuppositions may be regarded as an informal kind of entailment, but it holds only between a proposition and a question, not between two propositions.

A final corollary is that truth is not a property of propositions but of "complexes consisting of questions and answers" (A, 37). In such a complex, particular answers are not in themselves true or false but may be "right" or "wrong"—a "right answer" being one "which enables us to get ahead with the process of questioning and answering" (A, 37). Collingwood knows, of course, that his denial that propositions can be true or false is wildly divergent from the traditional practice of regarding individual statements, and only those, as true or false (even a "true story," in the usual analysis, is one made up of statements all of which are true); but he goes so far as to claim that his view is the correct account of the ordinary meaning:

> What is ordinarily meant when a proposition is called "true," I thought, was this: (a) the proposition belongs to a question-and-answer complex which as a whole is "true" in the proper sense of the word; (b) within this complex it is an answer to a certain question; (c) the question is what we ordinarily call a sensible or intelligent question, not a silly one, or in my terminology it "arises"; (d) the proposition is the "right" answer to that question [A, 38].

Collingwood's proposed revolution in logic was, to say the least, not a timid one. He was not wrong to think it revolutionary. His mistake was to regard it as an attack on *logic*. It it were a substitute for traditional principles of logic, it would undoubtedly be open to serious criticism. Four main objections, in particular, can be distinguished, and these are worth brief discussion even though, in the following section, I shall try to show that on a different interpretation of Collingwood all of them are objections not to Collingwood's theory but to the way he chose to describe that theory.

a. Is it true that "every statement that anybody ever makes is an answer to a question" (EM, 23)? While this undoubtedly is often the case, many exceptions suggest themselves at once: pedagogical

statements, gratuitous narratives, persuasive claims, exclamatory assertions, statements offered as reasons for other statements, and
many others. Now it is of course true, but only trivially true, that
any assertion may be *regarded* as the answer to a question. One can,
that is, always construct a question to which a given statement
would be an answer (this is a grammatical fact about English and
most other natural languages). It also seems impossible to conceive
of a statement which cannot be regarded as the answer to more than
one question. But the very fact that questions can always be discovered or constructed seems fatal to Collingwood's view that the
meaning of the statement is a function of the question to which it is
an answer; for one must obviously understand the proposition in
order to construct a question which the proposition relevantly answers. Similarly, one could not decide to which of several possible
questions a statement is the relevant answer unless one could know
the meaning of the statement independently of those questions. But
in Collingwood's view one does not understand a statement except
as an answer to a specific question. To make the connection between
statements and questions one of *meaning* therefore results in a vicious circle: we cannot know what a statement means unless we
know what question it answers, but we cannot decide which question it answers unless we know what it means.

b. A similar argument applies to the doctrine that every question
presupposes one and only one proposition, which causes it to "arise"
(EM, 25). One may agree that questions do have presuppositions,
and that these are seldom made explicit. But as it is possible to construct alternative questions to which a given proposition is a relevant
answer, so it is possible to construct different propositions presupposed by the same question. "When do you intend to catch the train
for New York?" presupposes both that you intend to go to New
York and that you believe that it is possible to get there by train.
Now the second of these does not of itself give rise to the question;
we know of trains which we do not intend to catch. But on the other
hand, neither does the knowledge of the intention to go give rise to
the question apart from knowledge of the available means of trans-
portation. Collingwood might say that what the question presupposes, *à la fois,* is "You intend to catch the train for New York"; but
even so, this proposition does not uniquely give rise to the question
"When?" rather than, say, the question "Why?" Collingwood does

not deny that a question may presuppose more than one and very likely a great many propositions. But his view is that one and only one of these has uniquely the property of "logical efficacy." Now there is no apparent way of ascribing that property, in any given case, to one rather than another of the propositions jointly presupposed. One might say that a question can have different meanings, and that one presupposition gives rise to one meaning of the question while a different presupposition gives rise to another meaning. But in that case we are merely trapped into circumnavigating the vicious circle in the opposite direction.

c. It is not propositions, Collingwood says, but question-and-answer complexes which alone can properly be called "true" (A, 37–38; this doctrine is not explicitly repeated in EM). He does not discuss what might be meant by "falsity," nor, does it appear, could he. For how could a question-and-answer complex be "false"? It could not be because it contained answers which are false. Presumably one could say only that it would not be a question-and-answer complex at all; but then "it" would not be false. Collingwood might be willing to bite the bullet and deny that question-and-answer complexes are ever false (presumably because there are only degrees of truth). But a concept of truth which has no opposite is not merely curious but impossible, since in the ordinary course of events we often arrive, even provisionally, at "truth" by processes which essentially involve the demonstration that other alternatives are false.

Collingwood recognizes this difficulty, but his attempt to escape it is not convincing. He is properly concerned to show that it is possible for the "right" answer to a question to be "false," in the sense that such an answer, like the hypothesis in a *reductio ad absurdum* proof, may be a "link, and a sound one, in the chain of questions and answers by which the falseness of that presupposition is made manifest" (A, 38). Notably, the quotation marks which Collingwood carefully puts around his other uses of "true" or "false" in their ordinary senses are omitted here; but the "falseness" of which he speaks cannot possibly be the opposite of "truth" in the sense stipulated in the Logic of Question and Answer. The falseness of the hypothesis in a *reductio* proof is shown by the fact that it leads to a logical contradiction; and the truth of its contradictory follows from that. But to admit this, it may be said, is to accept just those meanings of "true," "false," and "contradiction" which appear in the propositional logic which Collingwood claims to reject. It appears that Collingwood covertly presupposes the very view which he opposes, in the course of explaining his own view.

d. Finally, it might be objected that Collingwood's argument depends in a fundamental way on exploiting the ambiguity, which he explicitly recognizes, in such terms as "knowledge," "assertion," and "statement"; each of these terms may refer either to the *activity* of knowing, asserting, or stating or to *what* is known, asserted, or stated. Collingwood himself for the most part uses the term "proposition," which in the traditional vocabulary of logic is not at all subject to that particular ambiguity; but he then *gives* it the very ambiguity which it ordinarily escapes. As "assertion" means both the act of asserting something and what it is that is asserted, so Collingwood uses "proposition" to mean both the act of propounding something and what it is that is propounded. The effect of this innovation is that while most of the doctrines of the Logic of Question and Answer are acceptable but trivial in the first, unusual sense, they tend to be understood in the second and more ordinary sense, and it is only in this sense that they seem incompatible with "propositional logic."

An example of this is Collingwood's principle that no two propositions can contradict each other unless they are answers to the same question (A, 33). This is intended to controvert the principle of "propositional logic" that two propositions which are not answers to the same question *can* contradict each other; and what is more, Collingwood accepts and even brandishes the opinion that *these* two principles are incompatible. But quite apart from the question whether these two principles are answers to the same question, none of Collingwood's argument follows if "proposition" is an activity-word rather than an entity-word; because as an activity-word, "proposition" refers to the attempt by someone on a specific occasion to communicate a meaning in an utterance, and it may well be the case that two *propoundings* do not contradict each other although they result in propositions which (formally) do. Significantly, the main example which Collingwood offers refers to a *man,* not to a *sentence:* "It is therefore impossible to say of a man, 'I do not know what the question is which he is trying to answer, but I can see that he is contradicting himself' " (A, 33).

But no logician would claim that two sentences could be contradictory if they contained different terms, or the same terms but with different meanings. Whether or not terms are used ambiguously in a particular piece of discourse is not a question for the formal logician to settle; the most he can say is that if the terms mean the same thing in their different occurrences, then there is this contradiction or that implication. If Collingwood's claim is only that the meaning of an utterance is not wholly determined by the form of the utterance, then he is not asserting what anyone would deny, and his view correspondingly loses in interest what it gains in plausibility. It would still differ from other views insofar as it holds that the *only* way of determining the meaning of statements is to discover the questions they are intended to answer, but that returns us to the objections canvassed above.

3 · *"Logic" or Hermeneutics?*

What leads the Logic of Question and Answer into this tangle of difficulties? It is, I believe, Collingwood's claim that his views are incompatible with those of "propositional logic," although by his own account they could not be incompatible unless they are answers to the same question or questions. And he did not even attempt to show that this is the case. Nor is it. *His* question—in its most general terms—was: What are the generic features of the process by which we can correctly interpret the meanings of statements? The *logical* question is: What are the formal features of statements in virtue of which they can sustain logical relationships independent of their meanings? The Logic of Question and Answer is not a theory of logic at all, in any ordinary sense of that term, nor is it even a theory of semantics; it is a hermeneutics. And as such it supplements but does not replace formal logic.

Collingwood could not avoid regarding propositions as logical entities, but he wanted to regard them as something more, and it was on this "something more" that his energy and attention were concentrated. The question-and-answer complex is a model, not of a logical system of interrogative and indicative sentences, but of stages in the process of inquiry or of active thought in general. The emphasis on knowledge as an activity of asking and answering questions rather than as a "body" of "propositions" was a note which Collingwood struck early and never abandoned. It occurs in an eloquent passage in *Speculum Mentis:*

> A crude empiricism imagines . . . that to know and to assert are identical. But it is only when the knower looks back over his shoulder at the road he has travelled, that he identifies knowledge with assertion. Knowledge as a past fact, as something dead and done with—knowledge by the time it gets into encyclopedias and text-books—does consist of assertion, and those who treat it as an affair of enyclopedias and text-books may be forgiven for thinking that it is an assertion and nothing else. But those who look upon it as an affair of discovery and exploration have never fallen into that error. People who are acquainted with knowledge at first hand have always known that assertions are only answers to questions [SM, 77].

The view expressed here is clearly not a substitute for formal logic but an observation that the subject-matter of intellectual history is a process of thinking which is to be interpreted through but not identified with the documents—the series of statements—which provide the evidence for the reconstruction of the process. The Logic of Question and Answer might more properly have been called the *dialectic* of question and answer. This would make the fact clear, whereas Collingwood's rhetorical use of traditional logical terminology with unannounced shifts of meaning tends to obscure it, that the relation between question and answer, or between question and presupposition, must be understood as occurring in processes which are *prospectively open but retrospectively determinate*. This is the generic characteristic of any process dialectically envisioned. Its special features in the case of "question and answer complexes" (*sc.* "processes") could be summarized as follows:

a. Given a certain question, the answer to it must be discovered, not just inferred. In the case of empirical science, for example, the question must be put to nature; the question determines what will *count* as an answer, but which of alternative answers which *would* count is the "right" one must be settled by other criteria.

b. Given a certain answer (i.e., a "proposition" in Collingwood's sense), the question which it answers can be inferentially reconstructed from the proposition together with other evidence about the process of inquiry in which it occurs. Taken as having a specific meaning, the proposition is an answer to a *unique* question; but the interpretation of meaning and the reconstruction of the question are themselves parts of a single process and cannot be determined independently of each other.

c. Thus the possibility of answers, seen from the standpoint of the question, is multivalent; but the reconstruction of the question, seen from the standpoint of a given answer, is univalent.

Analogous features hold for the relation between question and presupposition:

d. Given that a certain presupposition is made, any of a number of questions may arise, none of which would arise in the absence of the presupposition. At the same time, none must, or automatically will, arise.

e. Given that a certain question arises, there is an indefinite number of presuppositions which are jointly necessary to the question's arising, but there is one presupposition which uniquely, taken together with the others, is sufficient. This is its "logical efficacy."

f. Sections d and e above are *prima facie* contradictory: according to (d), no presupposition entails the asking of any question, and according to (e), the asking of a question is entailed by a unique presupposition. The resolution of this apparent contradiction depends entirely on seeing the subject at issue as the dialectic of a question-and-answer *process* rather than as the logic of a question-and-answer complex. The difference between these is analogous to the difference between inference and implication. The former is a process—something done by someone—while the latter is a relation —something which exists whether or not it is recognized. Now one cannot describe a situation in which someone validly draws an inference unless one supposes that there is an implication which is correctly traced out in the process of drawing the inference. But on the other hand there are obviously many cases in which, although a certain implication plainly exists, it is drawn incorrectly or not at all: we see other people—and they see us—failing to "get the point." It is of course logically impossible to see oneself as failing to get the point, because one would have to get it in order to do so. Yet often we recognize that we *did* fail, but only after we have succeeded— when we have, so to speak, actually drawn the inference corresponding to the implication which was there all the time. Now such a situation has this peculiarity: *Before* we get the point, there is nothing whatever which can compel us to do so. A concerned friend may invent heuristic devices for increasing its visibility, but none of these can substitute for the act which we ourselves must perform, and in the end the only response to obtuseness is, "But don't you see? Just *try* to see." However, *after* we have correctly drawn the inference, it is no longer possible for us to re-enact the state of mind in which we *failed* to see it. We cannot pretend to ourselves that we cannot solve a problem whose solution we do know. *Before* we get the point, we cannot imagine what it might be. *After* we get it, we cannot imagine how we failed to see it.

Now it is in a way similar to this that one can say that a presupposition is not a sufficient condition of a question's arising, but that once the question *has* arisen it can no longer be thought of except as an inevitable consequence of the presupposition. The logical efficacy of a presupposition is not a force which causes a question to arise, just as the existence of a problem is not a sufficient cause of its solution. It is rather a property which accrues to presuppositions *in retrospective reconstruction,* in the same way that the reconstruction of the steps by which a solution was reached has a lucidity which did not characterize the confusions and false starts of the problem-solving process itself.

This is of course an emendation of Collingwood's view; for he did say that the logical efficacy of a presupposition *causes* a certain question to arise (EM, 27). But there is no reason to suppose that he meant by this that the making of a presupposition is the sufficient condition of a question's arising, and some evidence to suppose that he meant no more than that it is a necessary condition. What he is quite explicit about is that a question is related to a presupposition in such a way that the former cannot arise in the absence of the latter (EM, 25–27); and where one would expect him to raise the question whether a presupposition can be made which does not lead to a relevant question's arising, he discusses instead, and at some length, the entirely different point that the logical efficacy of a proposition does not require that it be asserted, but only that it be supposed, or "assumed" (EM, 27). Since Collingwood himself does not raise the question which leads to the present emendation, it can be regarded as supplementing and not contradicting his intent.

Understanding the process of question and answer as prospectively open but retrospectively determinate reveals that it is closely analogous to the structure of a scale of forms. For in the latter, too, each lower level or earlier stage is a necessary condition of the next, does not necessitate the emergence of the next level, but yet is seen from the standpoint of that level as leading to it and in fact incorporated in it. The scale of forms, as we saw, does not apply to all concepts and theories but to what in the *Essay on Philosophical Method* Collingwood called "philosophical" concepts and theories; the Logic of Question and Answer, on the other hand, does claim unrestricted generality. The present interpretation amounts to saying that this claim can be sustained only as applying to questions and answers occurring in a process of inquiry; it does not extend to all sentences of interrogative and indicative form. One simply cannot tell of an interrogative sentence separated from every possible context what question it would represent in an actual case of inquiry; in order to do that one must have some *historical* understanding of the features of that actual process. Hence the criticisms canvassed above of Collingwood's "logic" pass into irrelevance, since they all propose as counterexamples statements abstracted from the concrete situations in which they might be *actually* asked or asserted.

Now we do, it might be observed, distinguish readily between rhetorical and non-rhetorical or genuine questions; a rhetorical question is not a genuine question because, although it has interrogative form, it is not intended to leave open the possibility of alternative answers. But how do we decide *in practice* that a question is rhetorical? There is no *formal* difference whatever between "Are we decided?" (Perhaps; perhaps not) and "Are we downhearted?" (No!). Yet in most cases we have no difficulty in deciding that a question as uttered is rhetorical; it is simply clear from the context that it does not represent any process of *inquiry*. We might therefore say that the Logic of Question and Answer applies to, and only to, relations between questions and answers which are context-dependent; it calls attention to the fact that we do understand and use such context-dependency, and that this understanding cannot be exhausted by any formal analysis.

But even if one agrees to see what Collingwood has to say about the "logic of question-and-answer complexes" as answers to questions about the "dialectic of question-and-answer processes," an important problem remains. The import of his contribution to the theory of meaning remains that the meaning of statements cannot be understood except as answers to specific questions. But this does not seem to be true of many cases of knowledge, and especially of scientific knowledge; and it is an especially poignant difficulty in view of the fact that Collingwood is claiming in the *Essay on Metaphysics* to provide an analysis of scientific thinking. Consider this question:

does answering a question in any way modify the question itself? Collingwood answers, "By being answered a question does not cease to be a question. It only ceases to be an unanswered question" (EM, 25). What this statement obviously intends to reject is the possible objection to Collingwood's theory that although it may well be true that in a process of scientific inquiry statements *occur* only as answers to questions, they nevertheless, as contributions to knowledge, are detachable after they have been attained from the questions which led to their discovery. This is at any rate the most usual interpretation of most scientific knowledge. We can understand the meaning of "The earth rotates on its axis" without necessarily understanding it as the answer to the question, "Why does the plane of oscillation of a Foucault pendulum shift with respect to a fixed line on the earth's surface?" And we understand "Sound is the propagation of waves in a medium" without thinking of it as the answer to the question "Why is no sound heard from a bell ringing in a jar from which the air has been exhausted?" Moreover, it is a characteristic often noted of some scientific discoveries that they turn out to be answers to questions which had not yet been asked when they were discovered; and this could hardly be the case unless their meaning were understood apart from the questions which they antedate.

There is a second class of questions for which Collingwood does not account: those which by being answered do cease to be questions because they are *dissolved* as such; for example, "Is justice round or square?" In Collingwood's terms, of course, such a question could not arise unless it were presupposed that justice is a spatial object; but if that presupposition *were* made it could arise. And one would not want to say that it could, or should, survive as an "unanswered question," but rather that (as we think) it should be dissolved as a question by eliminating its presupposition.

Nevertheless, there remains an important class of questions to which Collingwood's account applies in an illuminating way. Although scientific answers are detachable from the specific questions which led to their discovery, and although category-answers often dissolve the questions which provoked them, there are other statements which become intelligible only when they are reconstructed as answers to specific questions. Such reconstructions predominate in intellectual history, and Collingwood's own work in intellectual history shows how consistently and extensively he applied his own principles. In *The Idea of Nature,* for example, he shows how the thought of the Ionian pre-Socratics whom Aristotle called "physio-logues" can be reconstructed as a series of questions, each growing out of the answer to the last. The first question of Thales and of Anaximander was "What is nature?" This is a question of the form ("What is x?") which Collingwood in *The New Leviathan* called "bogus" (NL, 11.12); but it was at once converted into the question "What are things made of?"—a question which prescribed in advance that a satisfactory answer must designate some universal substance. And this led in turn to further questions: "How can we form a clear mental picture of the universal primitive substance?" and "How, from the description of this primitive substance, can we deduce the details of the world of nature?" And Collingwood shows how such a reconstruction discloses a pattern of intelligibility in Ionian thought and simultaneously shows why it led to a dead end so far as its own aims were concerned.

Now Collingwood is surely right that the thought of the physio-logues, and not merely because of our fragmentary knowledge of it, is a hash of nonsense if we suppose that its key terms had anything like our contemporary meanings or that the physiologues were asking anything like contemporary questions, either scientific or metaphysical; their questions were neither "scientific" nor "metaphysical," as we understand those terms. On the other hand, it is not necessary to suppose that the fragments were merely lyrical flights of the sort which surprise and baffle even their creators. From the standpoint of our *historical* knowledge the pattern of question and answer is *the* pattern of intelligibility. The questions we know only by reconstructing them from the answers, but the answers would not make sense at all unless they are taken as answers to *some* question. Why else have the pre-Socratic fragments survived in the history of Western philosophy at all? Because (ever since Hegel), it was recognized that later and more sophisticated philosophers were asking questions which stemmed in various ways from, although they also differed from, the Ionian series. Collingwood, in effect, elucidates, in his theory of question and answer, the logic of *interpretation* which has become almost a matter of consensus in the historiography of ideas. Even those who believe that there is a standard repertory of "philosophical problems" have tended to agree that these are formulated in different ways over time, and that it is essential, in order to understand a particular view, to grasp the specific way in which the questions were formulated in that view.

Thus it appears that although in some cases questions are not answered but dissolved, and in even more cases there are questions whose answers are independently intelligible, there are also some questions whose meaning is correlative with that of the possible answers to them. The tendency of recent critical philosophy has been to regard the first type as the province of philosophy, to identify the second as the province of science, and to ignore the third entirely. Collingwood, on the contrary, ignored the first and sometimes spoke as if he intended to reduce the second to the third. But even if the distinction is reinstated, his question-and-answer formula holds good for a wide range of cases and brings them within the scope of philosophical inquiry; and it also contains recommendations for the scientist and historian as well as for the philosopher, insofar as science and history raise conceptual as well as empirical questions.

Like the pragmatists who were his contemporaries but of whose views he was unaware, Collingwood's contribution was not to the *logic of proof* but to the *theory of inquiry.* Unlike pragmatism, to which he attributed the vulgar interpretation that it scorned all problems not of immediate practical interest, Collingwood wished to distinguish between scientific thought and historical thought and to justify the latter as an intellectual activity with its own aims and methods. Hence the Logic of Question and Answer has a double reference which is absent in classical pragmatism; it looks backward as well as forward. It is not equally effective in both directions, however. Significantly, Collingwood compares the Logic of Question and Answer with the programs for method introduced by Francis Bacon and Descartes, and this in itself is evidence that he was proposing not a substitute for formal logic but a new *Organon,* that is, a set of canons for the prosecution of inquiry. But although his recommendations do in fact constitute a *novum organon* for historical thought, their consequences for scientific thought are less novel and illuminating. A way of seeing why this is so is to consider that our understanding of past scientific thought is itself a matter of historical reconstruction. When Collingwood refers to "science," he more often than not has in mind the *history* of science, that is, of completed processes of inquiry. It would be granted, I suppose, that the ability to make scientific discoveries is quite different from the ability to reconstruct the history of the way in which a scientific discovery was made. Einstein is supposed to have said, when asked how he discovered the theory of relativity, "I questioned an axiom." Now this accords with Collingwood's theory, but at the same time it makes clear that the secret of scientific discovery is to question the right thing at the right time. As it applies to science, the Logic of Question and Answer tells no one *how* to do this. According to Collingwood, the "right" question is the one which helps us to *get ahead;* this clearly is not a regulative principle which enables one to distinguish which is the right question to ask *now;* it is rather an interpretative principle which enables one to tell what *was* the right question after the inquiry has succeeded. Thus, where science is concerned, the question-answer formula does not tell one how to answer questions but only reminds one that that is what one is trying to do. It does not recommend a method of investigation but describes a stage of inquiry.

However, the situation is different for historical thought, for which the object of inquiry is itself a completed process of thought, and the problem is to show why a certain solution *was* successful or not. For Collingwood, of course, not just intellectual history but all history is the reconstruction of past thought; thus the question-answer formula is perfectly general with respect to history, although the limit of its application in science is precisely that immediate present in which the scientist does not yet know the answers to his questions nor even whether those questions are the right ones—that is, the ones which in the end will turn out *to have been* the "right" ones.

The double reference of the Logic of Question and Answer therefore reflects the asymmetry of dialectical processes in general, and specifically the asymmetry by which an open future becomes a determinate past. Both historical thought and scientific thought are processes of inquiry which proceed by raising questions and trying to answer them; but the former is, and the latter is not, also *about* such activities of mind, reconstructed from their evidence in the record of human action and expression. Historical inquiry is doubly dialectical, both in its procedure and in its subject-matter.[1]

4 · *The Theory of Absolute Presuppositions*

But even this is prolegomenon. I have argued that Collingwood intended his Logic of Question and Answer to provide a model for his conception of knowledge as essentially a process of inquiry and not an expanding body of true statements. This was a conception which he held unaltered from the time of his earliest work; but it was not until his last years that he saw that it also provided the foundation for what appears as his theory of presuppositions, and especially of "absolute presuppositions." The Logic of Question and Answer was first given shape in the lost manuscript of "Truth and Contradiction" of 1917; the theory of presuppositions, on the other hand, is not even mentioned before the *Autobiography* in 1939. But it would be surprising, even though Collingwood seems both in the *Autobiography* and in the *Essay on Metaphysics* which succeeded it within a year to have effected his "rapprochement between history and philosophy" by resolving all philosophical problems into historical questions, if the theory of presuppositions were a completely new departure rather than an answer to questions which he had been long in the process of reformulating. This is in the end the crucial issue in the interpretation of Collingwood. The theory of *absolute* presuppositions makes explicit and throws retrospective light on a great many ideas which Collingwood had sought to express earlier, including a number of the more curious ones, such as his attempt to describe the "categorical propositions" of philosophy in the *Essay on Philosophical Method,* and his doctrine of the "a priori imagination" in *The Idea of History.* Moreover, it is at this point that Collingwood becomes most relevant to current philosophical issues and proves to have illuminating affinities with contemporary types of philosophy which otherwise have seemed to have little relevance to each other. Yet, as in the Logic of Question and Answer, the theory of absolute presuppositions has been generally misunderstood —in large part because of the fact that Collingwood stated it in such a way that it also seems to be, although it is not, a rival to propositional logic.

Most of Collingwood's discussion of the Logic of Question and Answer consisted of an examination of the relations in which questions, answers, and presuppositions can stand to each other, and, as noted above, what Collingwood says implies that they constitute linear series, which move forward as an answer to the last question becomes the presupposition from which the next question arises. *Mutatis mutandis,* in the reconstruction of such a series, the recovery of a question to which a statement is an answer leads on to the discovery of the presupposition in whose absence the question would not have arisen, and this presupposition in turn is regarded as the answer to a prior question. The process of inquiry itself (i.e., both the attempt to make such a resonstruction and the process of thought which it seeks to reconstruct) has no *terminus ad quem;* its future will include questions which cannot even be guessed at before their presuppositions emerge as the answers to present and future questions. But at the same time any given process of inquiry does have a *terminus a quo;* this consists of a set of "absolute" presuppositions differing from "relative" presuppositions in that they are not, as relative presuppositions are, themselves answers to any questions whatever.

The spurious "axiomatization" of the Logic of Question and Answer and the Theory of Presuppositions which Collingwood attempted in the *Essay on Metaphysics* (it is a rhetorical device, not a logical one) says only two things about absolute presuppositions: they are presuppositions of some questions but answers to none, and they are not propositions, that is, not capable in principle of being true or false. But Collingwood had more to add to the theory quite apart from his *use* of the idea of absolute presuppositions in the *specimina philosophandi* of the *Essay on Metaphysics.* And, as is often the case with Collingwood's theories, although its import is difficult to assess, its outlines are easy to summarize.

a. Absolute presuppositions, like relative presuppositions, are presuppositions of *questions* rather than of, say *beliefs;* but while a relative presupposition gives rise to one question, an absolute presupposition gives rise to many questions (EM, 31); this is why it can be the *terminus a quo* of an entire question-and-answer process, while a relative presupposition is only one step in a given process.

b. Absolute presuppositions can be made not only by individuals but by groups—not, of course, in a sense which supposes that there is anything like a group mind but in the sense that individuals can share absolute presuppositions, and it is therefore possible to speak of the absolute presuppositions of a society (EM, 48 n.).

c. Absolute presuppositions, Collingwood repeatedly says, are the presuppositions of "natural science." Taken out of context, this can be misleading, since the term "science" has taken on a meaning much broader than it had in *Speculum Mentis* or the *Essay on Philosophical Method.* By the "science" of a given time he now means the inquiries undertaken by the people of that time into the details of what they regarded as the world (A, 66). Hence Locke's political theory, for example, is put forward as an instance of "science" insofar as Locke's conception of property presupposed a "state of nature" of which property is a feature, and an idea of nationality as also having a "natural basis" (EM, 97). By "science," in fact, Collingwood means in this context (and claims that this is its "proper" sense) any "body of systematic or orderly thinking about a determinate subject-matter" (EM, 4); and he elsewhere adds that this includes not only intellectual but practical thought, such as is involved in "making a table or organizing a secretarial staff or defeating an enemy" (EM, 85). Thus the theory is intended to be perfectly general; it applies to the entire history of human thought and action, including what we think of as the bounded field of natural science.

d. Absolute presuppositions do not occur, and cannot be analyzed, singly. Although they are not propositions, and therefore cannot form systems in the logical sense, they do occur only in sets or *constellations* of absolute presuppositions, "all made at once in one and the same piece of thinking" (EM, 66). And the absolute presuppositions in such a constellation must be *consupponible* in the sense that with respect to any one of them it must be *possible* to suppose every other one, although it is not *necessary* to suppose any. No absolute presupposition can be deduced from another or from a constellation. All this implies, of course, that with respect to a single absolute presupposition, there will be a class of possible constellations with which it is consupponible, and a class of possible constellations with which it is not consupponible.

e. Nevertheless, it does occur that constellations include presuppositions not consupponible with each other, and such constellations are in unstable equilibrium, or under internal *strain* (EM, 74). The constellation of absolute presuppositions operative in the thought of a person or of a society may not be—and in fact ordinarily will not be—perfectly consupponible; and absolute presuppositions which have been recessive may become dominant, exacerbating the strain. Hence there is a dynamics of absolute presuppositions, and it is possible to analyze the way in which strains occur, how they are taken up, and in the extreme case how one constellation, unable to compromise its increasingly disruptive internal strains, comes to be replaced by another. "Metaphysics," as Collingwood used the term in the *Essay on Metaphysics,* is the analysis of the absolute presuppositions made in the thought of a given time; but, although his illustrations in that book are limited to such analysis, it is also, as he recognized in the *Autobiography,* a way of following the "historical

process by which one set of presuppositions has turned into another"
(A, 66).

f. Absolute presuppositions, whether taken singly or as belonging to constellations, are not subject to proof or disproof. This follows directly from Collingwood's denial that they are propositions
and his acceptance of the usual view that only propositions are capable of being true or false.[2] But additional material reasons are
offered: absolute presuppositions are not subject to proof because "it
is proof that depends on them, not they, on proof" (EM, 173).
Clearly an absolute presupposition could not be proved by showing
it to be entailed by something more fundamental; for then it would
not be an *absolute* presupposition. But neither is any sort of empirical evidence relevant: an absolute presupposition is not derived from
experience in the first instance (EM, 197) and "cannot be under-
mined by the verdict of 'experience' because it is the yard-stick by
which 'experience' is judged" (EM, 193–94). In a different context
(PA, 8 n.), Collingwood had quoted the anthropologist Evans-
Pritchard to the same effect: "Let the reader consider any argument
that would utterly demolish all Zande claims for the power of the
oracle. If it were translated into Zande modes of thought it would
serve to support their entire structure of belief."[3]

g. Evans-Pritchard, Collingwood might say, had in fact analyzed
the absolute presuppositions shared in the Zande culture; but as a
modern western European man, and a scientist, his investigations
also reflected his own absolute presuppositions. Therefore, if he were
right about the Zande—or even if he *could* be right—it follows that
he was not prevented by his own absolute presuppositions from reconstructing their quite different constellation. This possibility helps
to explain Collingwood's insistence that the logical efficacy of presuppositions does not depend on their being true or even being believed to be true but only on their being supposed; Evans-Pritchard
did not need to accept Zande presuppositions, as he did his own, in
order to understand the way in which they gave structure to the
thought and experience of the Zande. One can, that is, think *about*
absolute presuppositions different from and not consupponible with
the absolute presuppositions of one's own thought. But can one make
one's own absolute presuppositions an object of one's own thought?

Collingwood suggests that such reflection is possible, even
though it rarely occurs. He was particularly concerned to deny that
we can be *directly* aware of our absolute presuppositions by intro-

spection. It is only by analysis that absolute presuppositions can be discovered (EM, 43); but the analysis by which one probes the absolute presuppositions of another could just as well be applied to thought by oneself or one's society. However, knowing what one's absolute presuppositions are neither eliminates nor reinforces them. Nor is it an easy matter, in any case. Collingwood slyly suggests an experimental method for deciding whether another person's presuppositions are relative or absolute: persons used to disciplined thinking, he observes, will consider with equanimity an invitation to justify or else abandon a presupposition if it is relative. But if the presupposition is *absolute,* the invitation will be rejected, and violently so. Now one cannot extend such an invitation to oneself in order to find out whether one feels threatened by it. But as Collingwood observes, such irritability depends on "a kind of virginity in the reflective faculties." Just so, Socrates irritated his accusers to the point of violence in the course of attempting to analyze his own presuppositions as well as theirs (and the irony is not mitigated by his conviction that they were the same). Self-analysis is possible—but the temptation to cheat is strong. Finally, however, analysis is itself a process of inquiry, and as such it is not presuppositionless: no matter what constellation of absolute presuppositions it may reveal in the object of inquiry, it proceeds from its own constellation, which includes, among others, the presuppositions of all consciously historical thought (EM, 63-64).

5 · *Absolute Presuppositions as A Priori Concepts*

This completes the main outlines of the theory of absolute presuppositions so far as Collingwood's explicit discussion of it is concerned. A perspicacious reader, however sympathetic, will remain dissatisfied. Despite all that Collingwood had to say about what absolute presuppositions *do,* and how they function, it remains unclear what they *are.* The temptation is very great—and it is a temptation to which Collingwood himself occasionally succumbed—to regard them as propositions, or as examples of a special kind of proposition, despite his repeated denial that they are. An interpretation on this assumption would be possible: absolute presuppositions can be regarded as assumptions, like the postulates of an axiomatic theory; their "consupponibility" would become a curious way of referring to their logical compatibility, "constellation" to a set of logically independent postulates, and "strain" to logical incompatibility, perhaps in the technical sense in which postulates may not be directly contradictory and yet, taken together with other postulates, entail contradictory theorems. All this would be familiar territory for anyone familiar with modern logic; and Collingwood's terminology of "constellation," "consupponibility" and "strain" even suggests that he had such an analogy in mind. But if it were more than an analogy, it would vitiate both the novelty and the application of the theory of absolute presuppositions. The logic of deductive systems is well developed, and Collingwood's theory makes no contribution to it even obliquely. Moreover, the main point of the theory would evanesce, since in deductive systems the postulates are never "absolute"; they are postulates relative to a particular system, but it is always theoretically possible to construct another system in which they appear as theorems (as the so-called "Laws of Thought" appear as theorems in the system of Russell and Whitehead's *Principia Mathematica*). If one interprets absolute presuppositions as propositions and their relations as the logical relations of propositions, therefore, one is dismissing the possibility that the theory of presuppositions is either novel or true.

But what else could absolute presuppositions be? They are neither assumptions nor beliefs, insofar as assuming and believing are attitudes which can take only propositions as objects and can be expressed only in propositional form. Moreover, assumptions can be denied and beliefs can be false, while absolute presuppositions, according to Collingwood, can be neither. In one striking way, absolute presuppositions are more like habits of thought or rules of inference: they are a necessary condition of every argument but are not parts of any one: and this, as Lewis Carroll's Tortoise said to Achilles, is the logical character of a rule of inference such as *modus ponens*. It cannot be stated as a step of a proof in which an inference is drawn from the assertion of an antecedent to the assertion of a consequent, because if it were itself a step, a *further* rule would be required to connect it with the other steps. Hence rules of inference, in modern logical systems, are regarded as belonging to the metalanguage in which one describes the proof rather than to the "object language" in which the proof is stated. Certainly in this respect absolute presuppositions resemble rules of inference; they are not capable of proof because all proof depends on them. But on the other hand, rules of inference for formal deductive systems are few and thin, although completely general, while the possibilities of constellations of absolute presuppositions are very rich; and with few exceptions there is little fundamental disagreement over rules of inference, as Collingwood believes there to be over absolute presuppositions.

What can it be, then, which fits the description of an absolute presupposition? Only one thing: an a priori concept. *Absolute presuppositions are concepts functioning as a priori; constellations of absolute presuppositions are a priori conceptual systems.* The theory of presuppositions, on this interpretation, belongs to that history of ideas which began with Kant and whose most recent manifestation is linguistic analysis; but it also differs from both, just to the extent that it is (as incorporating a dynamics of change) explicitly dialectical.[4]

Kant's a priori concepts, which he called "categories of the understanding," were regarded by him, as Collingwood regards absolute presuppositions, as providing the general structure of experience and at the same time, when "schematized" or applied over time to the raw data of the manifold of sensation, as yielding synthetic a priori truths which are the ultimate premises of scientific knowledge. Kant thought, moreover, that he had proved the categories of the understanding to be necessary conditions of the possibility of experience *überhaupt;* thus they jointly constitute, in his view, the formal structure of mind—not just of the modern mind, or of the Western mind, but of anything which could count as a mind at all. There is a remarkable, although little remarked, similarity between Kant's view and that of so-called linguistic philosophy stemming from the later Wittgenstein. For the latter, it is not the "human mind" but common language which incorporates a conceptual system acquired in the process of learning to speak ordinary language, and determining a priori what is *conceivable,* so that to depart (as in speculative philosophy) from the clear uses of common language is to start insoluble puzzles by pressing language beyond the limits of application of its constituent rules.

The idea that in all experience and thought a conceptual scheme is brought to the ordering of an intrinsically indeterminate congeries of data, and that such a scheme is a priori in the sense that it determines in advance at least part of what we appear to find in experience, is of course not original with Collingwood but is a view shared by otherwise quite disparate thinkers.[5] Even so radical an empiricist as William James occasionally wrote passages which might have come straight from Collingwood:

> All our conceptions are what the Germans call *Denkmittel,* means by which we handle facts by thinking them. . . .
> We . . . frame some system of concepts mentally classified, serialized, or connected in some intellectual way, and then . . . use this as a tally by which we "keep tab" on the impressions that present themselves. When each is referred to some possible place in the conceptual system, it is thereby "understood." [6]

James recognized that there can be many conceptual systems, including but not limited to that of "common-sense." He even gave a list of some of the more important concepts of the latter: Thing, Same or Different, Kinds, Minds, Bodies, One Time, One Space, Subjects and Attributes, Causal Influences, the Fancied, the Real.[7]

One could read the passage from James as Collingwood's by substituting "absolute presuppositions" for "concepts." But it is notable that the passage reflects the preoccupation with the epistemological analysis of perception characteristic of most philosophy since Descartes. James regards conceptual systems as "tallies" (compare Collingwood's reference to absolute presuppositions as "yardsticks") which assign a place to each presented "impression." Thus the partial list of fundamental concepts which he suggests includes those involved in recognition, identification, and classification; it includes Kant's "forms of intuition," space and time, and the more important of his categories of the understanding. These are the concepts which Kant claimed to "deduce" or justify, as the necessary conditions of all perceptual experience and, stated in propositional form, as the premises of all natural science.

Compared with this preoccupation with perception, Collingwood's emphasis is primarily on the conceptual systems involved in practical, social, aesthetic, and intellectual experience. He does not ignore perceptual experience (and addresses himself to it in his discussion in *The Principles of Art* of sensa and the relations among sensa); but he is more interested in the other kinds. Why? For one thing, he held that there is no *history* of perception (IH, 307) as there is of action. And he also believed that while the chief business of philosophy after the seventeenth century was to reckon with natural science, the chief business of twentieth-century philosophy is to reckon with twentieth-century history (A, 78–79). Hence his main interest was not in the conceptual systems presupposed in identifying and classifying physical objects but with the part played by conceptual systems in those activities of which there can be histories, or re-enactments. From the standpoint of this interpretation of Collingwood it is possible to see that when he spoke, in his *Autobiography*, of "metaphysical problems, concerned with the nature of the historian's subject-matter: the elucidation of terms like event, process, progress, civilization, and so forth" (A, 77), he was actually giving a partial list of the concepts associated in a constellation of absolute presuppositions with the concept of history itself.

It is at this point that the rapprochement of philosophy and history is finally achieved, not (as even Collingwood's friendly critics have thought) by the disappearance of the former into the maw of the latter but by the supersession of both. To put it concisely: philosophy (old style) is seen as the articulation and codification of the conceptual systems (constellations of absolute presuppositions) which determine the formal features of the experience characteristic of a society and implicit in its institutions as well as in its beliefs. Philosophers have always done this, although in the belief that they were doing something else. Philosophy (new style) is also the analysis of the structure of conceptual systems so articulated and of the process by which one conceptual system has changed into another; but it is also an analysis of contemporary conceptual systems and as such is conscious of being *part of the process* by which such systems become more coherent and comprehensive or else give way by piecemeal modifications to identifiably different systems. Collingwood calls the analysis of this process an "historical science," and this has often seemed to be what might be called a dissuasive definition; but he means no more than that the analysis of absolute presuppositions is an analysis of a process of conceptual systems subject to change in time, not of "timeless entities," and that the conclusions of such analysis apply to an historical milieu and not to "mankind at large" (EM, 57). At the minimum, this is not a proscription of "philosophy." It is a memento mori, a reminder to philosophers (as to scientists and historians) that what they now think may be the latest thing, but it is not the last. "I have made completeness my chief aim," said Kant in the Preface to the first edition of the *Critique of Pure Reason*, "and I venture to assert that there is not a single metaphysical problem which has not been solved [in this enquiry], or for the solution of which the key at least has not been supplied." [8] And

Wittgenstein remarked without immodesty to Norman Malcolm that "it was very unlikely that anyone in his classes should think of something of which he had not already thought." [9] Both were right if one understands their claims as relative to particular conceptual systems. But who will be to Wittgenstein as Wittgenstein was to Kant? Who, that is, will explore the absolute presuppositions of ideas which have not yet been thought? If this question makes sense, Collingwood's discovery is irreversible. One may go beyond it, but cannot retreat from it.

The theory of absolute presuppositions was Collingwood's final answer to a question whose series of reformulations is the history of his own thought; and the question is both existential and theoretical. In its existential form it is: How can one nerve oneself to engage in systematic and rational philosophical thought when one recognizes that at best one can achieve mention in the history of errors which will be written from the standpoint of an unforeseeable future? In its theoretical form it is: What is the validity of philosophical arguments which belong to a history in which the criteria of validity have their own history of change? It is a natural tendency to regard the history of a problem as culminating in one's own solution to it; but the historical viewpoint is that this, too, shall pass away; the present, as well as the past, is prologue. Historicism is itself a kind of Copernican revolution which dissolves the egocentric conviction that history pivots on the present, as Copernicus destroyed the geocentric conviction that the heavens revolve around the place on which we stand. The modern history of astronomy replaced a closed world with the open universe. In the modern history of thought, the analogue to the closed world of medieval cosmology is the Enlightenment faith in progress by closer and closer approximations to ideally exact and complete knowledge. What the analogue is to the open universe we do not know, and to discover what it may be is the unsolved problem of modern thought. Collingwood laid siege to this problem, and his strategy (in retrospect) consisted of the attempt to take up the "strain" which it reveals in the constellation of absolute presuppositions which gives rise to it by finding a way in which the concept of system (required by the idea of reason) and the concept of change (required by the idea of history) become consupponible.

We have met this problem before. In the *Essay on Philosophical Method,* as we saw at the end of Chapter 3, Collingwood developed the idea of a scale of forms as the dialectical logic of philosophical concepts, but came to realize that it applied as well to the history of the development of philosophical theories, each of which is an "interim report" or summation of a history of which it is the latest but not the last stage. The theory of absolute presuppositions is thus the explicit elaboration of possibilities implicit in the dialectic of concepts. It relates the concept of system and the concept of change by interpreting the former as the articulation of a constellation of absolute presuppositions and the latter as the dynamic process by which thought attempts to relieve the strains in its own constellations. But the origins of the problem lie even further back. At the end of *Speculum Mentis* Collingwood had already recognized it:

> In an immediate and direct way, the mind can never know itself: it can only know itself through the mediation of an external world, know that what it sees in the external world is its own reflection. Hence the construction of external worlds—works of art, religions, sciences, structures of historical fact, codes of law, systems of philosophy and so forth *ad infinitum*—is the only way by which the mind can possibly come to that self-knowledge which is its end.

But self-knowledge paradoxically requires self-deception:

> It is perhaps not possible to carry out this process [of construction of external worlds] in the full consciousness of what one is doing: the illusion of abstract objectivity is essential to it: it must be done in good faith, in the belief that one is now at last discovering the ultimate truth, coming into contact with a pre-existent and absolute reality.

If the mind could realize that it has been "tracing its own lineaments in a mirror," it would therefore realize that

> The truth is not some perfect system of philosophy: it is simply the way in which all systems, however perfect, collapse into nothingness on the discovery that they are only systems, only external worlds over against the knowing mind and not that mind itself [SM, 315–16].

The tension here is plain, and it is both existential and theoretical. How can one—how can *I*—continue to maintain the "illusion of abstract objectivity" once it has been recognized as such? Collingwood's ultimate answer is that the theory of absolute presuppositions explains the generic features of the "construction of external worlds": absolute presuppositions provide the armatures on which those worlds are constructed. But the theory also provides the technique for going on without being sustained by the "illusion of abstract objectivity"; to recognize oneself as participating in the process of conceptual clarification *and change* is not, like the consciousness of illusion, self-defeating.

In the history of Collingwood's own thought, the theory of absolute presuppositions as a theory of a priori conceptual systems also makes explicit what was implicit in the development of other earlier ideas, and it should not now be necessary to spell these out in detail: "absolute presuppositions" are identical with "philosophical" (as distinguished from "empirical") concepts, with the "a priori imagination" in *The Idea of History,* with the "first principles" and "categorical propositions" of philosophy in the *Essay on Philosophical Method.* But they are "identical" only in the sense in which an earlier stage of a dialectical process is continuous with a later one as seen from the standpoint of the latter.

6 · *Absolute Presuppositions and the Dialectic of Mind*

I wish finally to make good the suggestion that the theory of absolute presuppositions interlocks with and completes the dialectic of mind—that is, the dialectical order of levels of consciousness or series of mental functions—in a way which makes the conclusion inescapable that both theories represent the same underlying system of ideas. The interpretation I am about to suggest could be summarized by saying that the theory of absolute presuppositions is to the dialectic of levels of consciousness as the theory of the scale of forms is to the dialectic of forms of experience in *Speculum Mentis.* In each of these pairs, the latter theories represent a sort of *Phänomenologie des Geistes* (in the Hegelian sense) and the former a *logic* or theory of dialectic. Moreover, the later philosophy, although a reformulation of the earlier, turns out to be continuous and compatible with it and to have the same general structure. *The dialectic of mental functions in the later philosophy is isomorphic with the dialectic of experience in the earlier.* There is one exception to this description, and it represents a significant advance in Collingwood's recognition of the theory of dialectic itself.

It will be remembered from Chapter 4 that Collingwood identified four major stages in the dialectic of levels of consciousness: pure feeling or undifferentiated sensation with its *apanage* of emotion at the first level of consciousness, appetite and imagination in "conceptual" or second-level consciousness, desire and primary intellect (i.e., perception) in "propositional" or third-level consciousness, will (further divided into two kinds of choice) and intellect (further divided into two kinds of thinking) in "rational" or fourth-level consciousness. In *The New Leviathan* he expressly identified the Logic of Question and Answer with the third level (NL, 11.22). But he never explicitly raised the question about the level of consciousness at which absolute presuppositions function.

Since absolute presuppositions are not propositions, and since they are absolutely presupposed by any series of questions and propositional answers, it might seem that they belong to the activity of second-level consciousness; and assigning them to this level would also comport with the interpretation of absolute presuppositions as conceptual systems rather than unacknowledged propositional beliefs. Yet for several reasons this is too simple a conclusion. For one thing, the concepts which function at the second level are mainly those which inform modes of perception; and the conceptual systems of action and reflection, which Collingwood was chiefly interested in elucidating, must belong to higher levels which absorb but go beyond the appetites and perceptions of the second level. Moreover, it is clear that Collingwood calls second-level consciousness "conceptual" not because all concepts belong to that level but because that is the lowest level at which concepts function at all. There are second-level concepts but also concepts which appear for the first time at each higher level; and there are third-level propositions but also propositions of the fourth level. "Self" is an example of a concept which appears at the second and every higher level (NL, 8.17, 10.15); "time" and "possible" are examples of concepts which appear at the third and higher levels (PA, 223–24); and "intention" and "entailment" are examples of concepts which appear only at the fourth level.

It therefore appears that there are conceptual systems at every level of consciousness, and further that any such system is a priori with respect to its own level because at no level can a conscious act become its own object; on the other hand, there is no conscious act which may not become the object of a higher level. So it follows that in Collingwood's view there is no absolute, or in Kantian language, "pure" a priori. At any level, thought "apprehends or constructs" (PA, 216) relations among the data available to it from a lower level, and it does so by inquiry, i.e., by a question and answer process. The experience of a lower level provides the data which thought organizes into answers; the concepts of its own level determine the kind and limits of the questions which it can entertain.

Moreover, concepts of a lower level may carry over to a higher level not only as objects but also by being transformed into concepts of the higher level. The concept of self is an illustration of this. The contrast between self and not-self is implicit in appetite at the second level of consciousness; self and not-self, however, are not in themselves first-order objects of consciousness, but abstractions from the first order activity of "loving," the act of seeking relation with something which will alleviate felt dissatisfaction (NL, 8.16). This is, of course, the most rudimentary concept of self; Collingwood also says that self and not-self are abstractions from the activity of becoming *angry* (as a first-order object) and again that the ideas of self, of not-self and of their contrast are conceptual elements in fear (NL, 10.15, 10.26). In all these cases the concept of self implicit in second-level activities is made explicit only by third-level reflection. But of course third-level activities (e.g., desire and perception, or propositional thought) are themselves activities in which third-level concepts of self and not-self—now related to such concepts as happiness and power—include but expand the second-level concepts, as, in general, desire includes but expands and makes more specific the forms of appetite. Thus in the series of levels the concepts of self and not-self become increasingly complex by taking over the lower-level concepts but relating them more and more to higher-level systems of concepts. By the fourth level, the conceptual system is so integrated that every fourth-level act involves distinguishing between the self and the not-self (NL, 18.1). The differences between "utility," "right," and "duty," all of which as modes of fourth-level practical consciousness have to do with the effective reasons for action and belief, reflect differences in the conceptual systems at different levels to which the concepts of "self" and "not-self" belong.

So far, then, we have again the vertical series of levels of consciousness, each with its own conceptual system or constellation of absolute presuppositions implicit in the activities of its own level, each capable of becoming the object of higher-level consciousness, and each to some extent also surviving in the conceptual system of that level.

At the fourth level, however, a profoundly significant characteristic emerges for the first time: rational thought, as Collingwood says, is "capable of understanding both itself and other things (NL,

10.51; cf. PA, 166–67). Therefore the *vertical* series of mental functions stops at the fourth level. An act of conceptual thinking cannot be the object of another act of conceptual thinking but only of an act of propositional thinking; an act of propositional thinking cannot be the object of another act of propositional thinking but only of an act of rational thinking; but an act of rational thinking, although it cannot be its *own* object, *can* be the object of another act of rational thinking. Thus at the fourth level there is generated for the first time a *horizontal* series of fourth-level acts. At lower levels there can be a sequence but not a series; states of conceptual consciousness can succeed each other, for example, but only in the way in which one total here-and-now of sensation and emotion can succeed another. Even at the propositional level the sequence is that of the classic reading primer: "Look, there is Jane. Look, look, there is Spot. Jane has a ball. Run, Spot, run." Apart from such sequences, in which one experience is succeeded by another and carried away in the flow of consciousness (cf. IH, 284–88), lower-level acts can belong only to the vertical dialectical series of mental functions which differ in kind as well as in degree. But fourth-level acts may belong also to a series of intellectual change over time, in which the acts themselves belong to a dialectical scale of forms. At the fourth level, we might say, self-consciousness *crosses the T* of the series of mental functions. Henceforth development proceeds indefinitely along this line without passing beyond its level. And this horizontal series is the dimension of history.[10]

Fourth-level acts therefore have, uniquely, a double genesis: in part, like all experience, their origin lies in sensation and emotion, which continuously feed into the life of reason and will, from *below,* the raw material of the changing states of the body; but in part, unlike lower levels of experience, their origin also lies in antecedent rational activities, which feed into the life of reason and will, from *behind,* the energy and formal definiteness but also the strains and limitations of a particular question-and-answer process reflecting a particular conceptual system or constellation of absolute presuppositions.

The principle of double genesis helps to account for certain major differences among interpretations of the history of philosophy or of intellectual history in general. The history of philosophy can be read—as it is in most histories of philosophy—as a series of systems or of intellectual problems and solutions completely unrelated to the human experience of warfare, political change, technological innovation, etc. (Consider the standard treatments of Locke, Berkeley, and Hume.) Or it can be read—as it is by many intellectual historians, or by Marxists or in such philosophical interpretations as Dewey's *The Quest for Certainty*—as a series of epiphenomenal reflections or rationalizations of the underlying process of social change. The former way, so to speak, attends only to the horizontal dimension of fourth level consciousness; the latter recognizes only the vertical dimension in which rational thought reflects the subrational interests and problems of men. The implication of Collingwood's view is that each is right in what it asserts and wrong in what it denies or overlooks. And, as the following chapter attempts to show, most discussions of Collingwood's theory of historical knowledge have been of little value because they have ignored the double genesis of "reflective thought"; they have taken, so to speak, the fourth level as the only level, since in *The Idea of History* the vertical series is not discussed but taken for granted by Collingwood in his use of "thought" and similar terms.

Although an order of consciousness higher than the fourth level is strictly inconceivable, because the fourth level crosses the T of the series of mental functions, there nevertheless is reproduced in this new horizontal dimension a dialectical series of types of rational thinking. Collingwood himself distinguished three such types, which are represented as forms of theoretical reason by Greco-medieval science, modern science, and historical consciousness, and as forms of practical reason by the corresponding concepts of "utility," "right," and "duty." There is no reason why the species of the fourth level should be as many as they are, other than that the history of the concept of reason has been what we understand it to be. In distinguishing the three types of practical reason, Collingwood says, "I find that there are three of these. Why three I neither know nor ask" (NL, 14.65). It is therefore possible that the concept of reason itself may change, as it has changed in the past; what we are willing to count as an instance of "because" or "therefore" may vary as we find new things to think about and therefore new opportunities to reflect on the experience of thinking. But what a fourth type of rational thinking might be could not in any way be predicted. It would come into being as a major transformation from the constellation of absolute presuppositions ordering contemporary western European thought to a new constellation. When such a new constellation comes into being together with the profound change of institutions and ideas which express it, its development out of its own past will be intelligible from its own standpoint, but only by criteria of intelligibility which would themselves have been formed in that development.

But this question, in Collingwood's view, is not yet even academic. The problem of the present is the self-understanding of the historical consciousness, and that process is barely under way. The theory of absolute presuppositions finds its place as Collingwood's contribution to that process. As we have seen, the structure of constellations of absolute presuppositions in any actual process of experience is T-shaped: the order of absolute presuppositions has both depth, in the vertical order of levels of consciousness, and breadth, at the fourth level, the history of which Collingwood came to regard as the object of "metaphysics." His particular examples of metaphysical analysis, in the *Essay on Metaphysics,* are in fact analyses of absolute presuppositions functioning at the fourth level; and thus they are *par excellence* chapters in the history of philosophical thought. But this does not rule out other kinds of histories. The history of art reconstructs absolute presuppositions of the second level from the evidence of the forms of imaginative expression to which they give rise; the history of science reconstructs third-level absolute presuppositions of theoretical thought from the explanations of natural events which have been advanced; the history of politics reconstructs third-level absolute presuppositions of practical thought from the purposive actions of men and the structure of their institutions. But the varieties of human histories are not only distinguished by the levels of experience on which they focus; they are also connected as these levels are related to each other. In this respect, the theory of absolute presuppositions is a kind of transcendental deduction of the leading principle of the *Geisteswissenschaften:* that there are discernible patterns of imagination, belief and action in historical epochs, and that the analogies among artistic styles, philosophical theories, religious beliefs and social and political institutions which one detects in, say, the Renaissance or the Enlightenment, while they are neither adventitious nor *causally* explicable, are intelligible as exhibiting the complex structure of constellations of absolute presuppositions implicit at those times in men's interpretation of the world and of themselves. The vertical and horizontal relations of absolute presuppositions constitute respectively the armature of historical reality and the dynamic of historical change. The logic of thought, dialectically interpreted, is the secret of history itself.

CHAPTER 6

The Grammar of Action:
History

1 · Objections to Collingwood's Account of Historical Knowledge

THE BEST KNOWN OF ALL OF COLLINGWOOD'S VIEWS IS BEYOND
doubt his theory of historical knowledge. When *The Idea of History*
was published posthumously in 1946, it filled the virtual vacuum
surrounding an issue which had been almost completely ignored by
English-speaking philosophers, although it was increasingly plagu-
ing reflective historians: is history an autonomous mode of knowledge, or is it an imperfectly developed version of the kind of inquiry
more securely practiced in the successful natural sciences? Collingwood gave a definite answer to this question, and one which, if not
authoritative, was at least reasoned and provocative. Yet the essays
collected as "Epilegomena" in *The Idea of History* are in fact very
difficult to understand and elucidate, although the full extent of
their difficulty is concealed by the grace of their style and the often
compelling quality of the *obiter dicta* so often quoted from them.
They are, nevertheless, largely unintelligible unless they are interpreted in the light of Collingwood's dialectical theory of mind as we
have reconstructed it. There are at least three main reasons for the
almost universal failure to recognize this.

First, the seven essays were written at different times for different
audiences and were never revised as a whole. This is an especial difficulty where anything like a systematic theory is at issue. While Col-

lingwood did have a systematic theory in mind, whose publication he projected under the title of "The Principles of History," he left only a fragmentary manuscript of this work, and only two of the essays in the Epilegomena (on "Historical Evidence" and "History and Freedom") are from this unfinished treatise (IH, vi). In the *Autobiography* he said of his theory of historical knowledge that "the main problems are now solved" (A, 117); but in fact both problems and solutions were left in the wax and must now be reconstructed.

Second, if Collingwood were correct in holding that history is different from what is ordinarily called "science," there is bound to be a systematic ambiguity in his discussion, for the vocabulary in which we talk about inquiry has been developed almost exclusively in connection with accounts of "scientific method." In *The Idea of History* the vocabulary of "hypothesis," "theory," "fact," "verification," and the like is deliberately eschewed, but this tactic forces Collingwood into circumlocutions which are open to misinterpretation. Finally, as we have seen, Collingwood's books to an unusual degree complement and explain each other; and *The Idea of History* is far from complete, although it creates the illusion of being so. A brief example may serve to illustrate this difficulty. Collingwood is widely known to have held that "all history is the history of thought." As a formula, this is brief, simple, provocative, and *prima facie* untrue. But is it likely that anyone hearing this will understand by "thought" what we have already seen to be a complex and unusual theory of mind? *The Idea of History* itself contains only tantalizing and not wholly consistent intimations of the ways in which "thought" is connected with "action" and "emotion," rather than being distinct from and even opposed to them as is ordinarily believed or assumed.

These considerations may help to explain why Collingwood's theory of history is so often accepted in principle but disparaged in detail, especially by historians. In recent years historians have more and more been prodded into reflection on their discipline, as they have keenly felt the increasing pressure of an imperialistic "behavioral science," which is applied in allied disciplines of psychology, sociology, political science and anthropology, and which recommends to historians that they stick to the "facts" and leave *explanations* to the methodologically sophisticated social sciences. In this climate, many historians have welcomed Collingwood's view as a generally correct account and welcome justification of what they themselves understand as the historical way of thinking. As an attorney for the defense, Collingwood seems to say of historiography what most historians wish to believe of it: that it is "scientific" but at the same time radically distinct from the methods and concepts appropriate to natural science. Yet at the same time many historians have uncomfortably felt that these conclusions are reached by a number of strange arguments which unconscionably restrict the field of historical knowledge. The doctrines most frequently criticized—and, as I believe, misinterpreted—are six in number. I shall state them together with a brief indication of the objections to them, and in the sequel discuss the extent to which a reinterpretation can escape these objections.

a. *All history is [exclusively] the history of thought* (IH, 215).

But, the objection comes, that restricts history to intellectual history; and history may be about ideas but it is also about *facts*. The Black Death, the Lisbon earthquake, the plow that broke the plains and the barbed wire which fenced it in, the effect of cannon on stone walls, and the gold or lack of it in the New World are facts, not thoughts.

b. *Moreover, all history is the re-enactment by the historian of reflective thought in the past* (IH, 308).

But, the objection comes, this is even more restrictive: it excludes passionate, impulsive, obsessive, compulsive, mistaken, forced, and thoughtless actions, i.e., the very stuff of history.

c. *If history is the re-enactment of reflective thought, it follows that there can be a history only of individual purposive actions; for states, societies, cultures and institutions do not think.*

But, the objection comes, the thesis of "methodological individualism" amounts to a restatement of the dubious view that history is the incomprehensible sum of innumerable biographies. And even apart from Collingwood's inconsistent denial that biography is history (IH, 304), what then becomes of the history of economic and parliamentary institutions, of legal codes, of the relation of warfare and technology, and so on?

d. *The criterion of historical truth* (IH, 238) *is the "a priori imagination"* (IH, 245). *The idea of the past is an innate idea* (IH, 247).

But, the objection comes, the most bitter critic of history would be unlikely to accuse it of the subjectivity and idiosyncrasy which this view of it apparently advances in its defense. Whatever the a priori imagination may be, as a priori it could not distinguish history from fiction, and therefore could not possibly serve as a criterion of historical truth.

e. *In history we demand (and get) not probability but certainty* (IH, 270). Historical judgments must not merely account for the evidence but "follow inevitably" from it, i.e., be logically entailed in the way in which mathematical deductions are but even explanations in the natural sciences are not (IH, 254–55; cf. 262).

But, the objection comes, even the secret vanity of historians is hardly adequate to bear this fulsome praise, which in any case seems clearly inconsistent with Collingwood's own recognition elsewhere that in history "no achievement is final" and that every generation not only does but *must* "rewrite history in its own way" (IH, 248). Presumably what historians would like is a justification of the corrigibility of historical knowledge, not the ascription to them of a certainty which they do not feel, cannot conceive, and regard with contempt whenever it is claimed.

f. *When we understand what happened, we already understand why it happened* (IH, 214, 222–23).

But, the objection comes, this flies in the face of common sense. We know that Zimmerman acknowledged the authenticity of his intercepted telegram, that Hitler failed to invade England, that Christianity spread with incredible rapidity in the first century; in none of these cases do we understand why. The "facts" of history provoke questions; they could not do so if to know them at all were already to know their explanations.

There may well be other doctrines in *The Idea of History* which seem equally perverse or exaggerated, but these alone provide the basis for a perfectly understandable criticism of Collingwood: that he defends the autonomy of historical thought by barricading it in a castle keep which is indistinguishable from a prison. The subject-matter of history is overintellectualized by excluding from it natural events and processes (a), psychological determinants of human behavior (b), and the structure and development of institutions (c). And these artificial restrictions result in but do not justify the further confusion of description and explanation (f), the delusion that claims to historical knowledge are to be judged by a priori criteria rather than by evidence (d), and the illusion that what in fact are only plausible explanations are instead logically certain (e). The latter three theses, so to speak, overintellectualize the historian's process of thinking, while the former three overintellectualize his subject-matter.

The edge of these criticisms is sharp, because the theses on which they bear are not passing remarks of Collingwood's but his central doctrines. They are also among his most provocative; and as elsewhere the suspicion is hard to down that what makes Collingwood's views *interesting* is a quality of exaggeration and an air of paradox, neither of which will bear close examination. Yet, I believe, all of the criticisms can be answered, although some of the claims in *The Idea of History* may require modification in the process.

It should not be forgotten that Collingwood has certain aims and certain ways of asking questions which are not ordinarily familiar to historians. He asks about history two main questions, both of which are philosophical, and neither of which directly reflects the usual interest of historians in defining their *profession*. The first question is not "What is history?" but rather "How is historical knowledge possible?" This is an exact analogue to Kant's question, "How is [natural] scientific knowledge possible?" and, like Kant's argument in the *Critique of Pure Reason*, Collingwood attempts in *The Idea of History* to give a "transcendental deduction" of the concept of history, i.e., to show by analysis the necessary conditions of the possibility of knowing *now* something which happened *then*. Moreover, he claims to have discovered and to show that history—and not psychology—is the "science of mind," or the mode in which the human mind attains self-knowledge. His second question, accordingly, is not "What is history?" but "How can mind come to know itself?"

Both primary questions are difficult, but at least neither is impossible to answer, as "What is history?" cannot be answered if it is taken to mean "What characteristics are common and peculiar to everything that is called history (or that has been done by people called historians, or that is done by people who are professional academic historians, etc.)?" A question of this form is impossible to answer not just because such a wide variety of things have been called history—and even by people called historians—but rather because no matter how circumspect and carefully qualified your generalization, it can be confuted in an instant by a university president with original ideas and a post to fill—or even, for that matter, by an historian with original ideas. Moreover, in accepting the "principle of the limited objective" (NL, 31.61–68), Collingwood himself renounced questions of the form "What is *x*?" insofar as such questions admit only real (as opposed to nominal) definitions as answers. But Collingwood had always rejected *both* nominal and real definitions of philosophical concepts; for such concepts, definition is replaced by a scale of forms (cf. EPM, 98 ff.). It would beg the question to criticize as a definition of "history" what in fact is an answer to a different question, which cannot be answered by a definition. In fact, we already know enough of Collingwood to give some sense to the six odd theses listed above. The logic of question and answer implies that their sense depends upon the questions to which they purport to be answers; the theory of absolute presuppositions implies (as Part I of *The Idea of History* undertakes to illustrate) that the concept of history, like the concept of nature, itself *has* a history, which shows it to be a number of different concepts belonging to different a priori conceptual systems; and the dialectical theory of mind reminds us that if the question is "How can mind come to know itself?" it is not to the Oxford Dictionary that we should go in the first instance for clues to the meaning of "mind" and "know."

2 · The Second Objection: Does Collingwood's Theory Ignore the Real Motivations and Causes of Human Action?

We may begin with the second thesis, since it is the most restrictive characterization of historical knowledge. "All history is the re-enactment in the historian's mind of past reflective thought." The question, of course, is what Collingwood means by "thought." The answer to this lies in the complex dialectic of mind which we have already examined, but *The Idea of History* itself contains only hints and shards of that theory. It refers to thought "in the widest sense of that word" (IH, 282), but what is that "widest sense"? Apparently it is wide enough to include some activities of some animals (IH, 216), but at the same time it excludes those aspects ("irrational elements") of human mental activity which are properly the subject-matter of psychology: "sensation as distinct from thought, feelings as distinguished from conceptions, appetite as distinct from will" (IH, 231). Although this is not an orderly classification, it at least clearly implies that "will," as well as conception, is associated with thought. In yet another place there are excluded from thought "feeling, sensation and emotion" (IH, 205); and "emotion" is again, in an obscure description of the difference between biography and history, distinguished from the "thought" which is the subject-matter of the latter alone (IH, 304).

Now it should be clear why all this poses a problem for anyone who reads *The Idea of History* alone. What history is about is *res gestae,* "actions of human beings that have been done in the past" (IH, 9); and, even though we go on to grant that actions have "outsides" and "insides" (IH, 213–14), we would ordinarily want to say that the "inside" of an action includes not only deliberate intent, calculated policy, and rational inference, but also, at least sometimes, fear, ambition, anger, love, pride, hatred, and other emotions. No doubt we should never understand Hitler unless his policies can be reconstructed, but on the other hand we should understand very little if we could reconstruct *only* those of his decisions which were the conclusions of purely ratiocinative processes. Yet Collingwood seems to hold not only that we can reconstruct Hitler's rational decisions, but that nothing else is possible or necessary for historical understanding. He insists, in the Epilegomenon called "The Subject-Matter of History," that only "acts of thought" which are "reflective" can become the subject-matter of history (IH, 308–309). It is at this point, I suspect, that historians have found Collingwood's conclusions more agreeable than his arguments.

But it is also at this point that we are recognizing only one arabesque in the figure in the carpet. The sections of *The Idea of History* which support the interpretation at which the above criticism is directed were, as we now know, written earlier than *The Principles of Art* and *The New Leviathan.* Collingwood had already elaborated in detail the series of functions of practical consciousness leading from feeling to will; but in his consideration of the problems of moral action he had not elucidated the concept of emotion: this was done only in *The Principles of Art.* In *The Idea of History,* therefore, Collingwood is quite clear about the connection of thought and action. "All history is the history of thought" does not mean or even seem to mean that the subject-matter of history is limited to thought given verbal expression in writing or reported speech; it also includes the thought which is the initial stage of action and can be reconstructed from the evidence of the action itself and its consequences. On the other hand, *The Idea of History* is not clear about the connection of thought and emotion; on this issue Collingwood tends to slip into the confusions embedded in ordinary language and hence seems to assimilate emotion to sensation and feeling (as we often do) rather than recognizing, as in his more developed reflections on the connections of mental functions, the extent to which emotion dialectically links levels of consciousness and appears, as sensation and feeling do not, in the higher levels, although it is rooted in the lowest. In his developed theory of mind, a distinction is made between "psychical emotions" of the first level and "emotions of consciousness" of the second and higher levels (cf. PA, 230–33; 266–67). The former can be expressed at the psychical level only in physical reflexes—cringing, groaning, fleeing, pursuing, and the like; but they can also become objects of consciousness and thereby transformed into emotions of second-level consciousness which can be expressed, for example, in gestures or in verbal language at that level. Emotions of consciousness themselves can be expressed "psychically" at a lower level (e.g., the blush of shame or the knit brows of hard thought) as well as consciously at their own level. Collingwood's account of this is immediately relevant to the elucidation of "thought" in his view of history:

> Why should emotions of consciousness be thus expressible in two quite different ways? The answer lies in the relation between any one level of experience and the next above it. The higher level differs from the lower in having a new principle of organization; this does not supersede the old, it is super-imposed on it. The lower type of experience is perpetuated in the higher type in a way somewhat like (though not identical with) the way in which a pre-existing matter is perpetuated when a new form is imposed on it. . . . [In a metaphorical sense] a mode of consciousness like shame is thus, formally, a mode of consciousness and nothing else; materially, it is a constellation or synthesis of psychical experiences [PA, 232–33].

The relevance of this passage to determining the scope of "thought" which the historian can re-enact should be obvious: so far as the historian can re-enact past thought, he thereby *does* re-enact the emotion (and, one could add, even the sensory experience) which survives in and is transformed by consciousness in becoming an object for it. So far as such emotion does not thus survive, it cannot be recalled even by the person who felt it, and no theory of historical knowledge could possibly account for it.

It has sometimes been supposed that in holding that only acts of "reflective thought" can be subject-matter for history, Collingwood was employing a sense of the term in which a scientist, say, is reflective but a craftsman is not, or a philosopher is reflective but a politician is not; but the defining characteristics of reflective activity are only (a) that it is performed in the consciousness that it is being performed and (b) that it can fail or succeed and be known to have done so (IH, 308). "Reflective thought" is thus exactly as broad as Aristotle's notion of "intellectual virtue," which includes not only the capacity for logical reasoning but also the practical wisdom (*phronesis*) of the politician and the skill (*techne*) of the craftsman. (It does not, however, include *art,* whose essential activity of imaginative expression is *not* one "which we are enabled to perform by knowing in advance how to perform it" [IH, 308].) The difference between "reflective" and non-reflective activity, it is clear, is not that between ratiocinative and practical thought but that between *conscious* and *unconscious* thought, the former of which can be re-enacted, the latter of which cannot (IH, 308).

Now by "unconscious" thought Collingwood meant *memory* and *perception,* both of which can properly be called "thought" insofar as they are modes of consciousness which have the data of experience as their objects, but are "unconscious" insofar as they are not objects for themselves but are potentially objects for a higher level. At the level of perception, for example, an hallucination is as much a perception as any veridical experience; it is only at a higher level that I can analyze and criticize it as incompatible with the rest of my structure of perceptions and beliefs. Hence the term "hallucination" belongs to the vocabulary of "reflective thought" but does not exist at all in the vocabulary of the perceptual level.

"Conscious" and "unconscious" were not concepts of Collingwood's own theory; and in using them he fell into ordinary habits of thought, according to which they are mutually exclusive in meaning;[1] hence the inference that "acts of reflection" are what we can, and *all* we can know through "re-enactment." But as we have seen, the levels of consciousness are in Collingwood's developed theory of mind not mutually exclusive at all; the third, for example, survives in the fourth, which comes into being only insofar as the third is its object and even contributes something (e.g., emotion) to it as a mode. Hence Collingwood's view of the "subject-matter of history" can be emended without important repercussions where his other views are concerned. And in fact, he even suggested the line of emendation in admitting that there can be a history of art although not a history of artistic problems (remember that this does not refer to problems of technique, but to problems of *expression* [IH, 314]). In *The Principles of Art* he insisted that "art" is not a special class of artifacts but *expressive* activity in general; and "every utterance and every gesture that each one of us makes is a work of art" (PA, 285).[2] It follows that if there can be a history of the special class of expressive activities recorded in what we call "works of art," there can be history of expressive utterances and other actions *in general*. This does not contradict the principle that historical inquiry is the re-enactment of reflective thought, but shows rather that "reflective thought" is to be understood as incorporating those lower levels of mental functions to which it is usually thought to stand opposed. It is, I think, an interesting comment on the nature of philosophy that in thinking about art Collingwood was, and very probably without realizing it, resolving some of the conceptual problems he had left unsolved in his unfinished work on history.

To oversimplify: Collingwood's true view was that the fourth level of consciousness can be re-enacted *simpliciter;* and the second and third levels can be re-enacted so far as (but no farther than) they have survived as objects of third- and fourth-level acts. What this means, practically, is that the historian is not limited to reconstructing Caesar's policy while ignoring his ambition. On the other hand, he cannot, as historian, deal with Caesar's ambitiousness as a *psychological* characteristic. "Upon what meat does this our Caesar feed?" is not an historical question, insofar as it purports to suggest a bio-psychological explanation of individual personality characteristics. *Ambitiousness* belongs to the second level of *appetite* (vague hunger for something); *ambition* belongs to the third level of *desire* (hunger for a specific object); *ambitious decision* belongs to the fourth level of *will*. In re-enacting the latter, the historian can and must re-enact ambitiousness and ambition as far as they survive in it.

Now it is beyond argument, I think, that the first and second levels of experience could not be re-enacted simply in themselves. We cannot even revive our own past feelings and appetites, much less re-enact those of someone else. Moreover, the third level cannot be re-enacted, either, in the sense of identical repetition. I remember badly wanting a tricycle when I was a small boy, and I remember too the frustrated longing which occupied my thoughts and to some extent governed my actions; but clearly I do not, need not, and cannot now yearn to have a tricycle and feel the frustration of not having it. Yet I can, I think, reconstruct (partly from memory but partly from the testimony of others) what I said and did, which would be unintelligible apart from the particular desire. The desire is re-enacted not *as such* but in a surrogate way, so to speak, by appearing in my re-enactment in the same way that desire as a level of practical consciousness survives in but is transformed by will.

The dialectical structure of Collingwood's theory of mind thus provides the requisite background for understanding the terms "re-enactment" and "[reflective] thought." Experience at the first, second, and third levels of consciousness consists of temporal sequences. The contents of consciousness come and go, and states of feeling succeed each other in the same way as do states of the body. We may, from a higher level, regard them as correlated or causally connected over time, but no state of feeling intrinsically *refers* to another, and in the same way no state of feeling is conscious of itself as such. Appetite and imagination are modes of consciousness *of* feeling, but again these states of second-level consciousness come and go like reveries, and although they can be known to form sequences from the higher standpoint of third-level consciousness, even at that level the succession of desires and perceptions do not *refer* to each other;[3] they are activities with objects, but they do not apply this distinction to themselves (as they do to second-level acts); they do not know themselves to do what in fact they do. Only fourth-level consciousness forms a self-referential *series* rather than a transient *sequence* of conscious states. Hence only fourth-level acts—inferential thought and intentional action—can be re-enacted, but *as* re-enacted they carry with them their freight of lower-level states modified by the activity of each higher level. To re-enact Caesar's decision to enter Rome is not merely to rehearse the logic of a practical syllogism from which the passion of life has been pressed out; it is to apprehend, in the only way in which they can be apprehended, the ways in which caution was mastered by ambition, and ambition was expressed in decision. How Caesar's decision *felt* to him is something which not even the aging Caesar could have remembered; and for us as historians it is not something which we unfortunately fail to know, because it is not something which we could possibly succeed in knowing.

However, even on the interpretation suggested, it may still be objected that on Collingwood's theory there can still be no history of actions with *unconscious* motivations in the Freudian sense. "An act of reflective thought," Collingwood says, is "one which is performed in the consciousness that it is being performed, and is constituted what it is by that consciousness" (IH, 308). But according to some versions of psychoanalytic theory, many actions are symbolic enactments of unconscious wishes, and the agent's own description of his action and his reasons for it are "rationalizations," unrelated to an understanding of what the act really was or to his real motivations. Now I am not at all sure that an account of historical understanding is obliged to accommodate itself to a theory whose great influence on modern thought has not yet downed the suspicion that it is the boldest of modern myths. But even without raising this question, two observations are possible on the basis of Collingwood's theory.

First, it is worth noting that while there are psychoanalytical explanations of mere *behavior* such as tics and stammers, which are observed and described as physical processes, the crucial cases for psychoanalytical explanations are those of *action,* that is, of behavior believed by the agent to be conscious and purposive. Psychoanalytic theory holds that what a man thinks he is doing may not be what he is really doing. But even were this so, one could never discover what he is "really" doing without *first* discovering what he thinks he is doing. Otherwise, one could not even *describe* the act to be explained. Hence, the objection from psychoanalytic theory presupposes the possibility of the re-enactment of the *thought* of an agent in Collingwood's sense; so it turns out to be not an objection to the theory at all but to rely on historical understanding as a necessary condition of psychological explanation.

Second, it is a principle of psychoanalytical explanation that even though an agent may be unaware of the real causes of his action, nothing can be regarded as a cause of his action of which he cannot *in principle become* conscious; and to bring about such awareness is precisely the aim of psychotherapy. It does not appear that Collingwood understood this. He bitingly classified and dismissed Freud's work (mentioning only *Totem and Taboo*), along with every other psychological attempt to be a "science of thought" rather than a "science of feeling," as the "propaganda of irrationalism" (EM, 118, 142); but it must be said that the provocation for this in Freud's work, and in the interpretation of that work in the 1930's by Freud's own disciples, was very considerable. From a larger perspective, it is remarkable how closely the interpretation of neurotic behavior as unconsciously purposive, of the analyst as reconstructing unconscious thought as it would be if it were conscious, and of the analyst's attempt to bring the patient to his own conscious re-enactment of his unconscious thought, conforms to Collingwood's general account.

By the time of *The New Leviathan*, Collingwood had had second thoughts about Freud's concept of repression, and they took the remarkable form of finding full agreement between Freud and himself. Already in *The Principles of Art* he had pointed out the resemblance between the concept of repression and his own discussion of the "corruption of consciousness," the disowning of feeling (PA, 218–19). In *The New Leviathan* he flatly identified Freud's idea of repression as, in his own terms, the "negative side of attention," that penumbra of feeling which attention neglects by focusing on something else. As a result, he credited Freud with having agreed with him that "if all a man can find out about his feelings is derived from his consciousness of them, . . . no man can know (and a fortiori no other can know about him) that he has feelings of which he is unconscious" (NL, 5.82). The implication is that Freud did not hold that feelings can be unconscious and is generally thought to have held this only because he expressed his ideas unclearly.

But even if this curious interpretation of Freud were accepted (and it is incompatible with Freud's own distinction between the "preconscious" and the "unconscious" to which Collingwood himself appeals for support; NL, 5.9), there would still be a major difference: Collingwood repeatedly insists that it is a necessary characteristic of "reflective thinking" and of purposive acts that in such activities we are not only thinking but are *aware* that we are thinking; it is this self-consciousness which constitutes the fourth level of consciousness. The root notion of psychoanalytic theory is that there are unconsciously purposive acts in which there is no reflective thought in Collingwood's sense, although they *may* be re-enacted as the objects of reflective thought.

To accommodate this notion would entail a modification but not necessarily the rejection of Collingwood's view. Very roughly, the modification could be made by dividing the fourth level into two strata, one which has an apparent object or goal and a different real object or goal, and a second level in which these two coincide. (And the ground for this distinction is already laid in Collingwood's distinction between "capricious" and "rational" choice at the fourth level of will.) But there is another alternative: so-called existential psychoanalysis in effect rejects the concept of the unconscious altogether, and regards all actions whether "neurotic" or "normal" as chosen courses; the neurotic or psychotic is not the victim of a disease but the author of a drama in which he plays the leading role, and he knows this even in the course of denying it. This theory is not only compatible with Collingwood's as it stands but has not yet been supported by a theory of mind more developed than Collingwood's. However, I would not presume to debate the psychological issue; and the point of this discussion is only to show the conceptual compatibility or incompatibility of Collingwood's view with the grounds of the objections brought against his theory.

3 · The First Objection: Can Collingwood Account for the Effects of Natural Events in Human History?

"All history is the history of thought." This formula does seem to exclude from the subject-matter of history all natural events and processes, as the former principle seemed to exclude all so-called "irrational" springs of human behavior. But relevant to understanding this formula is the important distinction between history and chronicle (IH, 202–204). Chronicle is "the past believed upon testimony but not historically known." It includes both what is elsewhere called "scissors and paste" history and "critical history" (IH, 257–59). The former merely extracts and puts together statements from the received records of the past; the latter critically assesses recorded testimony for credibility, but can reach no conclusions of its own other than to accept or reject each bit of testimony available to it. True or "scientific" history is the practice of an autonomous kind of inferential thinking concerned not with testimony but with evidence; and evidence is defined not by the fact that it is received, or even by the fact that it is received and withstands critical examination, but by its relevance to the process of asking and answering historical questions (IH, 280–81).

So far, Collingwood has been discussing differences among concepts of the method of historical *inquiry;* but his distinctions have counterparts, although he does not emphasize them, in different concepts of historical *subject-matter*. The counterpart of chronicle is the view that the subject-matter of history is the aggregate of past facts and their connections. The counterpart of "scientific history" is the view that the subject-matter of history is human actions (including thought). The latter is of course Collingwood's view: what history is about is *res gestae* (IH, 9). But the lives of men are of course responses to their situation in nature as it impinges in one way or another on their activities.

Now if one accepts at all the distinction between history and chronicle, the objection that Collingwood neglects natural facts rests only on a misunderstanding. It is like objecting to a theory of planetary motion that it does not mention transits or telescopes, or to an account of scientific method that it does not mention test tubes. The *prima facie* justification of the objection is that history books do include references to the spices of the East, the precious metals of the New World, the effect of the Alps on European trade, the effect of natural boundaries on the development of nations, etc. But Collingwood's point is simple: these natural facts are relevant to history *only* to the extent that they enter the consciousness of men. Strictly speaking, the geographical location and configuration of the Alps have not been the cause of anything in human history; it is men's awareness of and beliefs about the Alps which have been the constraining and effective factors in human events. That this is so is shown by the fact that a false belief about natural fact does not differ in the least from a true belief so far as action is concerned (IH, 317), although action based on assumptions which include factually false beliefs is much less likely to succeed. (In some cases, such as Columbus's first voyage, an action based on false beliefs may be successful from the standpoint, retrospectively recognized, of a possible intention which no one in fact possessed.) But even in the case of failure, the failure cannot even be described apart from someone's consciousness of failure. Columbus did not discover the isthmus of Panama, but he did not *fail* to discover it, since he did not try. He did fail to discover the spices of the Indies, because in that case he knew both his intention and its lack of success.

Natural facts, one may say, always enter historical explanation only in the mode of indirect discourse; that is, if "*p*" is a proposition describing natural fact, then historical discourse proper never contains statements of the form "*p*" but only of the form, "It was known that *p*," "It was believed that *p*," "X said to Y that *p*," and the like. This of course does not deny to the historian the right to say "the Alps are impassable during much of the winter," so long as the context makes clear that someone believed this or found it out. If no one believed it or found it out, in what conceivable context could an historian relevantly display his bit of information?

Even so generally sympathetic a critic as Alan Donagan, however, has found it impossible to accept Collingwood's refusal to "concede that historical explanations might incorporate some of the results of natural science." [4] Historical explanations, Donagan claims, normally rely implicitly on explanations of physical fact but neglect to include such explanations because they are familiar and elementary; but in some cases—such as the explanation of why a particular method of farming exhausts the soil—the explanation is not elementary, and therefore the historian "must explain to his readers . . . certain advanced theories about the fertility of soils." But although an historian *may* explain this, in his lust to instruct at all costs, in what context of historical questions *must* he do so? Must he explain the aerodynamics of sailing as an essential part of his account of the defeat of the Spanish Armada by the swifter and more maneuverable English men-of-war? If so, we should have to say that this event is still not historically understood, to the extent that the physics of sailing against the wind has only recently been investigated and is still imperfectly known—and historians could most appropriately pursue their research into the English victory by conducting wind-tunnel experiments. The fact is that for Collingwood the question, "Why did this method of farming exhaust the soil?" is not an *historical* question, though couched in the past tense. "Why did people adopt and retain this method?" *is* an historical question. To make this point it is not even necessary to offer a clear criterion for distinguishing historical from non-historical questions; it is necessary only to observe that, if Donagan's criticism were valid, it is difficult to see how there could be any such criterion at all, other than the formulation of historical questions in the past tense.

What these considerations show, I believe, is that it is not very profitable to look for counterexamples against Collingwood's main theses. The reason for this is that his enterprise is not to arrive at true generalizations about the range of things called "historical writing" or "historical explanation." If it were, counterexamples would be relevant. But what he is actually undertaking is a conceptual revision of the received constellation of absolute presuppositions associated with the concept of history. As with any transformation of absolute presuppositions, in the process of transition some statements will be references to the prior constellation (that is, they will be or seem to be answers to questions to which the prior constellation gives rise); but other statements will be attempts to capture and express the new constellation, and these will seem, from the standpoint of the old, to be false or unintelligible. Since the issue is one of meaning, what is from the old standpoint a relevant counterexample may be from the new standpoint simply irrelevant.

What Collingwood means by "history," accordingly, cannot be understood as the class of things called by that name. His concept is both broader and more restricted than the usual meanings of the term. Very little of what appears in some history books may be "history" in his sense; on the other hand, things not usually recognized as historical inquiry may turn out to be so, parts of philosophy, for example, or the activity of clinical psychologists. The second of his original questions, we may recall, is not "What is history?" but "How can mind come to know itself?" The description of the complex activity to which he gives the name "history" is his answer to that question; and one significant thing about it is that it is a kind of thinking in the attempt to understand human actions which is different from the kind of thinking appropriate to the explanation of natural events. Now this view will surely be offensive to anyone whose constellation of presuppositions determines a priori that an action is just one kind of event, analyzable into the same order of temporal sequence, subject to the same type of causal explanation, and so on. Collingwood's conclusion is unintelligible to anyone presupposing such a constellation because from that standpoint his question cannot even arise. With such presuppositions, the only possible interpretation of Collingwood is that he must be trying to answer some *other* question, and making a bad job of it.

4 · The Third Objection: Does Collingwood's Theory Leave Nothing for History but Biography?

We come at last to the question of the history of institutions and of the essentially historical characterization of periods ("Renaissance"), styles ("Baroque"), institutions ("common law"), "national character," and the like. All of these have in common the fact that statements can be made about them which *prima facie* are not statements about individual persons or even groups of identifiable persons and hence cannot be analyzed into the re-enactment of individual thoughts and actions. Collingwood does not even consider this problem in *The Idea of History*. But it is easy to see why he does not: the first of his original questions is, "How is it possible that we can know the past?" and the initial answer to this is, "Only if the past can in some way be or be made present." If we ever *do* know the past, it follows that it *can* be made present. How? Only by, in some sense, re-experiencing it. How can the past be re-experienced now? Only if it, or some aspect of it, can survive through time and be revived. What is it that is capable of survival and revival? Only thought (in its wider sense); physical objects survive, but their past states do not; experience at its lower levels is transient and does not survive at all. Conscious thought alone can be identical and known to be identical in two different moments, and hence is alone capable of being re-experienced by way of being re-enacted.

So the sequence of question-and-answer itself leads to the conclusion that the *only* objects of historical knowledge properly so called are the thoughts of individual persons uttered in words whose record survives or expressed in actions whose descriptions survive. Yet if the development of institutions and the like is not analyzable without remainder into a sequence or class of individual thoughts, what answer then will be given to the question, "How is knowledge of the past possible?" To say that there *are* histories of institutions is not an answer to that question. Yet Collingwood himself never draws the inference that institutional history is either spurious or a sort of shorthand for an aggregate of individual histories. And he speaks with evident approval and no criticism of Vico's discovery of the "completely modern idea of what the subject-matter is," namely "the history of the genesis and development of human societies and their institutions": language, custom, law, government, etc. (IH, 65). Apparently, if there is a problem here, Collingwood did not see it. Why not?

One possible reason is that institutions may be regarded for most purposes as wholly analyzable into the thought of typical *but anonymous* individuals.[5] One may, for example, read a charter as evidence of the colonial policy of a government, meaning by "government" *any one,* not this or that particular one, of a group of individual persons with similar understanding of policy and of the situation; thus one can "re-enact" the thought of "whoever wrote that charter" without necessarily identifying the author in any other way. Collingwood explicitly appeals to the notion of the typical but anonymous individual in justifying his conclusion that there can be a history of economic activity: "If we are told that there was a strike at the factory or a run on the bank, we can reconstruct in our own minds the purposes of the people whose collective action took those forms" (IH, 310). But his only examples are of collective *events,* and it is at least not clear that the same account could be given of *institutions.*

Another reason why Collingwood may have overlooked the problem is that to the extent that institutions can be regarded as independent of any particular individual, they function exactly like natural facts in being relevant to historical explanation only to the extent that they enter the consciousness of individuals. (A law which was never repealed but was totally forgotten, like some Blue Laws, is technically part of the institution of law but is irrelevant to the historical explanation of anything during the period when it is forgotten. But *why* it was forgotten may be a good historical question.) Collingwood's individualism is compatible with either of these ways of connecting institutional features with individual thought. But it is *not* compatible with any attempt to regard human institutions as having a life of their own, or as instancing laws or patterns of development which make it possible even theoretically to explain changes in them by reference to causal factors which did not appear in the consciousness of the individuals whose institutions they were. And this is in fact the basis of the criticism which Collingwood directs against "philosophers of history" such as Spengler, Toynbee, and Marx.[6] Now it is true that his criticism begs the question: it depends on showing that an explanation of the development of human institutions which discounts the effect on these institutions of what people thought them to be is not an *historical* understanding of institutions because historical understanding *is* the history of thought. This is the form of all of Collingwood's arguments against "positivism." But the "positivistic" view is no less question-begging in its assimilation of history to nature. In such fundamental matters, can the impasse between incompatible and equally circular arguments be overcome?

No answer to this is provided or clearly implied in *The Idea of History,* I think. But if one considers what *The Idea of History* does, as well as what it says, it is clear that in tracing the *history* of the idea of history Collingwood is giving an account of the development throughout the history of Western civilization of a particular concept whose stages of development are not only exemplified in the thought of individual historians and philosophers but are at the same time characteristic of the way in which whole societies and segments of society have thought about themselves in relation to what they understood as their past and their knowledge of it. Notice, for example, the significance of the fact that the Enlightenment is discussed in Part II, "The Influence of Christianity," and Romanticism in Part III, "The Threshold of Scientific History"; and notice too the classification of modern "scientific" history by nationalities, with its quick but lucid sketches of the English, the German, and the French intellectual styles, and the perception of the connection between French philosophy, historiography, and attitude in international politics (IH, 189). In effect what Collingwood is trying to show is that what men think of themselves and their world reflects a constellation of absolute presuppositions—one which may vary from society to society and from epoch to epoch, and which includes an a priori concept of history. For a person or a society to be unhistorical is to have a very thin concept of history, and to be anti-historical is to have a logically indefensible concept of history; one cannot argue against every concept of history without presupposing *some* concept.

But at about this time Collingwood was making a similar historical analysis of the concept of nature, showing that there is not *a* world of nature about which different theories have been held, but that there have been different theories of what is to be *counted as belonging* to nature; that is, there is not only a history of theories about nature but a history of the concept of nature itself. Distinguishable forms of this concept are represented most clearly in the thought of scientists and philosophers but they can be discerned as well in the problems and ways of thinking of whole societies. Roughly speaking, the positivistic assimilation of history to nature, or, to put it differently, the attempt to regard human actions as complex kinds of natural events, represents a higher stage in the history of the concept of nature combined with a lower stage in the history of the concept of history. *And this conclusion is itself an historical statement.*

This may suggest that Collingwood's argument, although circular, is in a peculiar way self-justifying by being self-exemplifying, while no argument can be made for a "positivistic" conception of history which is similarly self-exemplifying; it may indeed be self-refuting. The error of Spengler or Toynbee or Marx is that they do not and cannot regard as belonging to the process of historical change the ideas in terms of which they characteristically explain the process of historical change. In Collingwood's view, at least, they have theories about the relation of historical events to each other but no historical understanding of the conceptual systems presupposed by their own theories. In Toynbee's case, for example, the relevant conceptual system does not consist of his well-known categories of affiliation and apparentation, internal and external proletariat, challenge and response, universal State and universal Church. These are, one might say, descriptive categories corresponding to such categories of natural science as vertebrate and invertebrate, acid and base, particle, atom, and molecule. Rather his absolutely presupposed conceptual system (cf. IH, 161–64) includes the a priori division of the field of data into *discrete* parts (e.g., "civilizations") related, if at all, by *external* relations, and an a priori concept of *individuality* which leads him to see individuals as sharply distinguishable from and only contingently related to their environments. These concepts, presupposed but not acknowledged or discussed by Toynbee, correspond logically to the a priori concept of conservation (of something or other!) in physics or to the a priori concept of mechanism in biology. It is historically understandable that Toynbee should presuppose such a conceptual system; but it is not historically *understood* by Toynbee that he does.

Now the key to grasping the nerve of Collingwood's criticism of Toynbee is the theory of absolute presuppositions. Toynbee, or "positivism" in general, is to be understood in terms of a constellation of absolute presuppositions which applies indifferently to history or to nature, even though the special concepts (which are not *absolute* presuppositions) employed in historical analysis (e.g., "internal and external proletariat") may differ from the special concepts employed in physical analysis (e.g., potential and kinetic energy). But it is only in a derivative sense that one can speak of the "absolute presuppositions" of an individual thinker. Absolute presuppositions are not idiosyncratic or personal, even though they are exemplified in thought and thought is always thought by *someone*. They are widely as well as deeply shared; they are ways in which men may think alike as well as be alike in what they think. In fact, the theory of absolute presuppositions is intended by Collingwood as a logical instrument for the analysis of the foundations of civilization and of the dynamics of historical change. If one employs this instrument, Collingwood promised in the *Essay on Metaphysics,* he will see that what philosophers have been doing throughout history is to elucidate the absolute presuppositions of the scientific knowledge of their own epochs; he will get a "hint of the way in which different sets of absolute presuppositions correspond not only with differences in the structure of scientific thought but with differences in the entire fabric of civilization" (EM, 72); and he can investigate the way in which the course of history reflects the conflicts and concourses of changing constellations of absolute presuppositions. The historical understanding of civilization thus requires the analysis of the a priori conceptual schemes implicit in the dominant thought of an epoch, and of the structure of conflicting conceptual systems and fragments of systems within an epoch. What men have done can be understood only in terms of what they have thought. What they have thought can be understood only in terms of the questions and problems to which they sought answers. And what their questions and problems were can be understood only in terms of the conceptual systems in whose absence these questions and problems could not even arise and be formulated.

The theory of absolute presuppositions thus provides the link between individual thought and action on the one hand and human institutions on the other. A priori conceptual systems are essentially corporate, because they are the basis of communication, and even, as recent linguistic philosophy has obliquely been demonstrating, of the use of language itself. They *are* the link between individuals and institutions, because they are both presupposed in the thought of individuals and exemplified in the structure of institutions. Consider, for example, the idea of hierarchy in medieval thought as well as in the institutions of medieval society—not propositions *about* hierarchical forms of order but the *concept* of hierarchy implicit even in contexts in which there are no specific references to it. Medieval men did not merely believe that nature is and society should be hierarchically ordered but literally could not perceive nature or society in any other way than as exemplifications of this general form. The cardinal who refused to look through Galileo's telescope did so, one might even say, not because he was afraid that what he would see would disprove his beliefs but because he knew a priori that nothing he could possibly see would be relevant to his belief that the moon is a perfect sphere of quintessential substance. The identity of *that* moon with the image on the objective of a telescope was something which he could not see by looking but only by a conceptual shift. He could apply his eye to the telescope, but he could not conceivably see an irregular surface as an imperfection of the moon rather than as an imperfection of the instrument. Collingwood could say that the cardinal had a reasonably consupponible conceptual scheme; and so did Galileo, although a different one. Presumably others, more sensitive than the cardinal to the strains within that scheme and between it and other accepted fragmentary schemes (e.g., that required to understand the optics of the telescope in terrestrial use and to connect optics with the concepts of a theory of perception) could inch their way, in a manner fully intelligible only in retrospect, from the received constellation of the cardinal to the novel (but not wholly novel) constellation of Galileo.

Similar examples, more thoroughly analyzed in detail, have only recently led many historians of science to the conclusion that, from an historical point of view, not only the data and explicit theories of science but the intellectual methods by which theories are constructed and confirmed are subject to change over time; and Stephen Toulmin, for one, has expressed his sympathy for "Collingwood's vision of philosophy as a study of the methods of argument which at any historical moment have served as the ultimate Court of Appeal in different intellectual disciplines." [7] (Such "methods of argument" would be related to what Collingwood called the "logical efficacy" of a particular constellation of absolute presuppositions.)

But if intellectual history, such as the history of science, provides the clearest examples for analysis of the ways in which absolute presuppositions are attained, employed, and abandoned, Collingwood clearly did not intend to limit the idea to its applications in intellectual history alone. An early version of his notion of absolute presuppositions was his distinction between the "philosophical" and "empirical" elements in economics and politics, regarded as the study of forms of action governed respectively by the concepts of utility and rightness as forms of value. In economics, he held that wealth, exchange, supply, and demand are "philosophical" concepts, while capital, manufacture, money, and credit are "empirical" concepts. In politics, the concept of state is "empirical," while the concept of rules (or the concept of law in general) is "philosophical." The difference in general between empirical and philosophical concepts is that the latter are "universal and necessary characteristics of rational action as such," while the former apply to special kinds or classes of actions. It will be remembered that in the *Essay on Philosophical Method* a non-philosophical concept was described as qualifying a limited part of reality and observing the rules of classification, and a philosophical concept as escaping every imposed limit and breaking the rules of classification (EM, 35).

Now it would of course be a mistake to suppose that, in speaking of "universal and necessary characteristics of action as such," Collingwood was avowing anything like an absolute or categorical ethics such as Kant's. His analysis of Kant's theory of knowledge as making explicit the absolute presuppositions of Newtonian science applies *mutatis mutandis* to Kant's ethics as making explicit the absolute presuppositions of the Western institutions of law and regularian politics. The *source* of "universal and necessary characteristics" is always a constellation of absolute presuppositions; but absolute presuppositions as the *ground* of universal and necessary judgments are themselves neither universal (although they may be widely shared) nor necessary (although from their *own* standpoint explicit alternatives are literally inconceivable). Collingwood's early distinction between philosophical and empirical concepts therefore has its own history. The detailed investigation of the concepts of nature and of history in the books of corresponding titles led directly to the theory of presuppositions in the *Essay on Metaphysics* and this, combined with the dialectic of mind, to the final reformulation of the connection of thought and action in Chapter XVIII in *The New Leviathan*.

Collingwood's last affirmation of the continuity of thought and action is simply stated, although among its consequences is a completely general view of the range of history. The primary function of thought, he holds, is practical, the activity of explaining and justifying one's own actions, i.e., of asking and answering the question, "Why am I doing this?" (This is of course an act of fourth-level consciousness.) The secondary or derivative function of thought is theoretical: the activity of asking and answering questions about the world. But the absolute presuppositions of practical thought are also the absolute presuppositions of theoretical thought. Hence the conceptual schemes in terms of which men come to understand their own actions are also the conceptual schemes presupposed in all objective inquiry; and changes in practical consciousness therefore bring in their train changes in the organization of theoretical thought. The utilitarian conception of action has the same presuppositions as the teleological conception of nature; and the regularian conception of action has the same presuppositions as the conception of nature governed by universal laws.[8]

The connections between individual thought and institutional change are thus multiform. In some cases institutional history records the direct influence of individual thought. In still others it discloses changes in the collective purposes and beliefs of a "public" of anonymous but typical individuals. But in any case there are absolute presuppositions of the structure and change of institutions as there are of individual thought and action. What these absolute presuppositions are in any given case is a matter for investigation: Collingwood's discussion of the forms of civilization and of barbarism in Books III and IV of *The New Leviathan* is one such investigation. But that institutions and individual thought may have the same presuppositions is itself a necessary proposition; it is a corollary of Collingwood's view that "when an historian says that a man is in a certain situation this is the same as saying that he thinks he is in this situation" (IH, 317). Institutions are constituted by the way in which they are thought of by the people living under them (cf. Collingwood's comments on Herder; IH, 92). Hence it was quite natural that, in illustrating the investigation of absolute presuppositions, Collingwood should have referred to institutions as readily as to individual thinkers and spoken of "an historical inquiry in which . . . the beliefs of a given set of people at a given time concerning the nature of the world are exhibited as a single complex of contemporaneous fact, like, say, the British constitution as it stands today . . ." (A, 67).

To connect individual thought and institutional history by the presence in both of absolute presuppositions, however, requires a further emendation of *The Idea of History*. Collingwood supposed there that one can consciously and reflectively re-enact the conscious and reflective thought of another and claimed to show how it is possible to do so. But he did not clearly explain how we are to understand these cases in which one tries but *fails* to achieve re-enactment. He suggested, rather mysteriously, that not only must the object be "of such a kind that it can revive itself in the historian's mind; the historian's mind must be such as to offer a home for that revival. . . . A man who at one time of life finds certain historical studies unprofitable, because he cannot enter for himself into the thought of those about whom he is thinking, will find at another time that he has become able to do so" (IH, 304–305). But why at one time he cannot do so, and what, specifically, changes in order to enable him to do so, are not even acknowledged as problems by one of Collingwood's brusque instructions to the reader to figure it out for himself.

The theory of absolute presuppositions can answer these questions, and exactly as if it were designed to do so, although Collingwood nowhere says or hints that it is. For consider: if absolute presuppositions *were* propositions, then the only sense in which they could be absolutely presupposed is by being *believed* beyond the possibility of doubting them, either because one was not explicitly aware of believing them or because one could not succeed in doubting them even if one were aware of them. In such a case, one could not re-enact another's thought unless one happened to believe all those and only those absolute presuppositions which he believed. Otherwise, one could not even reconstruct his thoughts of what his actual situation was, since these would reflect his absolute presuppositions about what counted as belonging to his situation. But if absolute presuppositions are not propositions but a configuration of a priori concepts, the historian can make explicit and disclose the logical efficacy of the concepts implicit in the original thought, without either adopting or rejecting them as his own. If he has not made this analysis, he may adventitiously be able to "enter into" the thought because its absolute presuppositions are in fact his own; but if he has analyzed the concepts presupposed, he need not share them but only be able to *suppose* them in the special way in which a conceptual scheme can be supposed. His own thinking will of course still reflect his own absolute presuppositions in a way which makes it in turn a possible object of subsequent analysis. This is why there can be—and must be, once the possibility is recognized—a history of historical thought which exemplifies its own principles. The historian is always—or always can be—one up on the past, but is always one down to the future. When it arrives, he will belong to its history. But until it does, it has no history for him to belong to.

5 · *The Fourth Objection: How Can the Criterion of Historical Truth Possibly Be A Priori?*

Good historical novels often seem "truer" than scholarly histori- cal monographs. Historical narratives are in any case more like fic- tion than like scientific treatises; like fiction, they are stories. But his- torical narratives are supposed to give a true account of something that really happened; if there is a "truth" of fiction, it lies in the co- herence and vividness of imagination, not in any correspondence to fact. But "correspondence to fact" cannot be the *criterion* of histor- ical truth, for the well-known reason that we can have no knowl- edge whatever of past facts except as historical knowledge. One his- torical claim can be compared only with another historical claim; a criterion of historical truth must justify the acceptance of one and the rejection of another. According to Collingwood, the criterion of historical truth is the "a priori imagination"; but this seems, *prima facie,* completely incapable of distinguishing history from fiction, and incompatible with the empirical nature of historical research and argument. Yet here again, I believe, we can give sense to Col- lingwood's argument if we keep in mind the development in his thinking of the theory of mind and the theory of absolute presup- positions.

The essay on "The Historical Imagination" (written in 1935) is best understood as a commentary on F. H. Bradley's essay on "The Presuppositions of Critical History." [9] Collingwood elsewhere (IH, 134–41) credits Bradley with having seen that the historian cannot accept the testimony of "sources" as incorrigible data but must bring to the criticism of sources a criterion of interpretation. But Bradley concluded that this criterion is the historian's *scientific* knowledge which compels him to reject all testimony about alleged happenings (e.g., miracles) which are discrepant with his own understanding of the laws of nature. Bradley correctly stated the principles of "criti- cal" history as an advance over "scissors and paste" history; but he failed to pass on from critical history to "scientific" history. What

Collingwood means by the latter—and the name is unnecessarily misleading—is historical interpretation on a criterion derived not from natural science but from the experience of historical thinking as an "autonomous form of thought with its own principles and its own methods" (IH, 139-40). "The Historical Imagination" is an attempt to elucidate this criterion, and thereby to give an account of the new historical consciousness as Bradley did for "critical history."

Collingwood's ostensible thesis is that "historical thinking is its own criterion" that is, that "there is nothing other than historical thought itself by appeal to which its conclusions can be verified" (IH, 243). The circularity of these statements is only partly mitigated by the fact that Collingwood includes under "historical thought" such matters as the establishment of dates and the authenticating of documents, which elsewhere he regards as belonging not to "history" proper but to "chronology." The escape from circularity is achieved by identifying as another part of historical thought the activity of a priori imagination. The historian comes to his materials already equipped with a picture of the past, a "web of imaginative construction" to which he implicitly refers both in criticizing evidence (Caesar could not have been one day in Rome and the next in Gaul) and in interpolating among the evidence (if Caesar was at one time in Rome and later in Gaul, the journey between can be interpolated, although not fanciful details of that journey).

So far there is nothing to distinguish Collingwood's view from the common opinion that history, like any other empirical inquiry, builds up a body of knowledge on securely attested facts and judges new claims by their coherence with what is already known. But Collingwood takes one step further: the a priori imagination, he says, is not just a schematic summary of the historian's knowledge to date, nor is it based on a body of well-attested facts. On the contrary, "so far from relying for its validity upon the support of given facts, it actually serves as the touchstone by which we decide whether alleged facts are genuine" (IH, 244). History differs from fiction because the historian's picture stands in a particular relation to evidence (IH, 246). But Collingwood apparently does not see that by his own account, even though evidence may be used to fill in details of the historian's "picture," he has ruled out the possibility that evidence could either confirm or disconfirm the outlines of that picture.

Now I would suggest that the mystery of these descriptions is dispelled if we recognize the "a priori imagination" as an early and imperfect attempt to bring out the notion of a "constellation of absolute presuppositions." Like absolute presuppositions, the historical imagination is said to be a priori; and as they are later said to be "the yard-stick by which 'experience' is judged" (EM, 193–94), so the imagination is "the touchstone by which we decide whether alleged facts are genuine." We might also recall that in the dialectic of mind which was only later fully worked out, "imagination" is the cognitive side of second-level or *conceptual* consciousness; it is the level at which experience is informed by concepts not yet organized into propositional beliefs. Finally, Collingwood gives one striking clue to what he was trying to think through. As his example of the function of imagination in interpolating among evidence, he says that when we perceive a ship and later perceive it at a different place we necessarily infer that it has occupied intermediate positions in the interval. Now this cannot be "already an example of historical thinking," as Collingwood calls it (IH, 241), because the ship's motion has no "inner" side of thought to be re-enacted. The illustration is in fact the example given by Kant of the a priori concept of causation, which together with other categories of the understanding determines the form of ordinary perception and of scientific thinking, exactly as Collingwood says that the imagination determines historical thinking a priori. The illuminating mistake of choosing this example shows that Collingwood was on the way to recognizing that *all* thinking is informed by absolute presuppositions, but for the time being could regard this only as the unique character of historical thinking. Four years later, in the *Essay on Metaphysics,* he transposed the same example into a new key, and said that not the perception of the ship but Kant's *analysis* of its presuppositions is "historical" thinking; what Kant really achieved was the elucidation of the absolute presuppositions of eighteenth-century science (EM, 245 and Ch. XXVII).

The doctrine of a priori imagination, then, was an attempt to show that historical knowledge is not *merely* empirical but is based on an "innate idea" which is "the idea of history itself . . . , an idea which every man possesses as part of the furniture of his mind, and discovers himself to possess insofar as he becomes conscious of what it is to have a mind" (IH, 248). But Collingwood had not yet generalized the notion of absolute presupposition implicit in this statement, and he had not yet "crossed the T" of the series of mental functions. The doctrine of the a priori imagination is a stage on the way to those developments; it was absorbed into them, but also superseded insofar as it still supposed that there is a single concept of history, universal and necessary in all thought, as Kant believed his categories of the understanding to be. Even in Part I of *The Idea of History,* it is clear that the main theme is the history of *concepts* of history. The *historical* concept of history (which in the dialectic of mind is the horizontal dimension of fourth-level consciousness) is there contrasted throughout with the *positivistic* concept of history (which belongs to the central stratum of fourth-level consciousness corresponding to "Science" and is exemplified, for instance, by Toynbee). The later development is foreshadowed when Collingwood speaks of "a second dimension of historical thought, the history of history: the discovery that the historian himself . . . is a part of the process he is studying . . . and can see it only from the point of view which at this present moment he occupies within it" (IH, 248). But this is as far as he could go at that time; there is as yet no distinction between the relative presuppositions which are involved in any imaginative picture of the past and the absolute presuppositions including a concept of history, which provide the structure— one might almost say, the style—of those detailed pictures.

Collingwood's doctrine of the a priori imagination can thus be seen as an attempt, as yet dimly conceived, to lead the reader *and himself* from one concept of history to another, from one constellation of absolute presuppositions to another. It is part of the effort, as he said later (A, 79), to "reckon with twentieth-century history" as philosophy in the past has reckoned with natural science. But since it is as yet partial, the claim to state "the criterion of historical truth" is unsupported. For even the historical concept of history does not enable us to distinguish between a true history and a false history; rather it is what is presupposed in recognizing the difference between anything which truly has the *form* of history and other things (e.g., chronicle, or chronology) which are pseudo-histories, or examples of an earlier stage of development of the concept of history itself.

6 · *The Fifth and Sixth Objections: How Can Historical Explanations Claim Certainty? And How Can Understanding What Happened Leave Nothing to Be Explained?*

The view that there is a history of the concept of history itself justifies anew the ancient maxim that each generation must rewrite history in its own way (IH, 248). Yet Collingwood paradoxically goes out of his way to stress that an historical construction must be not merely a plausible but a necessary account, and that it "involves nothing that is not necessitated by the evidence" (IH, 241). This is strong language for a philosopher, and it is not inadvertent, since it is reaffirmed in the section on "Historical Evidence" (IH, 268, 270), which was written as late as 1939. What could Collingwood possibly have meant by it, and what could justify his claim that there are historical arguments which "[leave] nothing to caprice, and [admit] of no alternative conclusion, but [prove their] point as conclusively as a demonstration in mathematics" (IH, 262)? When it comes to the issue, Collingwood indulges in special pleading: he merely asserts that historians do have experience of such arguments, and that the only way of knowing whether an historical argument is demonstrative is to learn to think that way; and to anyone who is still not convinced, he says, "I am not arguing; I'm telling you" (IH, 263). The ensuing discussion shows rather neatly that neither "scissors-and-paste history" nor "critical history" can yield conclusions which have the character of demonstrations; but nowhere is there any positive account at all of the logical compulsion supposed to result from the series of questions and answers which Collingwood calls "scientific history." It is not unknown for readers to be left with the impression, in this as in similar cases, that scientific history has somehow been shown to produce incorrigible conclusions because the other types of history have been so forcefully shown to be incapable of any such thing.

Can we provide the argument which Collingwood failed to produce? The issue can be clarified, I believe, only if we combine the claim to logical compulsion with the remaining strange thesis that when the historian "knows what happened, he already knows why it happened" (IH, 214). This, in turn, Collingwood regards as a restatement of the principle that, if the object of the historian's inquiry is the thought expressed in an event, to discover that thought is already to understand it. He clearly does not mean that a statement about a past event somehow entails other statements which constitute an explanation of the event, but that the process by which the historian comes to re-enact past thought is identical with the process by which he comes to understand it. For Collingwood, it is a necessary proposition that he could not re-enact it without understanding it and that he could not understand it without re-enacting it. This is a perfectly acceptable principle of intellectual history; it states the difference between critically interpreting the meaning of a text and dealing with that text in a purely philological way. It makes sense to say that, with respect to rational processes of thought, when we know what happened (e.g., the discovery of a solution to a problem) we already know why it happened (e.g., what the problem was and why it occurred as a problem). It is not so clear, however, that the principle is readily applicable to, say, political or military history. It is in such kinds of history that we seem to have many more facts than explanations; we may have the dispatch, for example, in which a foreign office ordered one of its ambassadors to communicate an ultimatum to the government to which he was accredited; but we may be completely puzzled as to why this policy was adopted. Even if we are not puzzled, it would still be true that the evidence for our knowledge that the ultimatum was issued is different from the evidence for any explanation of why it was issued, and that the former could be in principle complete whatever the state of our knowledge of the latter.

Now the weakest position Collingwood could adopt toward such an objection would be to restrict further the scope of his principle and to say that such examples simply do not fall under what he means by "history." This tactic would of course empty his position of most of its interest. The alternative would be to deny that our knowledge of what was done could possibly be *complete* apart from our knowledge of why it was done. And this answer is the only one compatible both with the Logic of Question and Answer and with his conception of the continuity of thought and action, one expression of which is his statement that "an action is the unity of the outside and inside of an event" (IH, 213).

Suppose, for example, that one is puzzled by the apparently mindless waste of British lives in the mass attacks repeatedly ordered by Marshal Haig against German strong points on the Somme long after any rational hope of victory had disappeared. In one sense we already know what Haig was doing—issuing orders for assaults. But in another ordinary sense we may still ask, "What was Haig *doing?*" And a satisfactory answer to this question would also answer the question, "Why did Haig do it?" The question calls for a more *complete* description of the series of actions of which "issuing orders" is only a very abstract and partial description. One fuller description might be "He was repeatedly attacking in the hope of victory." Another may be, "He was repeatedly attacking, without expectation of success, in order to force the commitment of German reserves and exploit the numerical superiority of Allied manpower by massive exchanges of casualties." The problem is not in the first instance to "explain" Haig's actions (psychoanalytically, say) but to say fully what they were, to describe them correctly. To the extent that they are described incompletely, they will *seem* to call for an explanation which cannot be forthcoming; to the extent that they are described correctly, *the description leaves no questions unanswered which arise from the description itself.* Attacks of attrition are perfectly consistent with all the evidence that Haig knew that the German positions were relatively stronger than in previous attacks which failed; attacks to capture and hold territory are not. Of course such a description does not explain why a policy of attrition was adopted. It answers the question, "What was Haig doing?" not the different question, "Why did Haig (and others) decide to do what he was doing?" But neither does a causal explanation of a natural event explain how the cause itself came to be. In its general form a scientific explanation shows that a state of a system is connected with an earlier state of the system according to general laws; it does not thereby explain either the occurrence of the initial state by referring it to a still earlier state, or the relevant laws, by deducing them from a more general theory. In science and in history, different questions call for different answers.

Hence the correct description of an action can show the unity of its "inside" and "outside." It is not Collingwood's view—although it has often been attributed to him by critics whose idea of interpreting his statements was to ask themselves what they meant by "inside" and "outside"—that "thought" is the "inside" of an action and facts of behavior the "outside" in the sense in which there is a pencil inside my drawer and a handle outside; the sense is much more like that in which the inside of a curve is concave and the outside convex. In the latter case, as not in the former, it makes sense to speak of the "unity of inside and outside"; moreover, in the latter case, as not in the former, we cannot know one without knowing the other, and the inference from one to the other is direct and immediate. It is not Collingwood's view that we first establish a description of someone's behavior and then use this description to confirm or disconfirm various hypotheses about what "thoughts" inside his head were the "mental causes" of that behavior. It is not his view that some actions have mental causes and others do not; thoughts do not cause actions but are expressed as aspects of activity and in no other way. It is for this reason that the correct or complete description of an action already says everything about the thoughtfulness of that action which can be said. The "thought of an agent" is describable because it is observable; "re-enactment" is not a privileged way of gaining access to otherwise unobservable mental processes, but rather a necessary part of the observation and description of actions.

With this in mind, it is now possible to say that the *necessity* of an historical account arises not in relating the description of an event to its (scientific) explanation but in arriving at the correct description. One might still understand Collingwood to mean that there is only one correct description of an event, and further that if we possess it we can be assured that it is correct, and that no future evidence could lead to its modification or abandonment. But this clearly indefensible view is not his. It seems to be so only to the extent that one takes for granted Ranke's famous ideal of representing the past *wie es eigentlich gewesen.* The past is *there,* we think, infinitely rich in detail but fixed and unchanging, while our knowledge of it is *here,* piecemeal and corrigible but approximating, more or less closely, to the independent reality of historical fact. This belief, with its obvious analogy to common-sense views of the perception of an external world, reveals as its presupposition, however, precisely that a priori concept of history which Collingwood rejected by implication in his Logic of Question and Answer. As we have seen in Chapter 5, this "logic" is really a theory of inquiry, and its import is that, although history may be a re-enactment, it is nevertheless not a *representation* of the past. A consequence of the theory, we saw, is that truth, "in the sense in which a historical narrative is called true," is not a property of a proposition or of a set of propositions but of a complex consisting of questions and answers. To every question there is an answer which is not by itself "true" (since its meaning is a function of the question to which it is an answer), but "right" in the sense that it helps us to get ahead in the process of asking and answering questions. It is the question-and-answer complex which is true in the "proper" sense of the word.

Now it is very difficult, but not impossible, to rid ourselves even hypothetically of the assumption that a correct description or true narrative account must deserve that title because it *corresponds to what really happened*. Yet of course if this were so, we could never know whether an account were true, since we cannot compare it with what happened to see whether they correspond. Nor can we simply compare it with some standard or normative account, since the latter would be in exactly the same predicament. Does Collingwood offer a genuine alternative? It does not seem so at first glance. Consider: "What color was her hat?—Blue." It is easy to see that "Blue" must be understood as an answer to a question, and its utterance on this occasion correctly understood only as an answer to *that* question. But how could one tell that "Blue" and not "Red" is the *right* answer in the particular sense of "helping us to get ahead"? And even if it were the right answer in *that* sense, what could it mean to say that the complex of question and answer is "true," without reference to something else (memory of the hat, memory of statement made by someone about the hat, etc.)? Now Collingwood might say that not this but some larger complex warrants the attribution of truth, e.g., the continuation, "How do you know it was blue?—Because I saw her wearing it," etc. And at each stage, the "right" answer is the one which leads to the larger complex which is true, that is, which does not draw a blank by causing to arise a question which admits of no answer. But it seems clear that the series either continues indefinitely or has a terminus; and if it has a logical terminus, that could only be an answer which does not lead to a further question because it announces a fact which cannot be further questioned, for example, "Because I remember seeing her wear it." ("How do you know you remember, etc." is senseless.)

But it is not immediately obvious how this analysis would apply to more complicated cases of historical interpretation. Even though an answer must be understood in terms of the specific question to which it is an answer, it does not seem that there is one and only one further question to which the answer leads as its unique continuation. As the Logic of Question and Answer was reconstructed in Chapter 5, it is possible from any point to trace a unique series *backward,* but there is no point for which there is only one series *forward.* (And if there were, Collingwood suggests no criterion for deciding which of the possible next steps is "right.") Yet just here, in the asymmetry of the series (like that of any dialectical series), may lie the clue. History is like this too: we can retrace, as it were, the logic of a random conversation, seeing in retrospect by what relevant associations it found its way from subject to subject, although we never could have predicted at any stage where it would be one subject ahead. *The Logic of Question and Answer does not tell us how to conduct the conversation but how to reconstruct it.* Similarly it could not be used by Haig as a model according to which he should arrive at decisions, but it can be used by the historian as a model for re-enacting Haig's thought. In the case of reconstructing the conversation, a "wrong" answer is one which leads to a blank. The "right" answer is the one which shows us by what transition we got on to the next subject, and it may often also be confirmed by the recollection it calls forth. In the case of re-enacting Haig's thought, the right answer is the one which leads to the next question and is confirmed by *including* the evidence as part of its statement. To the question, "Why did Haig attack two days before fresh reinforcements were due?" the answer, "Because he was a stupid automaton" is the wrong answer, not because it is "false" (he may in fact have been a stupid automaton, but even a stupid automaton goes through *some* process of thought) but because it leaves no further question to be asked. (We could not believe that he had no reason at all.) "Because he was obeying strict orders" may not be "true" but is not wrong because it leads to the further question, "Whose orders?" (It may also be "right" in the sense that it leads to inquiry which results in its disproof.) And "Because he did not wish in any case to drive the enemy into disengagement" is possibly right because it leads in turn to questions about the conduct of the entire campaign which may make sense out of otherwise incoherent and apparently unrelated actions.

I think that now it is possible to give a partial elucidation of Collingwood's strange emphasis on "necessity." What results from the historian's series of questions and answers is not a theoretical explanation but a *narrative* (the "convincing narrative" which for the scissors-and-paste historian becomes more rather than less difficult as evidence accumulates; IH, 278–79). The narrative is not a story *supported* by evidence, but the statement of the evidence itself, organized in narrative form so that it jointly constitutes the unique answer to specific questions. That evidence might indifferently confirm different theories (e.g., that Haig was mad, or sane) and could at best confirm (not prove) a theory even if the theory had no rivals. But the story is the uniquely necessary answer to the question what Haig was doing, because it *shows* him doing it. (This is one of the legitimate senses of "demonstration.") And in this respect it has a kind of incorrigibility or immunity to the threat of new evidence, which at best could serve to answer some other question or questions in conjunction with some or all of the evidence which answers *this* question.[10]

It is important to realize, however, that its incorrigibility does not mean that it is "*the* true story," and that its completeness does not mean that history can be the replication of the past. Necessity, incorrigibility, and completeness are all relative to the specific question asked, as it occurs in a specific question-and-answer sequence. And this is no mere addendum to our understanding of how historians think, but a radical critique of historical knowledge.

What Collingwood calls "scientific" history is not just a technical improvement on critical history, as critical history is an improvement on scissors-and-paste history. It results from a dialectical shift from one level of consciousness to another, from one constellation of absolute presuppositions to another, *with the awareness of that shift*. Many concepts are transformed in this shift—not only the concept of history itself, but the concept of knowledge, the concepts of action and of event, the correlative concepts of subjective and objective, and even the concept of evidence. For the scissors-and-paste historian, or for the critical historian, his subject becomes more difficult as evidence accumulates because he thinks of history as the use of *all* the "facts" to verify a single coherent and complete representation of the past. But this is the idea of history which in *Speculum Mentis* was called "the crown and the *reductio ad absurdum* of all knowledge of an objective reality independent of the knowing mind" (SM, 238). For the scientific historian, on the other hand, "the whole perceptible world is potentially and in principle evidence for the historian" (IH, 247), but it is not an embarrassment of riches because his understanding of inquiry affords a principle of selection: potential evidence becomes actual evidence only in relation to specific questions.

To give sense to Collingwood's claim of certainty for historical knowledge has required a long *excursus*. Certainly it would be simpler to regard it as merely a wilfully provocative statement, one of the scrappy exaggerations with which Collingwood teased his readers and sometimes himself. But to dismiss it so easily would be to overlook the fact that Collingwood was not in the least haunted by the ghost of the belief that the aim of history is to tell the truth and the whole truth, *wie es eigentlich gewesen*. He had exorcised that ghost as early as 1924, in *Speculum Mentis*. The job of the historian, he was quite clear even then, is not to reduplicate the lost world of the past but to ask questions and to answer them. There is no finite limit to the number and kinds of questions which can be asked nor to the amount and kinds of relevant evidence; the process of inquiry is itself an historical process. Whatever the merits of the answers I have suggested in this chapter to the objections lodged against his account of historical understanding, it is at least clear that he did not think that historical knowledge is the slow but steady accumulation of answered questions, because since it itself has a history it is constantly abandoning its old questions for new ones (IH, 248). There are, historically considered, no universal and necessary presuppositions which determine once and for all what questions may be asked; there is only the career of absolute presuppositions which by provoking us to ask questions insure their own mortality. Thought dies to its own life.

CHAPTER 7

The Rhetoric of Civilization: Art

1 · The Origin and Relevance of Collingwood's Philosophy of Art

THE UTILITY OF RECONSTRUCTING COLLINGWOOD'S DIALECTIC of mind with the degree of definiteness attempted in earlier chapters does not lie in its answer to such formal questions as whether there are four and only four levels of consciousness. One could conceivably interpolate more, or as in the fourth level find more than one stratum at a given level, just as Collingwood often found it sufficient for his immediate purpose to refer to fewer than four. There should in this respect be no "disciples" of Collingwood, loyally defending his interim report as a completed system. But while the *interior* stages of the dialectic of mind are subject to compression or expansion, the *terminal* stages represent stronger and more definite philosophical claims. These stages are of course "Art" and "History"; and the philosophy of art and the philosophy of history are accordingly both more important and more developed in Collingwood's thought than his views on religion and on science. (Philosophy, of course, stands apart from all of these as the activity of reflection on them.) We have already traced the development by which Collingwood solved the problem of the *terminus ad quem* by "crossing the T" of the series of mental functions and thereby giving new meaning to the phrase "historical consciousness." I propose in this chapter to turn to the problem of the *terminus a quo,* which Collingwood attempts to solve by a philosophy of art which identifies in the aesthetic transformation of first-level consciousness the origin of all those modes of thought and action which culminate in the historical consciousness.

The unique importance of origins for a dialectical philosophy should be evident even to someone who shares not at all that philosophical style; for the essence of the dialectical standpoint is to interpret processes of development as transformations in which later stages incorporate earlier stages and are not fully intelligible considered in abstraction from them. In the present inquiry, moreover, there are two kinds of origins to consider. Most importantly, of course, there are the origins of thought and action in the rudimentary forms of consciousness; this is what Collingwood's theory is *about*. But since to understand this theory requires an interpretation of it, there is also the question of seeing how the development of Collingwood's ideas can be related to its own origins. I do not think that this must take us back to the history of aesthetics or even to Croce and Gentile, although Collingwood unquestionably owed an especial debt to the "idealist aesthetics" of those contemporary but senior Italian philosophers. The extent of that debt is a question for intellectual history; but it could not be assessed at all apart from a prior interpretation of Collingwood, and such an interpretation is not much less difficult in the case of his philosophy of art than for his philosophy of history. It is possible to take as a given, therefore, Collingwood's *own* understanding of the problems of aesthetics; and that takes us back once again to *Speculum Mentis.*

In *Speculum Mentis,* Collingwood said that "the paradox of art is that it is both intuitive (pure imagination) and expressive (revelatory of truth): two characteristics which contradict one another" (SM, 87). The classical view of art, and the dominant one through the Renaissance, was that art is a way of communicating knowledge which cannot be acquired or uttered in any other way. The "newer doctrine," derived from Vico and the eighteenth century, is that art is the pure construction of imagination as a separate and independent mental faculty. Hegel tried to synthesize these two views in his aesthetics, but failed to do justice to all the consequences of the theory of art as imagination (SM, 74); Croce also tried to synthesize them but failed because he collapsed "expression" into "intuition"; that is, he interpreted the cognitive claim of art as simply its knowledge of its own imaginative constructions. And this tactic does not *resolve* but only "pricks" the contradiction between the view that art reveals truth about the world and the view that art is the free activity of fantasy; Croce's synthesis of expression and intuition is just intuition twice over (SM, 87). It defends the cognitive claim of art by trivializing it.

Collingwood boldly tried in *Speculum Mentis* to succeed where Hegel and Croce had failed. But he was justifiably modest about his success, and later, in *The Principles of Art,* he tried again. The difference between the discussion of Art in the earlier book and the theory of art in the later one is an instance of the difference between the dialectic of experience and the dialectic of mind; it shows, among other things, that the corresponding change in Collingwood's vocabulary from "spirit" to "consciousness" was not merely a semantic substitution but a complex conceptual development. The earlier dialectic of experience interpreted the lower orders of experience in terms of the higher orders toward which they are driven by internal necessity to unfold; and this dialectic ends with the visionary prospect of mind liberated from all its abstractions and from all its differences from other minds and from the natural and social world. The later dialectic of mind, on the other hand, interprets the higher levels of consciousness in terms of the lower levels which they assimilate and transform, and it ends with the description of contemporary civilized man conscious of his own historicity and of the perpetual and precarious self-creation of his own nature. In *Speculum Mentis* the importance of Art is entirely that it is a stage of development, corresponding to childhood in human life and primitivism in human society, which is superseded as conceptual thought develops. In *The Principles of Art,* this view of art survives but is greatly transformed by its combination with two new views: first, that art—or aesthetic activity or imagination—is the process by which the sensuous-emotive flux of feeling, the rudimentary consciousness of our bodily states and changes, is converted into self-conscious emotions capable of being expressed; and second, that conscious activity at *every* level has its concomitant emotions of which we may or may not become fully conscious by successfully expressing them. The first of these views is elaborated into Collingwood's version of an expression theory of art; the second extends the notion of art (thus it "escapes" the attempt to impose limits on its range of application, as in the *Essay on Philosophical Method* all philosophical concepts were said to do) to connect it with the entire dialectic of mind.

These are not, I think, merely the changes which one would naturally expect from someone who goes on thinking for a decade and a half without rereading his earlier works. Rather they correct what is, as the dialectical phrase goes, "partial and one-sided" in *Speculum Mentis,* while restating what was true. In *Speculum Mentis* Collingwood treated Art as a form of experience to be superseded by higher forms. In *The Principles of Art* he treats it as an aspect of consciousness which is the primary activity of second-level consciousness, but which also runs, like a scarlet thread, through every level; it appears in the tone and texture of the most abstract thought, and is the basis, at every level, of the activity of abstraction itself.

The particular problems which arise in the process of giving sense to Collingwood's theory of art thus are most intelligible as indicating, not a change in Collingwood's view of what art *is,* but a change in his view of its scope and value. The former does not significantly change; and *The Principles of Art* is his final answer to the same question which in *Speculum Mentis* was posed but not satisfactorily answered: how is it possible for art to be both imaginative and expressive? Or, in different language, how is it possible to reconcile, from the standpoint of the audience as well as from that of the artist, a view of art which regards it as the free creation of fantasy with one which regards it as cognitive or "revelatory of truth"? But the new answer to this question transforms the scope and value of art: art is no longer regarded, like Art in *Speculum Mentis,* as a self-transcending failure in the adventures of the mind, an experience "pregnant with a message that it cannot deliver" (SM, 110); rather it is recognized as *successfully* expressing something which cannot be asserted or described. Its importance is both individual and social: individual, because it is the agency by which the character of our most primitive and powerful feelings is recognized and by which their energy can be subjected to conscious control; social, because there is no society without discourse, all discourse is expressive, and expression is art. Hence Collingwood can say, "The aesthetic activity . . . is a corporate activity belonging not to any one human being but to a community (PA, 324). . . . The artist . . . tells his audience, at risk of their displeasure, the secrets of their own hearts. . . . The reason why they need him is that no community altogether knows its own heart; and by failing in this knowledge a community deceives itself on the one subject concerning which ignorance means death" (PA, 336). Art is the rhetoric of civilization: not in the sense in which rhetoric may clothe truth and falsehood alike in appealing and persuasive garb, nor in the sense in which rhetoric is the superior amusement of elegant style, but as a function of language which to the extent that it succeeds in expressing the emotional side of all conscious activity is also the most fundamental and indispensable form of self-knowledge.

Collingwood's theory of art can be regarded as an exploration of the relations among three concepts: expression, imagination and language. Each of these, in the meaning which it acquires within the theory, is a characteristic of art. Art *is* expression; art *is* imagination; art *is* language. Each of these formulae provides the conceptual link between the other two, when they are interpreted against the background of the dialectic of mind. As in the case of Collingwood's philosophy of history, his philosophy of art seems to contain many perverse claims when it is isolated from the larger system to which it belongs; but at least some of the objections to it evanesce when it is restored to its rightful place. I shall consider each of the concepts in turn, beginning with the concept of expression, because it is that which is linked in the most complex ways with the dialectic of mind, and ending with the concept of language, because it is that which Collingwood arrived at latest in his attempt to solve the "paradox of art" recognized in *Speculum Mentis*.

2 · *"Art Is Expression": Collingwood's Account of the Genesis and Expression of Emotion*

We have no names for feelings, although we *think* that we do because we confuse feelings themselves with the ways in which we become conscious of them, which is to say the ways in which we express them. Feeling at the first level of consciousness, or what Collingwood calls the "psychical level," is not, however, something *of* which we are conscious although we may become conscious of our expression of it. In its own right, psychical feeling is a sensuous-emotional flux—although of course it can be called "sensuous" and "emotional" not because we *find* these aspects separately in it but from the standpoint of higher levels of consciousness within which they are distinguishable: it is like calling a human infant a rational animal. One can think, to use a contemporary model which might not have recommended itself to Collingwood, of psychical feeling as having an input and an output. It receives its input *entirely* from the states and processes of the body, its sensory responses, glandular secretions, and so on. More precisely, it is the way in which these states and processes are *felt,* and it includes subliminal and unconscious feelings insofar as we may find it necessary to postulate such feelings in order to account for behavior. The output of the process of psychical feeling has two forms: first, it consists of "evincing" or "betraying" feeling in involuntary physical ways which we call "natural": in the tension and relaxation of muscles, in grimaces, grunts and screams, in the rush of blood to the face, in the sudden drying of the mouth or increased perspiration of the palms. Such natural discharges of feeling Collingwood calls "psychical expression"; but another word than "expression" would be useful as making clear the difference of such behavior from the second kind of output, or expression proper. The difference between the two is not that the physical effects of psychical feeling are involuntary but that they are not, as such, objects of self-consciousness. At the psychical level there is and can be no introspection of what we are feeling or what our bodies are doing. The distinction between "voluntary" and "involuntary" expression itself rests on a more fundamental difference. Involuntary expression is, so to speak, simple and direct, like a linear chain of cause and effect. In fact, if this were the only kind of expression with which we had to deal, the concept of feeling could be replaced, as it is in psychological theories of behavior, by the concept of overt response to external stimuli; for such theories, feeling is at most an "intervening variable," a concept useful in theory construction but one which does not denote or postulate any real state or process. There is no reason to refer to the physical signs of feeling as "expressions" except by extension of the concept of expression from its application to less simple and direct cases of expression proper. These cases are, in Collingwood's view, duplex. The voluntary expression of feelings is always accompanied by a *new* emotion attendant on the specific activity of expressing feeling. The occurrence of this new emotion is identical with the conscious expression of feeling.

To put all of this in a different way: it is usually held, and is probably the view of "common sense," that emotions are things that we *have,* that are *there* in our personal histories, and whose interest from a practical or philosophical point of view is that they are effects of causes in our experience and in turn are causes of effects in our behavior. It is not often thought that emotions are something we *do,* as thought is something we do. Language itself has no active intransitive verb for emotion—except the barbarism "to emote," which significantly means "to dissemble emotion"—as it does for thought, nor even a transitive verb as it does for perception, sensation, imagination, and feeling. Even less is it thought that emotion is something, like thinking, which can succeed or fail, or be done more or less well. Yet just this, I believe, is Collingwood's view. Emotion is neither a state nor an object of consciousness, but a kind of conscious activity. Moreover, it is an activity at which we can succeed or fail, and which, in a given instance, can be better or worse performed. *That aesthetics is a normative science, like logic and ethics, rests ultimately on the fact that emotion is an activity which can fail or succeed.*

The strangeness of this view is removed—or at least transferred—if we remember that for Collingwood emotion is identical with the expression of it; for it would be granted, I presume, that expression is an activity which may succeed or fail. This is not true, for Collingwood, of psychical feeling and psychical expression—and this is another reason why "expression" is misleading when applied to the physiological effects of psychical feeling. Psychical feeling *is* something that we have, that is just there, and psychical "expression" is always complete, automatic, and adequate to feeling. But feeling is not yet emotion. The simplest form of *emotion* consists of becoming conscious of feeling by successfully expressing it in a non-psychical way. "The expression of emotion is not, as it were, a dress made to fit an emotion already existing, but is an activity without which the experience of that emotion cannot exist. Take away the [expression], and you take away what is expressed; there is nothing left but crude feeling at the merely psychic level" (PA, 244; cf. 274). Expressing an emotion is thus the same thing as becoming conscious of it (PA, 282); and becoming conscious of it is the same thing as having it. To adapt a distinction originally invented for a different purpose, Collingwood's theory of the expression of emotion is a "one-termed" rather than a "two-termed" theory.[1] The usual view is that emotions may be expressed or may go unexpressed. This implies that the occurrence of emotion can be distinguished from the expression of it (even though we may have no reason to assert its occurrence in the absence of any expression). Collingwood's view is that having an emotion and expressing an emotion are identical; and this entails that there are no unexpressed emotions. There are, of course, feelings not expressed in any other way than psychically; but these cannot even be identified as individual occurrences.

Now when we add to this view of the identity of emotion with the activity of expressing it the other doctrine that the activity of expressing emotion not only *consists* of becoming conscious of that emotion but is accompanied by a new emotion, it is evident that the situation is complex. Collingwood did not make it easier by sometimes using "feeling" and "emotion" interchangeably; but it is clear that the dialectic of mind enables Collingwood to distinguish three separate activities within what in common language is lumped together as indifferently "feeling" or "emotion." First, there is first-level consciousness as such, which in one sense contains sensation *and* feeling but in another sense is all feeling insofar as it is throughout suffused with feeling-tone which can be abstracted from it only by a higher conscious activity. First-level feeling is always "psychically expressed" or discharged in physiological behavior. Second, there are second-level emotions or "emotions of consciousness." These consist of first-level feeling as we transform and become conscious of it by expressing it in a non-physiological way. Second-level emotions, however, *also* may themselves have physiological expressions, as shame (which for Collingwood is the "consciousness of weakness") can be expressed by blushing or stammering as well as in the high poetry of Job after the epiphany. Third, the *expression* of second-level emotion is itself an activity, and as such it is attended by a *new* emotion. The emotion of expressing feeling differs from the emotion which is feeling expressed. It is a quality of second-level consciousness, not its object; hence we become conscious of *it* only by expressing it in a *further* act. The duality of expression therefore survives at every level of consciousness, and the highest forms of intellectual activity themselves have the emotional tone appropriate to thinking in just this way. "Lucidity," "elegance," "turgidity," and the like, are terms which recognize the expressiveness of fourth-level rational thinking. As a consequence, poetry may express how it feels to think as well as how it feels to feel; there is, properly, no poetry of *ideas,* if that means the assertion of propositions sugar-coated with vivid images irrelevant to their truth, but there can be a poetry of *thinking* which expresses how it feels to think in a certain way quite apart from the truth of conclusions. What is *expressed* by "Euclid alone hath looked on beauty bare" is not affected by doubts about the axiom of parallels. Or, in Collingwood's illustration, Dante "fused the Thomistic philosophy into a poem expressing what it feels like to be a Thomist" (PA, 295).

At every level (above the first) it is necessary to distinguish between the emotion *expressed* and the emotion attending the activity of *expressing*. The activity of expressing makes us conscious *of* the former, and simultaneously brings the latter into being as something of which we *may* become conscious only in a further expressive act. The raw flux of feeling is thus linked with the most abstruse of theoretical systems not only by a dialectic of conceptual abstraction (as we saw in Chapter 4) but also by a dialectic of emotion and expression. Yet what carries the energy of primordial feeling through the higher levels of consciousness is *successful* expression; and, as we have seen, the expression of emotion may fail as well as succeed. How are we to account for failure?

It may be recalled from Chapter 4 that every act of second-level consciousness is an act of selective attention, which focuses on some part of the sensuous-emotional flux of first-level feeling and converts it into second-level consciousness while at the same time ignoring other parts of that flux. Thus some parts of pure feeling become expressed while others are unexpressed and vanish forever. (This does not contradict the principle that there are no unexpressed emotions, since feeling is not yet emotion and becomes so only in being expressed). But there is also a third possibility: we may attend to a part of pure feeling and yet fail to bring it to expression; it may, that is, be disowned or repressed. In such a case consciousness does not grasp the nettle but avoids it. Collingwood calls this disowning the "corruption of consciousness" (PA, 216–21). It reflects the bipolarity (missing from pure feeling) of second-level consciousness, which does not formulate the explicit opposition of truth and falsehood or of good and evil, but is the relatively indeterminate matrix out of which such conceptual oppositions are constructed by abstraction and differentiation. The corruption of consciousness is psychologically very common: "Coming down to breakfast out of temper, but refusing to allow that the ill humour so evident in the atmosphere is our own, we are distressed to find the whole family suffering agonies of crossness" (PA, 218). But it is also theoretically important, since as we shall see it is only as a corruption of consciousness—a failure of expression—that there can be bad art. And it seems clear that if emotion and the expression of emotion do indeed run through all the levels of consciousness, a corruption of consciousness at its lower levels will infect the forms of development at the higher levels.

With this brief sketch of Collingwood's speculative psychology in mind, we may go on to ask about its specific bearing on art. The question cannot be fully answered before following on to the mutual relations among expression, imagination and language; but at least some reasons for pursuing the fine distinctions among feeling, emotions of consciousness, and emotions attendant on expression can now be brought out. Four specific applications to problems of aesthetics are of particular importance, either because they undercut objections frequently advanced against Collingwood or because they underline advantages of his theory. The first of these is the continuity of "art" with every kind of expressive activity; this is the basis of the most common objection, that Collingwood holds that a "work of art" exists only in the artist's subjective experience. The second is the difference between Collingwood's theory of expression and romantic views of "self-expression," a distinction which enables him to avoid the "intentional fallacy" of judging art by reference to the artist's intentions. The third is the ability of the theory of expression to account for the experience of ambivalence in the experience of art. And the fourth is the consequence of the idea of "corruption of consciousness" for the distinction between good art and bad art; this distinction is the usual basis for the objection that on Collingwood's view there can be no principles of criticism.

a. Collingwood says at the beginning of *The Principles of Art* that he proposes to arrive at a definition of the term "art." But quite apart from our knowledge that for him a philosophical definition of a concept consists in exhibiting it as a scale of forms, it should be clear from *The Principles of Art* alone that he is not asking, much less presuming to answer, the question, "What properties are common and peculiar to works of art (or: to *good* works of art)?" It is a presumption of most contemporary aesthetics that an aesthetic theory should afford an answer to this question, and even that this question is logically prior to all other questions of aesthetics—for until it is answered, it may be said, we cannot even be sure what is to be *counted* as an instance of anything else we say about art. The first presumption is shared, if not the second, even by those who hold that there are no common and peculiar properties of works of art: such a view at least acknowledges the relevance of the question. But Collingwood does not grant even so much. His question is rather: "In what ways is the experience of creating and enjoying works of art continuous with all experience?" His aim is not to discover the *differentiae* of works of art as a species of artifacts but rather to discover the ubiquitous characteristics of experience of which art so-called provides only one kind of instance, even though an especially intense and concentrated one.

The difference between these two questions is plain enough. Whether the second question is truly Collingwood's may be disputed. *The Principles of Art* does begin with the question "What is art?" and the *prima facie* strategy of all of Book I is to distinguish "art proper" from different kinds (there are six, all told) of pseudo-art, or "art falsely so called." Its main conclusion is that art proper is nothing seen nor heard but exists only in the imagination of its creators. This is enough to outrage anyone who supposes that Collingwood is purporting to state the generic and specific properties of members of the class "works of art"; for of course the critic knows perfectly well that he goes to galleries and concert-halls to see or hear works of art, and that he cannot see or hear the "imaginative experience" of painters and composers even though he believes that paintings and sonatas are in some sense *products* of such imaginative experience. It would be charitable to suppose that Collingwood knew what the critic knows, and that in holding that "art proper" is neither seen nor heard he was not denying that one can go to the Uffizi to see the Botticellis. To meet simple outrage with a plain answer, "art proper" is one thing, a "work of art" another. (The very phrase "a work *of* art" suggests this.) Those who demand before all a statement of the defining properties of works of art should not cavil at this point but at another. For Collingwood also holds that "every utterance and every gesture that each one of us makes is a work of art" (PA, 285), and this is intended neither as metaphor nor as hyperbole. It is not the doctrine that "art proper" differs from what we see and hear which is incompatible with the demand for defining properties of works of art, but rather the doctrine that so-called works of art do not differ in kind from other human productions which ordinarily would never be given that name. Collingwood does not deny that "work of art" has a lexicographical meaning different from his. Normally, we would not call anything a work of art which is not *property,* and we are also reluctant to call anything a work of art which is primarily identified by its utilitarian functions. (It is hard to say how many theories of art have been confused by the fact that we expect a work of art to have a *price* but no *use.*) Collingwood ingeniously exploits our tendency to identify "fine" art with "useless" art in his argument that a great deal of so-called art is not "art proper" because it is deliberately produced *for the sake of* arousing certain emotions and therefore does have a "use" as amusement or magic. Nevertheless, it is the continuity of art and experience, or the aesthetic element in all experience, to which the doctrine of art as expression uniquely calls attention and which it attempts to account for.

I have tried up to this point to suggest that while Collingwood does not even try to state the defining properties of the class of "works of art" he had good reasons for not attempting to do so. Ultimately they rest on the claim made in the *Essay on Philosophical Method* that a philosophical concept "leaks or escapes" out of any limits imposed on its application, as by the rules of classification; and he is giving an account of the philosophical, not of the classificatory concept of art. But while I have tried to distinguish his question from other questions which he does not ask, I have reserved most comment on his extension of "art" to coincide with all expressive activity, because his argument for that extension connects expression with imagination; and we can therefore postpone a consideration of that connection to section 3.

b. A second consequence of Collingwood's theory is that as art does not differ essentially from other expressive activities, so artists do not differ in kind from other mortals. Expression is not self-expression, as a century of romantic aesthetic theory has tried to make out. While it is true that creativity in art is the expression of emotion, the important thing is that emotions are expressed, not that they are possessed; the emotions of artists are not (necessarily) deeper, more powerful or more complex than those of others. It is simply that they are—or may be—more lucidly and completely expressed. The intensity and nature of Beethoven's attitudes toward Napoleon are connected in Beethoven's personal history with the *Eroica* symphony; but for Collingwood, as much as for the most formalist of critics, they are irrelevant to the expressiveness of the

Eroica. Nothing in Collingwood's theory implies that what a work expresses can be better understood or explained by reference to the biography of the artist—including the intentions or meanings which he may have imputed to himself. Although artistic creation is a primordial kind of thought (i.e., second-level consciousness), it cannot be brought under the rubric of question and answer, and therefore cannot be re-enacted in historical reconstruction. A work of art is in a sense a solution to a problem; but in any given case that problem, which is to find a way of uttering the significance of feeling, cannot be *formulated*. If it could be formulated, it could in principle be solved. But since it cannot be formulated, it can only be expressed.

Artists do differ in one respect, however, and that is that painters paint, poets write, and so on. They engage, that is, in productive as well as imaginative activity, and they control or try to control a definite medium. A painter sees not only his subject but his painting in process, and he feels not only the handle of his brush but his own fluid, slashing or choppy gestures with it.[2] Collingwood has been generally faulted for ignoring the significance of technique in art;[3] on the contrary, he often emphasizes it: "Unless [the total sensuous-emotional experience of a man at work before his easel] were actually present there would be nothing out of which consciousness could generate the aesthetic experience which is 'externalized' or 'recorded' or 'expressed' by the painted picture" (PA, 307). The sense of this statement is that the *total* life of feeling which is expressed in art and of which art is the only way of becoming conscious is one which includes the practical activity of artistic creation. If "every utterance and gesture that each one of us makes is a work of art," one could imagine a society in which individual feelings were successfully transformed into emotions of consciousness by being expressed, but in which no acts were set apart from others as specifically "artistic." Yet it is clear that we could not understand the sense in which every utterance *can* be regarded as a work of art unless we had learned to use the term "work of art" in situations in which only some are identified as such. But Collingwood's theory as sketched above can account for the difference: the "artist," in the narrower sense, expresses two kinds of emotions: some are emotions, in feeling and expressing which he does not differ from others, and others are emotions peculiarly attendant upon the activity of painting, dancing, composing, etc. In the wider sense, every expression of emotion is a "work of art"; in the narrower sense, works of art express the specific emotions of expressiveness achieved in a specific medium. The peculiar joy of art in the narrower sense, one might say, is that we learn from it not only what we seek to express, but how to live expressively. This accounts, I believe, for the otherwise baffling phenomenon of the pleasure we find in tragedy: our satisfaction is not in tragic emotions themselves but in the expression of them, in bringing the dull and inarticulate burden of feeling into the clarity of consciousness. Only expressive life is *felt* as life worth living, and art is its celebration.

c. A third advantage of Collingwood's conception of expression is that it enables him to account for a notable feature of the experience of art which leaves alternative theories in a state of dull embarrassment. Often (although by no means always), our emotional response to art is one which forces us into verbal paradox in the attempt to describe it, although the experience itself is not *felt* as contradictory or as containing the unresolved tension of conflict." Tragic joy" is one such description, and there are many others, from the mixture of farce and pathos (not in sequence, but all at once) in Charlie Chaplin's art to the suffering, unredeemed but exalting, which has frustrated the critical powers of every interpreter of *King Lear*.[4] In poetry, the device of oxymoron presupposes and exploits our ability to distinguish between verbal contradiction in expressive language and the clarity and coherence of *what* is expressed. Our logical instincts may lead us to try to elucidate "cruel kindness" as denoting something which is truly kindness and only apparently cruel, or which is immediately cruel for the sake of being ultimately kind. But the birth of logic is the death of poetry; and anyone who asks of oxymoron an analysis which *removes* the contradiction or incongruity is clearly asking for the elimination of its expressive power.

This is, of course, a large subject and a Pandora's box of problems. Philosophers of art may be excused their habit of ignoring it; they have, one might say, enough problems of their own in applying logic to the analysis of art without having to regard what Vico called "poetic logic" as anything but a contradiction in terms and a confusion of thought. Nevertheless, one might ask of aesthetic theory that it be capable in principle of acknowledging, even if it does not undertake to explain, those aesthetic experiences which can be *described* only in contradictory language although their *expression* is of a complex emotional state, memorable precisely for its clarity and felt coherence. No theory is adequate to this task which, even though it acknowledges expressiveness as an important feature of art, assumes that it is legitimate to assert that *"x expresses y,"* where *x* is a "work of art" and *y* an emotion (or even an idea), *only* when *y* can be independently described in terms which make no reference to *x*. (An analogous assumption is often made about the "meaning" of works of art; its implication is that *if* a work of art has a meaning, the meaning should be capable of independent statement. But of course the critical claim that "What the poem means is as follows . . ." is open to the retort final, that "If *that's* what he meant, why didn't he *say* so?")

Collingwood explicitly recognizes that what would be paradoxical in *description* need not be in *expression*. Two separate arguments converge in supporting the distinction. The first is that consciousness at the second level is not concerned with the "relations between things," such a concern belonging only to higher levels of consciousness.

> A poet will say at one time that his lady is a paragon of all the virtues; at another time that she has a heart as black as hell. At one time he will say that the world is a fine place; at another, that it is a dust-heap and a dunghill. . . . To the intellect, these are inconsistencies. . . . On the poet's behalf it may be replied, to some one who argues that a lady cannot be both adorably virtuous and repellently vicious, or that the world cannot be both a paradise and a dust-heap, that the arguer seems to know more about logic than he does about ladies, or about the world [PA, 287–88].[5]

The second argument, which stems from the view stated originally in *Speculum Mentis* that art is "monadic," is that in second-level consciousness all the distinctions and differences which appear at higher levels may be reabsorbed as felt qualities of the imaginative experience rather than as relations of its parts. The indivisibility of the imaginative object *fuses* into a single qualitative experience not only emotions and sensations but memories, and even ideas lose their discrete and characteristic features as they are transformed into aspects of a single although complex imaginative object (PA, 252–53; cf. PA, 223, 237). Shelley's line, "I spin beneath my pyramid of night," attributes to the earth as speaker an expression of "what it feels like to be a Copernican" (PA, 295). Now it could not do so apart from an understanding of the theory which it invokes, but at the same time it would be naive to regard it merely as a pedagogical illustration which asserts the theory in the form of an especially engaging image. The complex idea of the geometrical shape of the earth's solar umbra is fused with the personification of the earth and the suggestion of a whirling dance to express an emotion which is completely independent of the truth of the theory although it could not exist apart from an understanding of its meaning. What is expressed is not a belief but the feeling of belief.

Collingwood never refers to the "ambivalence of emotion." Yet his theory also affords the possibility of a uniquely illuminating account of that ubiquitous and puzzling phenomenon. Ambivalence is of course not ambiguity; most markedly, the former is definite where the latter is vague, determinate where the latter is indeterminate. In the classic instance of ambivalence, the combination of love and hate for the same object, it is notable that the ambivalence lies in our *description* of it. Love and hate, we believe, are somehow, whatever they are, incompatible. There is nothing puzzling about the knowledge that love can turn into hatred, or hatred into love; what is puzzling, if we recognize the possibility at all, is that hatred and love may be felt simultaneously and in such a way they are interdependent; if one were to disappear or be modified, the other would too. Why do we speak of *two* distinct emotions? Because there is no other way in which they can be *described;* in general, we cannot speak of ambivalence unless two separately identifiable emotions can be described, as we cannot speak of ambiguity unless two separately stateable meanings can be attributed. But it may be that the problem of ambivalence is not how incompatible emotions can be simultaneously felt but why a single complex emotion is describable only in contradictory ways.

Collingwood's theory implies that a single complex emotion can be successfully and completely *expressed,* and that its expression is not equivalent to any description or set of descriptions. Freud is supposed to have said that not he but Sophocles discovered the ambivalence of love and hate in the Oedipal relation; but he thereby affirmed the relation of theory and art at the expense of ignoring their difference. It would be better to say that Sophocles, by successfully expressing it, brought into the light of consciousness what "oft was thought but ne'er so well expressed" about the complex form of feeling. Yet neither love nor hate is *described* in *Oedipus Rex,* which is a work of imagination or second-level consciousness. It is in the third-level *description* of emotions that we find ourselves forced, like

Aristotle inquiring into the pleasure derived from the feelings of terror, to speak in paradox if we are not to fall into an insensibility
whose only virtue is the avoidance of inconsistency. But then at the
fourth level we introduce the concept of ambivalence in order to
bridge the gap between the emotional congruity of second-level expressions and the verbal incongruity of third-level descriptions.
Unfortunately, however, the problem is not solved by giving it a
name. On the other hand, if expression is distinguished from
description on the one hand, as it is from "betrayal" of psychical
feeling on the other, the problem does not arise, and yet it is
possible to say why it seems to arise.

   d. We come at last to the consequences for a philosophy of art of
Collingwood's claim that in the corruption of consciousness feelings
are attended to and then disowned. It may be granted that it is more
difficult to be honest about our own emotions than about our beliefs
and intentions. A man who will publicly acknowledge his beliefs at
great risk to himself and his career may well be incapable of admitting his true feelings even to himself. There are many cases in which
we are uncertain what we believe, but none in which we conceal
from ourselves what in fact we do believe; this is necessarily true,
because nothing can be believed which is not asserted, and we cannot be ignorant of assertions which we do make. They are *constituted* as assertions by our consciousness of them. But art is not assertion: this was the burden of *Speculum Mentis* and is worked out in
detail in *The Principles of Art*. Art is expression; and expression and
assertion are not two modalities of the same content. Whatever an
assertion asserts is not something which can be or could have been
expressed; whatever can be expressed is not something which could
otherwise be asserted. But the present point is that, as we saw in the
sketch of the theory of expression, something in principle capable
of being expressed, namely the result of attention directed on the
sensuous-emotional flux of feeling, may fail of expression. This
failure occurs at the threshold "which divides the psychical level
of experience from the conscious level" (PA, 283). Because artistic
creation is only a special case of expressive activity in general, anyone can be guilty of corrupt consciousness insofar as he disowns
his own feelings; but because art *is* a special case, the corruption of
consciousness in the process of artistic creation has a special and
relatively enduring consequence: it gives rise to bad art (PA, 282).

   It sounds as if at last we have extracted from a reluctant Collingwood a criterion of art-criticism, but not so. Whether a given work of art is "bad," can on this account be decided neither by a biographical account of the course of its creation nor by any analysis of its observable features. Collingwood is as insistent as the bitterest critic of the concept of artistic expression that there is no possible way of discovering what an artist "intended" to express apart from the work of art itself; no way of distinguishing what he *intended* to express from what, if anything, he did express; and no way of stating what the *work* expresses as distinct from the work itself. These impossibilities are not empirical or technical difficulties. It is not that we have no way of finding out whether an artist is correctly reporting his intentions, as we have no way of finding out whether he is accurately reporting a dream. Where expression is concerned, intentions cannot *possibly* be reported for the same reason that, as we argued above, they cannot be *described* at all: they exist only in their expression. When an artist says that he intended to "express" such-and-such, we can know a priori that he has not expressed such-and-such, although he may have expressed something else. One of the more memorable of the uncountable number of cartoons about artists in their studios shows a painter, bundled like his wife and child against the cold in a bare loft, stepping back from the inept imitation of Mondrian on his easel and saying, "There! It's finished! A message of good will for all the world!" I forbear to dissect the humor, and observe only that other "messages" which could be better transmitted by Western Union than by painting—for example, "the alienation of the artist in a technological society"—would make the cartoon less funny but no less absurd.

The inseparability of what is expressed in a work from the work itself as it is experienced is often urged as a criticism of the concept of expression itself: for if what is expressed cannot be independently described and confirmed, our understanding of a particular work does not seem to be increased by adding to a description and analysis of its observable features the supererogatory addendum, *"and* it is also expressive." Only obscurantism would insist on ascribing to a work a nonobservable quality which is *ex hypothesi* not even connected in any regular way with any of its observable properties (e.g., that it is linear or painterly, drawn in strict perspective or not, of such and such a palette, representational, semi-representational, or abstract, etc.). We might as well, and as fruitlessly, argue whether or not it is "inspired," a "work of genius," or "immortal."

But we must revert to the distinction with which we began: Collingwood's inquiry is into the connection of art with experience, not into the defining properties of works of art or of "good" works of art, and he has not *failed* to deliver a manual for critics, because it was never within the scope of his inquiry to produce one—if, indeed, it is within the power of anyone. That "good" art expresses feelings and "bad" art disowns them is not a rule for arriving at critical verdicts but a way of interpreting our own experience; and it makes, one would think, some difference to recognize as the perception of expressiveness what otherwise we might interpret to our own confusion as "aesthetic pleasure," an "intention of transcendent truth," a "sublimation of repressed wishes," or any of the other ways by which we bring—or let someone else bring—the shock of recognition within the reassuring confines of our familiar vocabularies.

Yet something is left over for critics, even if it is not a "criterion." Collingwood held that the philosophy of art is divided into two parts, or stages: art-criticism and aesthetic theory, in that order (PA, 3–4). Significantly, however, he makes no reference whatever to the vast variety of analyses, descriptions, evaluations, and recommendations which we have learned to count as "criticism," presumably on the ground that criticism is anything which is published by a "critic." The *only* judgment which Collingwood recognizes as a "critical" judgment is: "This is art; that is not" (PA, 3–4, 88–89). When they are not corrupted by the attempt to justify as art what in fact is "genteel amusement," critics are justified by their capacity to *recognize* art when they see it: their qualification is the sensibility to experience it as expressive or inexpressive. It follows that critics, insofar as they can discern expressiveness, are authoritative, like prophets and wine-tasters. Collingwood draws this conclusion explicitly, and goes even further to assert that whether or not a given object is art or sham art is a "matter of fact, . . . valid for everybody at every time and place" (PA, 92). But he does not say how, if we cannot tell a poem from a sham poem and therefore must seek the authoritative judgment of a critic, we can tell a critic from a sham critic. The search seems to be the pursuit of the ineffable by the insensible.

The perplexity, however, is academic. I think that the *process* of criticism can be sketched in a way which goes beyond Collingwood but requires no significant emendation of any of his views. The concept of an authority who is acknowledged but cannot be understood, we may assume, is as moribund as the Muses. But so, on Collingwood's view, is the notion that the function of art criticism is judicial. The critic's function is not to pronounce a verdict for any purpose other than to engage our attention. We can make up our own minds, and, indeed, if *expressiveness* is the uniquely relevant characteristic of art, we *must,* for unless we directly experience it, even the unanimous testimony of others may only arouse suspicion that they are stirred to rapture by the emperor's new clothes. The problem, however, with any given work of art is what is meant by experiencing *it.* We cannot assume (and in practice we do not), that good vision is all that is necessary to experience a painting, or that everyone with good hearing at a concert experiences the *same* music. In any concert-hall there are the tone-deaf fulfilling social obligations, conservatory students inspecting the technique of instrumentalists, a fair number of romantics lost in reveries of pastoral idylls or the clash of arms, sophisticates rehearsing the comments they plan to make at intermission; and of the disinterested friends of music some will bathe in the sensuous flow of musical movement while others struggle to grasp the larger forms, and so on. The sense in which they are all "hearing the same music," although no doubt there is such a sense, is of little more aesthetic relevance than the sense in which they are all enjoying the same weather. Yet it could hardly be denied that those whose hearing is informed by the sense of musical motion or the awareness of form, both of which are necessary although not sufficient conditions of expressiveness in music, are hearing music in a more typical or normal sense than those who are bored during quiet passages because they admire most the acrobatics of the conductor.

It is in such a "normal" sense that one may *try* to hear music and *fail* or *succeed* in doing so. The critic's function, Collingwood might therefore say, is to help those who wish to hear it as it can be heard, by calling attention to features (all of which *can* be heard, unlike details of the unhappy love affairs of the composer and of the politics of philharmonic societies) which otherwise might pass unnoticed. In this way, criticism can enrich perception, not by adding external details but by articulating internal complexity; and it is beyond some minimal level of complex perception that we can succeed in discerning for ourselves what the work succeeds, if it does at all, in expressing. Nevertheless, there can be no rules for critical discourse, as there are no rules for self-understanding. Criticism is a form of teaching, not of jurisprudence, and whether or not the rendering of verdicts can be reduced to rules, teaching is no science but itself an art.

3 · "Art Is Imagination": Artistic Creation and

Communication, and a Correction of Collingwood's

Thesis that Art Is Knowledge

Expression and emotion, in Collingwood's theory, are correlative terms: what is expressed is emotion and only emotion, never concepts (although the *feeling* of conceptual thinking can be expressed) or propositions (although the feeling of propositional assertion can be expressed); and emotion can in the first instance be *only* expressed (not described), because it is only in the expression of emotion that we become conscious of it at all and conversely.

At the same time, the emotion which attends activity at the higher levels of consciousness is entirely derived either from the emotional aspect of psychical feeling or directly or indirectly from the transformation of that aspect in the course of expressing it. And psychical feeling is an undifferentiated mass of sensation as well as emotion. To describe art as expressive, as we have done up to this point, isolates one side only of the sensuous-emotional states of first-level consciousness. The partial account of art as expression must therefore be supplemented by a parallel account of the conversion of the *sensuous* side of first-level consciousness into the imaginative objects of second-level consciousness. We have already canvassed, in Chapter 4, the major features of this process, which Collingwood usually relates to the classical epistemology of empiricism by calling it the conversion of "impressions" into "ideas." Ultimately, the theories of expression and of imagination are connected by the theory of language: for although expression and imagination can be conceptually distinguished, they cannot be actually separated; and it is only because language is both expressive and imaginative that linguistic activity can dialectically relate at higher levels of consciousness what only linguistic activity can distinguish at lower levels.

One of the most surprising features of recent philosophical aesthetics, at least to anyone familiar either with the history of aesthetics or with the vocabulary of contemporary non-philosophical discourse about art, is the almost complete absence of any discussion of imagination as such. Even when it does occur, concealed in discussion of equally protean concepts such as that of symbolism, or in Susanne Langer's analyses of "virtual" space, time, and action, the avoidance of the term itself is characteristic—and puzzling. The concept of imagination sometimes seems to have been relegated to the same limbo in which wander the shades of "spirit," "intuition," "sympathy," and "beauty" itself. Collingwood himself gradually abandoned many of these shibboleths of romantic philosophy. In his *Outlines of a Philosophy of Art* (1925), for example, he had defined "beauty" as "that quality of an object in virtue of which it satisfies the claims of the aesthetic spirit" (OPA, 30). In *The Principles of Art,* however, he says that "there is no such quality," and that "the words 'beauty,' 'beautiful,' as actually used, have no aesthetic implication," but refer to anything regarded as admirable or excellent in non-aesthetic as well as aesthetic respects (PA, 38 ff.). As his thought developed from a theory of "spirit" to a theory of "consciousness," so the concept of beauty came to be replaced in his thinking by the concept of imagination. The latter is broader in its application than the former, and it indicates something we *do* rather than something we apprehend.

The central emphasis of the theory of imagination corresponds to that of the theory of expression: it *connects* what we commonly call "art" with experience in general rather than seeking the essence of art in what distinguishes it from other kinds of experience. The term "art" itself thereby acquires an extended meaning whose function is to call attention to an aspect of all experience rather than to summarize the *differentiae* of "works of art." Just as "every utterance and every gesture that each one of us makes is a work of art" because utterances and gestures are *expressive,* so every conscious state is a work of art because it is the product of an imaginative process. Collingwood follows Kant in arguing that the perception of a physical object itself always and necessarily involves the imagination of properties of the object which correspond to nothing in sensory perception as such. We never see the other sides of objects (while they *are* the other sides) but would not see *objects* at all if we did not imagine them (PA, 192). Moreover, the ability to fix our attention on an object presupposes the ability to recognize the identity or at least the similarity of, for example, the colors and shapes of which we are aware at any moment with the colors and shapes seen at just preceding moments, and these latter survive for comparison only in imagination. Collingwood does not undertake to solve the "problem" of so-called sense-data except insofar as he makes the point that all perceptual experience includes as constituents data which are imagined as well as those which are directly sensed. No detailed theory of perception can be fathered on Collingwood; but in any case the special problems of perception are not immediately relevant to his purpose of explaining art. The question is whether the alleged ubiquity of imagination does not pay for the breadth of its application by being too thin to sustain aesthetic relevance.

It would be a mistake, I believe, although a tempting one, to suppose that Collingwood is merely straining for the paradox that we are artists whenever we look out of the window. The point of insisting on the ubiquity of imagination is related to the reason for adding to the theory of expression a theory of imagination at all: *through the description of art as imagination there is reestablished the contact between art and audience, between the creation and the enjoyment of art, which in the description of art as expression seems to be broken.* It is the artist, not the spectator, who expresses feeling; the spectator, to be sure, must recognize it, but to say that his experience as a spectator is itself expressive directly leads to the unpalatable consequence that such experience may be completely irrelevant to the expression of the artist or the expressiveness of the art.[6] On the other hand, the spectator's experience might be regarded as not irrelevantly self-expressive but as not expressive at all: an attitude of quiet contemplation, as one might say, which neither consists of nor leads directly to "utterances and gestures." But imagination is otherwise: art can be neither produced nor enjoyed except as an object of imaginative activity. This is quite clear in the case of the so-called "temporal arts"; music, dance, theater, and literature can *prima facie* be experienced only serially. Each moment of a dance, each line of a poem is an element of that dance or that poem only to the extent that the dance or the poem can be grasped—as it cannot be directly experienced—as a complex whole, and in this sense *the* dance or *the* poem is an object of imagination for anyone who could be said to be experiencing *it* at all. A similar account can be given of the plastic arts, which all take time to see, although they do not, as does music, impose a determinate order of serial experience. In each of the several arts, the result is the same: the experience of art is an imaginative experience. What distinguishes Collingwood's view, however, is that he takes two further steps, which he regards as supported by the same arguments which show that aesthetic experience as well as artistic creation is imaginative. The first is that the work of art "proper" is an imagined rather than a perceptual object; the second is that the imaginative activity of the spectator is expressive in the same way as that of the artist. The former thesis has been more commonly recognized and criticized than the latter, but both are major propositions in Collingwood's theory of art, and both have a paradoxical air. The first has often been taken as showing Collingwood to be essentially restating Croce's aesthetic, but the second could equally well be regarded as showing that he is not.

Why does Collingwood say that "the work of art proper is something not seen or heard but something imagined" (PA, 142) and that a work of art may be a thing "whose only place is in the artist's mind"? (PA, 130; later discussion makes clear that Collingwood would expand this to read "in the mind of artist or audience"; cf. PA, 139–40). It is such statements which have caused Collingwood to be classified as an "idealist" by people who already know all the refutations of philosophical idealism. But he clearly does not intend to make these statements bear any metaphysical weight; they are not part of a strategy first to win assent to the proposition that paintings and sonatas exist only in the minds of those who create and perceive them and then to lead by degrees to the conclusion that the same is true also of picture frames and violins, and in fact of all physical objects. He rejects out of hand the "metaphysician" who has decided that the things we call real are only "in our minds" or that "the things we describe as being in our minds are thereby implied to be just as real as anything else" (PA, 131). On the contrary, his argument necessarily assumes that we are capable of distinguishing between imaginary objects and real objects; and it also assumes, although not so evidently, that real objects include things which we correctly call "works of art" although they are not works of art proper. Collingwood thus holds, among his *reasons,* views which are the opposites of the positions aften attributed to him by a mistaken interpretation of his *conclusions.*

Collingwood's argument is a simple one. A composer in creating a melody has clearly created the melody when he has succeeded in imagining it in its entirety, and to this extent it exists in his imagination. It may or may not be written down, and if it is it may or may not be performed. But no one would say that he has not composed a melody unless it is performed, or even unless it is written down. There is nothing logically contradictory, implausible, or even odd about a composer's saying, "I worked out the first sixteen bars of a mellophone concerto in my head last night, but it didn't satisfy me and I've put it out of my mind." Now it is beside the point that we cannot tell whether he is telling the truth; the point is that we know what he *means,* and that therefore "composing music" does not entail writing it down or performing it although it does entail creating in imagination something of a sort which *could* be written down or performed. Imagining that one has composed a sonata differs from having composed a sonata in imagination; and an imaginary sonata (like one attributed to a composer in a work of fiction) differs from an imagined sonata.

As something created, therefore, music may be completely created, and yet exist only in the composer's imagination. Whether music is always or for the most part complete in imagination before it is committed to manuscript is irrelevant. Certainly in most cases it is not, and the gift attributed to Mozart of imagining an entire symphonic movement interests us because of its rarity as well as because of its possibility. The simpler case of an imagined melody suffices to establish the logical priority of imagination. In the most typical case, however, composition begins with fragments of theme, harmony, and form, and there is a constant interplay between new material and the development to date, often with revision and elimination of what has already been incorporated in the work in progress. But this is perfectly compatible with Collingwood's view and he explicitly acknowledges it. As early as *Speculum Mentis* he said that an aesthetic act "may last for five years at a time" (SM, 70), and in *The Principles of Art* he made clear that the activity of imagining and the activity of making go on simultaneously and not successively. In the case of painting, for example, "there is no question of 'externalizing' an inward experience which is complete in itself. There are two experiences, an inward or imaginative one called seeing and an outward or bodily one called painting, which in the painter's life are inseparable, and form one single indivisible experience, an experience which may be described as painting imaginatively" (PA, 304–305).

Emphasis on the simplest case, where there is imagination without making, is therefore not a complete *description* of the activity of artistic creation but part of an argument that an adequate description must recognize not the temporal but the logical priority of imagination. It may be called "logical" because it bears on our concepts of artistic creation, imagination, and technical production. It is often believed that our concept of "art" is derived (in some way) from our experience of works of art as public objects and our knowledge that these have been produced by technical processes such as the shaping of stone and clay, the production of sounds from vibrating strings and columns of air, and so forth. Then, the received analysis goes, we introduce as *explanatory* ideas concepts such as imagination in order to account for features of such objects such as their comparative novelty; but such ideas are hypothetical and can be eliminated if we can otherwise explain, without reference to them, everything which they seem to explain. According to this account, the primary meaning of "art" refers to observable characteristics of public works of art, "artistic creation" is understood as the process of which such works are the products, and "imagination" is a concept belonging to some but not all theories of artistic creation. Now Collingwood's view is that this account, although it may be a true account of the order in which we come to learn the meanings of these terms, is false as an account of their logical priority. Imagination is not an eliminable "intervening variable" in the explanation of art but a necessary element in the concept of it. Collingwood's way of putting this is that the production of a work of art as an artifact is necessarily connected with "the aesthetic activity, that is with the creation of the imaginative experience which is the work of art" (PA, 305).

The issue cannot be settled or clarified by appeals to experience or to common language, for experience is ambivalent and language equivocal on this point. We speak of the "art" of chimpanzees, and put the term in quotes to indicate that we are unwilling to call it *really* art. And what are we to say of the objects produced by Jean Tinguely's "painting-machines," or in aleatory music? On the one hand we are moved to call such objects "works of art," because they resemble in appearance and social function works of art with which we are familiar; on the other, we are moved to deny that they are works of art, because art without artists seems logically inconceivable. (Asked "How can you call this stuff music?" the composer John Cage once mildly replied, "Well, it seems a better word than 'sculpture.'") At the same time we are unwilling to "close" the concept of art in such a way that genuine novelties become forever excluded *by definition;* too often, we know, *les fauves* have become, in retrospect, the masters. But we are unwilling to say with Humpty Dumpty that art is whatever anyone chooses to call it. If we define art as whatever artists produce (quite apart from the obvious circularity of the attempt) they will trundle a baby-buggy with a wheel missing into a gallery and list it in the catalogue; if we stick to the accepted classics and define art as anything which shares with them certain characteristics, we are sure, as Collingwood observed of aestheticians who stick to the classical artists, to "locate the essence of art not in what makes them artists but in what makes them classical, that is, acceptable to the academic mind" (PA, 4).

No one knows anything about the imaginative activity of artists apart from the objects with which they furnish the world; hence it seems strange to say that the music is in the composer's head, or the painting in the artist's mind. But it is equally true that we know nothing about music or painting except through our own imaginative experience of it. It is therefore the awareness of our *own* imaginative activity which is the primary meaning of the term "art." Subsequently the application of the term may be extended to the class of objects in whose presence we regularly discover this awareness, then to the people who produce these artifacts, then to other objects produced by "artists" whether or not they make us aware of our own imaginative activity (e.g., Matisse's rugs or Picasso's pots), and finally to any objects, including *objets trouvés,* which have such an effect whether or not they are produced by "artists." If this is not the actual order in which meanings are learned, it is a reconstruction of their order of logical priority consistent with Collingwood's theory. To put it shortly: it is only because we are artists ourselves that we come to relate the term at all to a special class of artisans; and it is only to the extent that we rediscover our own imaginative activity in the contemplation of objects merely as such that we explicitly recognize that we are artists ourselves. There should be nothing baffling or disturbing about the fact that chimpanzees paint and computers produce poetry. It is we who are the artists in our perception of such products, for the same reason that it is we who wonder whether to call it "art."

Such an account of imagination, however, raises fresh doubts about "communication" in art. Formally, the relation of artist to audience seems in Collingwood's view to be analogous to the relation of historical agent to historian. In each case, a conscious activity, of imagination or thought, results in a product—a work of art or an action—which is intelligible to the extent that it is re-imagined or re-enacted. The parallel quickly breaks down, however. The general pattern of thought and action is that of problem and solution. The historian can re-enact only the thought of agents who knew what they were doing, as he reconstructs that thought from the evidence of their actions. But the artist quite literally does not know what he is doing; this is what distinguishes him from the craftsman who deliberately applies known techniques as means to an envisioned end. If an artist could "know what he is doing," he would know what emotions he was trying to express; but emotions can be known *only* by being successfully expressed. The spectator, unlike the historian, cannot understand the product by re-enacting the process. But in this he is like the artist himself, who can no more re-enact his own process of bringing confused feeling to articulate expression than a mathematician can re-experience the state of not being able to solve a particular problem once he has discovered the solution.

It apparently did not occur to Collingwood that in *The Principles of Art* he was dangerously close to assimilating art to the conceptual model of historical re-enactment which had already occupied so much of his thought. In *The Idea of History* he had struggled to make clear that the artist's "problem" is not one which can be clarified by reflection but is the "unexpressed significance" of his "immediate sensitive and emotional life" which "lies on his mind as a burden, challenging him to find some way of uttering it. . . . [Art] is the phase of that life in which the conversion from unreflective to reflective thought actually comes about. There is therefore a history of art, but no history of artistic problems. . . . There is only the history of artistic achievements" (IH, 314). In *The Principles of Art,* however, he attempted to explain the relation between artist and audience as the production ("we need not ask how") in the spectator by a work of art, say a painting, of "sensuous-emotional or psychical experiences which, when raised from impressions to ideas by the activity of the spectator's consciousness, are transmuted into a total imaginative experience identical with that of the painter" (PA, 308). This account, however, cannot be true. It is plainly inconsistent with Collingwood's own emphasis on the spontaneity of selective attention in the transformation of first-level feeling by second-level consciousness: "Attention is in no sense a response to stimulus. It takes no orders from sensation" (PA, 207). There is thus no guarantee that even if the same sensuous-emotional experiences were produced in two different spectators their own imaginative transmutations of these experiences would be identical. Collingwood does not note this difficulty; but he does consider a second one, namely the difficulty of *deciding* whether the imaginative experience of the spectator is identical with that of the artist. His answer, however, is inadequate: art is like conversation, he observes, in which we can have no absolute assurance that we can understand each other but only an empirical assurance which becomes stronger as conversation proceeds. The analogy, however, is imperfect in its most crucial respect. In conversation we can adjust our comments and questions for the sake of eliciting *new* responses by which we test our mutual understanding. In the case of our experience of art it is just this which is impossible. Reading is no more a conversation with great authors than paleontology is a conversation with brontosauri. Neither will answer our new questions, nor can we suppose that art is a cryptogram which encodes in advance the answers to all the questions we may ask. Collingwood acknowledges this when he admits that "the imaginative experience contained in a work of art is not a closed whole" and that *no* penetration into the complexity of a work can extract " 'the' meaning of the work, for there is no such thing" (PA, 311). This implies at least that the artist's "total imaginative experience" is not "the meaning" (since nothing is) and further that it is not the criterion, wholly inaccessible and unapplicable, of communication.

If these criticisms are sound, what is their force? If Collingwood's theory is emended to correct for them, how many of his striking and novel conclusions must be abandoned or modified in the direction of commonplaces? Not much, and not many, I believe. The notion that any meaning can be ascribed to the "identity" of the experience of the artist and that of his audience must be foregone, and so must offhand remarks such as the comment that in the case of a "great artist" we can catch his "meaning" only "partially and imperfectly" (PA, 309). But what must mainly be given up is Collingwood's attempt, no doubt an uncritical reflection in his thought of his sympathy for Croce's aesthetic, to claim for art the status of knowledge. It is, to be sure, an unusual sort of knowledge, the knowledge of "perfectly concrete individualities, . . . from which nothing has yet been abstracted by the work of intellect" (PA, 288). What these "individualities" might be is not explained, but we know that they could be nothing other than states of psychical feeling, modified by becoming objects of consciousness. Now the objection to calling art a form of knowledge is not that in the *Essay on Metaphysics* Collingwood restricted the application of "knowledge" to the asking and answering of questions (an act of third-level consciousness), and that having repeated this in *The New Leviathan* (NL, 11.11) he restricted "knowledge" still further to fourth-level reflection on propositional thinking (NL, 14.21). In the dialectic of mind, the concept of knowledge, like other concepts such as the concept of abstraction, will necessarily have an eminent sense at the highest level of consciousness but also an undeveloped sense at the lower levels out of which it grows. At the second level we would ordinarily call it "direct awareness" or perhaps, in Kantian language, "intuition"; but there is nothing wrong about calling it "knowledge" if we remember that it is second-level consciousness we are speaking of.

The difficulty is rather that in the sense in which there can be second-level knowledge, we do not know our own emotions. The artist knows what he is *creating,* but not what he is *expressing.* He is directly aware of the imagined object which he is in the process of fashioning, but although in this activity he is expressing emotion he is not in the same way directly aware or becoming directly aware of that emotion. If this is so, then becoming *conscious* of emotion by expressing it is not in any proper sense coming to *know* emotion, as we might say that in becoming conscious that one is hearing a foghorn in the distance one is coming to know that one is hearing a foghorn. One reason why we can become conscious of emotion without having it as an object of consciousness must wait until we turn to a consideration of the sense in which art is language; but another reason is itself sufficient to establish the point. Whenever we describe a work of art, we describe it as an imaginative object: a painting, for example, by the objects represented (if any), by colors and masses, form and design, and by such qualities as whether it is linear or "painterly." Or we describe music, as in the classic analyses by Tovey, by its musical material and its development, tonality and modulation, orchestration, and so forth. We *do not and cannot describe its expressiveness,* and if we try to do so we discover that there is no safe passage between the Scylla of inanity and the Charybdis of poetic evocation. In the former case one is trapped by the poverty of our language for describing emotion ("sad," "happy," "exciting," and the like), and in the latter one is seduced into metaphorical language (like all those program notes about Tchaikowsky's tortured cries from the depths) which, whatever its merits otherwise, is plainly not description. Anyone who is in doubt about this might try to describe the difference between the emotions of the pathetic and of the tragic without recourse to specific dramatic circumstances (e.g., the deaths of Little Nell and Antigone) supposed to evoke or express such emotions. Recourse to such a story as the "objective correlative" of emotion is itself the creation or recreation of that complex imaginative object which is a work of art, and we can be said to "know" such an object. But in such creation or recreation emotion is expressed, although in so becoming conscious of emotion we cannot be said to know it.

The peculiar feature of emotion, then, is that we become conscious of it by expressing rather than by observing and describing it; it was perhaps in oblique reference to this that in *The New Leviathan* Collingwood called feeling and the forms of feeling "apanages" rather than "constituents" of mind. Certainly it is presupposed in his observation, in *The Principles of Art*, that the lack of a vocabulary rich in words to describe a great variety of subtly differentiated emotions is no handicap at all to a poet, for if you describe an emotion, rather than *expressing* it, "your language becomes frigid, that is inexpressive, at once. A genuine poet, in his moments of genuine poetry, never mentions by name the emotions he is expressing" (PA, 112).

Nevertheless, Collingwood got himself into the difficulties we have observed by occasionally *identifying* imagination with expression, although his aim and obligation was only to relate them. We shall see in the following section that this inadvertent identification also creates difficulties, although remediable ones, in his theory of language. For the present we may observe that, since he believed that a work of art may be completely created as an object of imagination, it was not difficult to slip over into the assumption that its *expressiveness* is also single and complete although complex; and this permitted him to infer, for example, that we only partially grasp the "meaning" of a great artist although presumably *he* knew it completely and adequately. But if imagination and expression are not identified—and in the dialectic of mind they are not—this does not follow. Whatever is expressed could be expressed in no other way than by the creation of this specific work of art; in this sense imagination is both a necessary and sufficient condition of expression. But an artist may know completely and adequately what he has created (as an imaginative object) without knowing *in any other way* what he has expressed. It follows that there is nothing the artist knows which we as his audience do not. The artist is not a Fermat, leaving behind him theorems which challenge us to recover the proof which he alone has discovered. There may be more in the thought of scientists, philosophers, or statesmen than we have yet managed to understand, but in the case of artists we already have everything we possibly could have: the art itself. Our experience of it is not communion with them, but with ourselves, a discovery not of what they thought about life but of how our lives feel to us.

4 · *"Art Is Language": Collingwood's Final Synthesis Between Expression and Imagination*

Collingwood has so far argued that art is expressive and that art is imaginative; this enables him finally to conclude that art is language, since only language can be both expressive and imaginative. Thus the concept of expression is connected with the concept of imagination through the *tertium quid* of language, in its "original or native state"; of such language, "to call it imaginative is to describe what it is, to call it expressive is to describe what it does" (PA, 225).

This is already a notable change from *Speculum Mentis,* where language is never mentioned in connection with Art. But he had early almost succeeded in stating the central thesis of his later theory of language: that the most fundamental function of language is not to denote objects or to make statements but to express emotion. Reviewing in 1928 a book on aesthetics by S. Alexander, he observed that Alexander, like many others, regarded poetry as ordinary language plus a kind of magic, and therefore was at a loss to say how the magic gets in. The solution, according to Collingwood, is to recognize that poetry is the basis of *all* language. "Practical language" adds to the primitive poetic function of language a structure of logical implication in which the "magic" is overshadowed but never eliminated; hence "the magic of poetry . . . is nothing but the significance of language as such." [7]

What "the significance of language as such" might be, however, he could not then suggest. Nor had it yet become clear when in the *Essay on Philosophical Method* he described prose and poetry as overlapping species of a philosophical genus, both capable of "literary excellence," which is for poetry an end in itself but for prose a means to the communication of thought (EPM, 199–200). In *The Principles of Art* everything falls at last into place, and the early thesis that poetry is more fundamental than prose is elucidated by the entire dialectic of mind. The "magic of poetry" is explained as the capacity of language to express emotion; and the "literary excellence" which prose can share with poetry is also expressiveness, which in the language of third- and fourth-level consciousness increases the clarity of thought by expressing the new emotions which attend the activities of thought at these higher levels. Moreover, the concept of language itself is generalized to include all expressive activity, and thereby becomes coincident with the similarly generalized concept of art. In this development of ideas, the early insight that poetry is more fundamental than prose survives, much modified and expanded. The final view is that what we call poetry is but one instance of expressive activity, which as the generation of living language gives rise by a series of abstractions to the "intellectualized language" of higher levels.

The repetition of the schematic outline of the dialectic of mind from context to context should by now alert us to expect Collingwood's theory of language to reveal the same principles of organization. We might expect at least two features: first, that language will be analyzed as a series of activities corresponding to levels of consciousness, and second, that theories of language (since a theory is a product of rational thinking at the fourth level) should fall into classes corresponding to the three types of explanation and of value at that level. And one does find in fact that the discussion of language in *The Principles of Art* does fall into those patterns even though we must often spell out possibilities left implicit by Collingwood.

To consider the second feature first: Collingwood briefly considers what he calls the "technical theory of language" as exemplified by I. A. Richards in *The Principles of Literary Criticism* (PA, 262–63). The distinguishing feature of such a theory is that it regards language as something which can be "used" in various ways (e.g., for description or for evoking emotions and attitudes). The technical theory of language presupposes the same conceptual scheme of means-ends and cause-effect as the technical theory of art; and this conceptual scheme is the one associated with utilitarian justification and with teleological explanation. Collingwood does not discuss other theories; but we might go on to observe that recent philosophies of language, following Wittgenstein, have abandoned the "technical" or utilitarian interpretation of language and replaced it with the notion of language as a rule-governed activity. The main development of this so-called linguistic philosophy has come after Collingwood's death, and he did not discern its faint stirrings in his lifetime. Yet, and interestingly, a locus for linguistic philosophy is already established in the architectonic of his dialectic of mind, since a regularian conception of language would belong to that stratum of fourth-level consciousness at which "right" is the basic concept of value and nomological explanation the basic form of cognition. But it is the third stratum which Collingwood claims to have attained in the concrete ethics of "duty" and in historical explanation as knowledge of the concrete. The corresponding theory of language, one might guess, would regard the "ordinary language" whose rules are explored by linguistic analysis as an *abstraction* from the process of perpetual change in living language just as the ethics of duty regards the normative laws of regularian morality as abstractions from the concrete situations in which thought issues in action. Collingwood seems to say as much when he says that "the artistic activity does not 'use' a 'ready-made language,' it 'creates' language as it goes along" (PA, 275). The sense in which common language can be regarded as an "abstraction" and the sense in which Collingwood could hold a theory of "concrete language" may be partially clarified by some established distinctions of linguistics.

Linguists commonly distinguish, following Ferdinand de Saussure,[8] two elements of any natural language: one, which Saussure called *la langue,* is the system of signs inherited, held, and understood by members of a speech community, and capable of being described and analyzed without reference to any particular speaker or hearer. The other, which Saussure called *la parole,* is the active and individual use of language, the occurrence of particular speech-utterances. *La parole* is the element of innovation and individuation in language, as *la langue* is the institutional and social element. For Saussure, *la langue* and *la parole* together exhaust *le langage.*[9]

Both the "technical," or utilitarian, and the regularian theories of language take as their object *la langue.* Now any specific speech-utterance is clearly more than a particular instance of a language-system. We understand well enough a sentence like "I wouldn't do that," insofar as it belongs to *la langue*. But with stress on the first and last words it is a protestation of innocence and means (roughly), "I am not the sort of person who would do a thing like that"; with the stress on the third word, it is a warning, and means, "If you do that you'll be sorry." These differences still belong to *langage;* but there may be additional components of the total activity of utterance. Tone of voice and stress are properties of the spoken sentence; different from these are the slight shrug, the eyebrows raised or knit, the hands clenched or lifted palms outward. To account for the expressiveness of language, therefore, requires at least three categories, as is evident if we consider the ways in which an utterance may be heard or received. A speaker may be heard by someone who also observes him as part of "hearing"; he may be heard only, as by telephone; or an exact transcript of his words may be read. These differences have practical import as well as theoretical significance: Warren Harding won the Presidency with a "front-porch" campaign of press releases after his shrewd managers refused to let voters see or hear him.

With these differences in mind, we can see in Collingwood's theory of language the correspondence to the dialectic of mind which we have come to expect. By the generic term "language" Collingwood means a scale of forms corresponding to the three upper levels of consciousness and differing from each other like the three functions of language just discussed. *La langue* he calls "intellectualized language," referring both to natural language and to the constructed languages of mathematics and empirical science; it occurs only at fourth-level consciousness. *La parole* he calls "speech"; it occurs first in third-level consciousness although it carries over into the utterance of "intellectualized language"; and he calls "discourse" the total and continuous activity of expression of meaning or signifying anything (NL, 6.1, 6.11). It includes not only third- and fourth-level utterance but the expressive activity of second-level consciousness ("imagination") from which the higher levels develop. Intellectualized language is an abstraction from speech, and speech an abstraction from discourse; and although "language" is properly the name of the activity exemplified in the whole scale of forms, Collingwood seizes the opportunity to apply it not merely to the fourth and third levels, where it is supported by ordinary usage, but to the second as well, where it is not. Thus he can distinguish (as he claims that any-one accustomed to look after small children learns to distinguish) the automatic cry of a child in response to a stimulus from the child's cry of complaint and for attention; "the second cry is still a mere cry; it is not yet speech; but it is language" (PA, 236). This is as close as he comes, or could come, to giving an example of pure second-level language. Otherwise it is plain that we need not look for examples in the languages of primitive peoples, which are as much intellectualized languages as our own; and he specifically dis-avows speculation about the *origins* of language. To speak of lan-guage as imaginative or expressive in its "original or native state" (PA, 225), he explains, means only that "each one of us, whenever he expresses himself, is doing so with his whole body, and is thus actually talking in this 'original' language of total bodily gesture. . . . What we call speech and the other kinds of language are only parts of it which have undergone specialized development; in this specialized development they never come altogether detached from the parent organism" (PA, 246–47). Thus there are not three *kinds* of language, rather three aspects of living language in its actual oc-currences. It is "intellectualized language" whose syntactical struc-ture and semantical rules can be studied, and "speech" which en-virons the utterances of that language. In making these distinctions Collingwood is trying, not to make any contributions to the study of those levels (that is a task for linguistics), but to show their dialec-tical connection with the second-level "language" of incipient con-sciousness; and it is at *that* level that *every* expressive activity is called "language": not because it is like intellectualized language— there is no such "language" of painting or music, because the sets of conventions often so called are not syntactical-semantical—but be-cause it belongs to the functional matrix from which verbal lan-guage develops by abstraction.

There is thus especial significance in Collingwood's epigram that "the dance is the mother of all languages" (PA, 244). It survives in them all as the expressive gesture of which speech, painting, instru-ment playing, and the like are specialized forms. But such spe-cialization is necessary for the expression of what pure movement cannot attain. Collingwood unwittingly echoes Rilke: "And the artist is: a dancer whose movements are broken by the constraint of his cell. That which finds no expression in his steps and the limited swing of his arms, comes in exhaustion from his lips, or else he has to scratch the unlived lines of his body into the walls with his wounded fingers." [10]

Alone of all the arts, the dance has no medium. For this reason it is an embarrassment to theories of art which emphasize those aspects of art which Collingwood relegates to "craft," and to those theories which covertly or explicitly depend on a distinction of form and matter which Collingwood rejects. The absence of a medium, however, while it makes the dance a paradigm of "original language" which is *all* imaginative and *all* expressive, makes it that much more difficult to see how the other arts are specialized forms of the expressiveness of bodily movement. Collingwood does try to make these relationships plausible, in two ways. From the side of the artist, he correctly points out that painting is bound up with the bodily action of painting, music with the manipulative activity of playing, and even literature with the incipient movements of silent or imagined speech. From the standpoint of the audience, much the same can be said for the tactile values, as Berenson called them, of painting, images of utterance in the activity of reading, and of bodily motion in music and the dance itself. While Collingwood never mentions "empathy," he clearly is suggesting an explanation of *why* we find it natural to describe music or poetry as "soaring" or "plodding," or to regard Cezanne's still-lifes (as Collingwood himself does) as suggesting objects "that have been groped over with the hands" (PA, 144).

Such emphasis on the physical activity of artistic creation, of course, reduces to nonsense the standard criticism of Collingwood that, like Croce, he regards a painting as an imaginary object which the painter visualizes totally and completely and which he may or may not deign to record in pigments on a ground. According to Collingwood, it is sometimes said, one could be a painter without ever painting, and this is absurd. So it is, of course, for Collingwood too, since the "imaginary object" is not a picture in the mind's eye, but a total imaginative experience, including motor and tactile imagination as well as visual images. But it may be that his way of escaping this criticism leaves him open to a different one.

The attempt to give a *single* account of language of which the several arts are indifferently instances is constantly in danger of splitting in two, leaving on one side activities (like the dance) which are expressive but not verbal, and on the other those which are verbal but not *prima facie* expressive (like laundry lists, operating instructions, and essays on education). Somewhere between lie mixed arts like song, opera, theater, and film; acts and objects like the poetry of Gertrude Stein, which is verbal but has qualities of sound independent of sense; and features of nonverbal arts which resemble verbal language, like iconography. It is of course Collingwood's aim to undercut all such *prima facie* distinctions. In effect, he extends the application of the term "language" to include every bodily movement which is expressive as such or becomes so in a verbal context; and, conversely, he extends the application of the terms "bodily movement" and "gesture" to include all speech-utterances. In support of the latter extension, he cites the difference between languages, like French, in which sounds are formed relatively more with lip-movements and those, like German, in which sounds are formed relatively more in the throat, or those, like Italian, which are enriched and interpreted by highly differentiated gesture, and those, like English, which are not. But it seems both question-begging and false to call the movements of larynx, tongue, and lips "gestures" for the sake of including spoken language in "bodily movement." It is as if one were to call the vibrations of violin strings "gestures" as well as the movements of the player's fingers, wrists, and arms. The motion of tongue, lips, glottis, and larynx are not, like frowns, flinches, and raised eyebrows, directly *read* as expressive. Although the tone of voice in which a sentence is uttered may be an uneliminable part of what the utterance expresses, it is the tone and not the mechanics of its production which is expressive. However, it is not necessary, in order to regard all expressive bodily movements as language in the minimal sense of that term, to treat the mechanics of speech-production as expressive; the latter thesis can therefore be passed over without denying the former. And the former is all that is necessary to give the concept of language the same scope as the concepts of expression and of imagination.

We have observed that Collingwood's theory of language contributes nothing to linguistics and should not be compared with other studies of the elements and structure of language-systems. His interest, and the relevance of language to art, lies entirely in language as *parole* and in the matrix of expressive activity of which speech is one form of specialization; it is not at all in language as *langue*. The latter is something we collectively find, learn, share, and use; and the intimacy of our relation to it as well as its importance are well expressed by the fact that we call our own language our mother-tongue. The former is something we individually invent, vary, and recommend; poets, *par excellence,* but all men to some extent (and to that extent everyone who speaks is a poet) modify and transform the body of their language. Collingwood says of this that "the artistic activity does not 'use' a 'ready-made language,' it 'creates' language as it goes along" (PA, 275). This overstates the case, no doubt. The innovational aspect of individual utterance does not create a second aesthetic language independent of the utilitarian or "ready-made" common language; the former is rather a continuous modification of the latter. Joyce's *Finnegans Wake* is the most radical attempt by a poet to "create language" through deliberate individual innovation, but it is still a transformation of English. Nevertheless, Collingwood's statement is not a bad way of calling attention to two *aspects* of language. If there is a major flaw in his theory of language, it is not that it fails to be a science of linguistics.

The major difficulty, I believe, occurs elsewhere. Collingwood's theory of language perfectly reflects the confusion we noted at the end of the last section in his view that expressing emotion is a way, and the only way, of becoming conscious of emotion. He often failed to separate what are distinct and incompatible views; according to one, we become conscious of emotions through mental acts of a higher level of consciousness which have emotions as their *objects* in the same way that they have sensations as their objects; and as sensations are converted from "impressions" to "ideas" in becoming objects of second-level consciousness, so feelings are converted into emotions as objects of second-level consciousness. But at crucial points Collingwood seems to hold a different and more interesting view, according to which we become conscious of feelings not by coming to have them as objects of consciousness but by *expressing* them in imaginative activity whose *products* are objects of consciousness. In the language of the dialectic of mind, second-level consciousness is an activity of imagination which constructs and has for its objects imaginary objects. In the process of constructing and attending to them, feeling is expressed as emotion, but neither feeling nor emotion is an *object* of second-level consciousness. Third-level consciousness, in turn, may have as *its* objects second-level *activity* and abstractions from that activity. Although emotion is never, on this view, a direct object of consciousness, the activity of expressing it may be. What we think ourselves to be aware of as emotions are really our own expressive acts, and what we call emotions are abstractions from those acts.

The difference between these two theories can be summed up by saying that, for the first, emotions may be direct objects of consciousness, while for the second they cannot. And an exactly analogous difference appears in two different ways in which Collingwood speaks of language. The first theory appears to be most clearly reflected in Chapter VI of *The New Leviathan*. We become conscious of our feelings, Collingwood says there, by "talking about them," that is, by "naming" them; and there is no other way by which we can become conscious of them. He regards as an *hysteron proteron* fallacy the supposition that we are *first* conscious of what we feel and then find a name for it; but in any case, "the man who names his feeling thereby becomes immediately conscious of it" (NL, 6.36). To name a feeling is not identical with having it as a direct object of consciousness, but Collingwood seems to be asserting a necessary connection between the two. His thesis is that we are not conscious of a feeling until we name it; but it is evident that we could not name it were we not (in *some* sense) conscious of it. The only solution seems to be to deny the temporal priority of either: "the same consciousness which generates these emotions or converts them from impressions into ideas generates also and simultaneously their appropriate linguistic expression" (PA, 238).

However, this first theory seems plainly incompatible with Collingwood's recognition that "if you want to express the terror which something causes, you must not give it an epithet like 'dreadful.' For that describes the emotion instead of expressing it. . . . A genuine poet, in his moments of genuine poetry, never mentions by name the emotions he is expressing" (PA, 112). Moreover, the idea that emotions become conscious by being *named,* if that means being denoted by words or phrases, is controverted by Collingwood's claim that words and their syntactical combination into phrases and sentences are not the elements of language as an activity but "metaphysical fictions" devised in the course of analyzing that activity (PA, 254–59). Finally, even in *The New Leviathan* it is clear that Collingwood is speaking of names in an unusual sense, for an expressive shiver in the "language of gesture" is said to be as much a "name" for feeling cold as is the word "cold" in the "language of speech." Only haste or preconception could lead one to think that Collingwood is merely restating in all essentials Hobbes's view that "speech consists of

Names or *Appelations,* and their Connexion" (*Leviathan,* I, 3; quoted in *The New Leviathan,* 6.43).

Yet how is it possible to be conscious of emotions without having them as objects of consciousness and—if discourse is the activity of meaning something by something else (NL, 6.19)—without denoting them by words or other signs? It is not difficult to see how Collingwood came to lapse into this view. His dialectic of mind had recognized in feeling both a sensuous and an emotional aspect; his developed theory of imagination explained how the sensuous aspect of feeling becomes an object of (second-level) consciousness by being transformed from impression to idea. But although he occasionally spoke of *emotions* as also converted from impressions into ideas (cf. PA, 238, 283), he failed to recognize that the theory of imagination holds for, as in fact it speaks exclusively of, sensations or sensa. Although feeling as such is "sensuous-emotional," his theory of imagination can in fact be completely stated in terms of the relation between imagination and sensation alone. Impressions become ideas as they become objects of consciousness; so much is clear. But if emotions became objects of consciousness in the same way as sensations, there would be no necessity for any theory of *expression* at all; the products of imagination would all be objects of consciousness and therefore would all be *describable;* and if they were all describable nothing would be left over to express. Art, in fact, would turn out to be merely a way of being inarticulate, rather than a way of expressing what in principle cannot be described. The first theory of language therefore cannot be Collingwood's, since it leaves no place for art. It is only the second theory which explains how (as Collingwood knew) poetry expresses emotions which it never names.

Sensation and emotion, it will be recalled, are not two *kinds* of feeling, like seeing and hearing; rather emotions are "charges" on sensa (PA, 162; NL, 4.1). Sensa can, in a process of abstraction, be "sterilized" of their emotional charges, but Collingwood never suggests that the converse can occur, that is, that emotional charges can occur without any corresponding sensa. An emotional charge is not only, in psychological language, an *affect,* it is also, in old-fashioned philosophical language, an *affection,* that is, a property or attribute. It is misleading, if this is not remembered, to call feeling "sensuous-emotional," for the hyphenated phrase suggests that what is true of one is true of the other, insofar as both are feeling; and in fact Collingwood occasionally speaks of emotions as if they were like sensations in all relevant respects. But as feeling is the foundation of all consciousness, surviving in mental acts of whatever level, so must the difference between emotional charges and what they are charges on survive. And it is *this* difference which requires both a theory of imagination and a theory of expression. The theory of imagination chronicles the typical history of the sensuous side of feeling: by imagination it is converted from impression to idea, the latter becoming an object of second-level consciousness and abstractions from it the objects of higher-level mental acts. The theory of expression, on the other hand, chronicles the typical history of the emotional side of feeling: it is *expressed in* the activities by which imagination transforms into objects of consciousness the sensuous matter of feeling. But the connection between these two histories would be impenetrably mysterious were it not that language, or more precisely linguistic activity, *at every level,* is dyadic in the way in which original feeling is dyadic. It is throughout constructive and throughout expressive. It cannot convert the sensuous side of feeling into consciousness proper without at the same time expressing the emotional charge on feeling; and this is the sense in which "every gesture and every utterance that each one of us makes is a work of art." But at the same time it cannot express emotion except in the process of making us aware of objects; and this is the sense in which art can succeed or fail. An artist may well simply set out to make something and be expressive without intending to be; but no one creates anything merely by seeking to be expressive. Expressiveness, like happiness, is something which occurs in the process of seeking some other end. Collingwood's theory of art rests in the end not on the question-begging device of extending the meaning of "language" beyond all the limits of "ordinary language," but on recognizing that ordinary language has no limits. If logic is its father, its mother is poetry, and it is collateral with every art of expressive utterance.

Collingwood's theory of art is, like every expression theory, in an important sense "romantic," but it is also the exact opposite of those romantic theories which have claimed for the artist the capacity to soar on the wings of imagination and bring back supernal truths and exalted emotion from the top of the mountain which ordinary men cannot climb. For Collingwood, the artist has no authority at all but the lucidity of his work, and its lucidity is only a sign that we have found in the imaginative contemplation of it an expression of how our own activity feels. As the dialectic of experience in *Speculum Mentis* found Art at the lowest level of human experience, so the dialectic of mind finds in art the most rudimentary form of thought. Yet it also represents, just because it is rudimentary, the universal foundation of all conscious life. It is the basic form of the figure in the carpet to which every part of the rest of the design is related. The concept of art functions in Collingwood's thought, one might say, something like the concept of Eros in Plato's: not so much as a category in the conceptual scheme as the name of that intrusive and dynamic power which spurs the mind to further adventures. For consider: why should any level of consciousness be succeeded by another? Why should conceptual thinking be succeeded by propositional thinking and propositional thinking by rational thinking, appetite by desire and desire by will, utility by right and right by duty? Collingwood denies that any level *necessitates* a higher one, and spontaneity alone is hardly enough to account for the fact that we stand higher than the stages we discern.

Collingwood did not attempt an explanation, but he made one possible. Although nothing in any state of consciousness as such entails that it become the object of a higher state, every mental activity is accompanied by its own characteristic emotion, and this emotion may *remain unexpressed at that level*. Not only as the emotional charge on first-level feeling but as the emotional charge on *every* activity, this "unexpressed significance lies on his mind as a burden, challenging him to find some way of uttering it" (IH, 314). What drives the mind to a higher level is not the thirst for knowledge or novelty, but the need to express the emotion attendant on thinking at the lower. And at every level emotion attendant on that activity can be expressed only in an utterance at a higher level. Here is a recognizable transformation of the dialectic of implicit and explicit: it is in reflection that emotion becomes explicit, not as an *object* of reflection but by being expressed in the discursive *act* of reflection. The relation between emotion and thought therefore occupies in Collingwood's thought the conceptual locus which in other systems is occupied by a distinction between "subjective" and "objective." Emotion is, in all its occurrences, the felt ("subjective") quality of experience, thought the grasp of ("objective") structure in experience. Emotion never becomes an object of thought, but it is not opposed to thinking, as if every human act were a tactical victory for one over the other in a Manichean war for dominance. It is not emotion as such but *unexpressed* emotion which inhibits consciousness—which is to say, thought—from becoming self-conscious and therefore critical. And the failure to express emotion is the "corruption of consciousness" which in Collingwood's view is a disease of civilization as well as of individual life. The expression of emotion, on the other hand, is not just a catharsis which clears the way for thought nor a mode of sensibility gratuitously ornamenting a life of reason, but is the source of energy for all rational inquiry. Collingwood seldom uses the word "truth," but in whatever sense we wish to say that the life of thought is a search for truth, he would add that the truths we seek must not only satisfy the logical criteria of knowledge but also express the emotions which well up through the levels of consciousness. To that end art is indispensable, even though the "world of art" may be left behind; for art is education in expressiveness.

C H A P T E R   8

Conclusion:
The Philosophy of Philosophy

> *When I speak of a man's philosophy, I mean*
> *something of this sort. I see a man living a*
> *long and busy life; I see him doing a large*
> *number of different things, or writing a large*
> *number of different books. And I ask myself,*
> *do these actions, or these books, hang together?*
> *Is there any central thread on which they are*
> *all strung? Is there any reason why the man*
> *who wrote this book should have gone on to*
> *write that one, or is it pure chance? Is*
> *there anything like a constant purpose, or a*
> *consistent point of view, running through all*
> *the man's work?*
> —Ruskin's Philosophy (*1922*)

1 · The Philosophy of Philosophy as Part of Philosophy Itself

THE FIELD OF ACTIVITIES CALLED "PHILOSOPHY" IS OFTEN DI-
vided into philosophy *proper* on the one hand—logic, epistemology,
metaphysics, and ethics—and the "philosophy of" subjects on the
other. There seems to be a "philosophy of" every generic type of inquiry and activity: philosophy of science, of mathematics, of art, of
history, of law, of education, and so on. One is not surprised to hear
of a philosophy of administration or of social work; Hegel claimed
to have seen an English book on the philosophy of barbering. In
most such cases, "philosophy" means only theory as distinguished
from practice: whatever one can say about a type of activity as dis-

tinct from actually engaging in it. In well developed "philosophies of," however, the meaning is more complex. In part, a philosophy-of attempts to orchestrate the otherwise uncoordinated specialties of a field; in part, it concerns itself with the normative principles operative in a process of inquiry although not part of its subject-matter; in part, it is simply the attempt to give an intelligible account of the general features of inquiry in that field—something which even a successful practitioner may be unable to do; and in part, it is the analysis of concepts, both those peculiar to the field of inquiry and those which it shares or seems to share with other activities. Whether the same concept of causation is or can be used in both the natural and social sciences is not, for example, a question of physics or of psychology but of the philosophy of science.

It would seem, therefore, that there should be a philosophy of philosophy. Yet this is seldom identified as a field. The simplest way of explaining this—and the reason why answers to the question, "What is philosophy?" are not of the same *type* as answers to questions like "What is ichthyology?" or "What is econometrics?"—is that the philosophy of philosophy is part of philosophy itself, as the philosophy of history is not part of history or the philosophy of mathematics part of mathematics. Nothing in philosophy as such corresponds to the establishment of conceptual systems, principles, methods, and subject-matter which determines a field in all other cases. Other fields depend on some consensus about what is *not* problematic, on the basis of which problems can be identified and solutions pursued. In philosophy, even if not for any given philosopher, there is nothing which is not problematic. If there were, it would pass over into another field, and, of course, just this has happened as "natural philosophy" specialized itself into the natural sciences, "moral philosophy" into the social sciences, and "mental philosophy" into psychology, literary criticism, and the like.

But to say that philosophy of philosophy is identical with, or part of, philosophy itself falls far short of giving an account of just why and how this is so. Collingwood was unusual among philosophers in his preoccupation with this problem; perhaps since—unusually for a philosopher—he was also a working historian, he was particularly concerned to explain to himself the difference between what he was doing as an historian and what he was doing as a philosopher. T. M. Knox has observed, in explaining Collingwood's apparent abandonment of metaphysics for history in the *Essay on Metaphysics,* that

Collingwood tended to identify philosophy with whatever he was interested in at the time (IH, xv). This is true, but not enlightening. Collingwood always held that philosophy is "thought of the second degree," an activity of thinking about the principles involved in thinking about first-order objects (see pages 251–53, below). So it is not surprising that a discussion of second-order or meta-historical thinking, say, should contain a great deal of the first-order or historical thinking which it is about.

Yet Collingwood's philosophy of philosophy, scattered throughout his books and articles, exhibits to initial inspection that air of paradox which seems a natural feature of his style. Sometimes he says that philosophy has no methods of its own (RP, 16), or that philosophy "is the attempt to conceive reality *not in any particular way,* but just to conceive it" (IH, 152; italics added). But, on the other hand, the whole *Essay on Philosophical Method* is a discussion of the principles of philosophical *method* (see especially p. 147). As we have seen in other *prima facie* paradoxes, however, it is possible to pass beyond such apparent contradictions to discern the outlines of a consistent and illuminating set of theses about the philosophy of philosophy. From their earliest to their last statements, his sense of their relevance and application changed, but they provided the scaffolding within which his conception of dialectic and the shape it gave to his theories of absolute presuppositions, of the ordered levels of consciousness, of historical understanding, and of art, slowly came to fruition.

2 · *Collingwood's Constitutions for the Kingdom of Knowledge*

It was virtually impossible for Collingwood to write a book or essay without at some point drawing up, even partially, a constitution for the Kingdom of Knowledge which would assign to religion, science, mathematics, history, and philosophy their respective fields and functions. *Speculum Mentis* is only the most extended essay in this enterprise. In earlier articles and in *Religion and Philosophy* there is often a curious kind of distortion: he discusses philosophy as if he were not in fact engaging in it, and there seems no place left over, once the fiefdoms of the Kingdom of Knowledge have been parcelled out, for precisely the sort of thing he is doing in drawing up the constitution. As we saw at the end of Chapter 2, there is an uneasy tension in *Speculum Mentis* between the claim that philosophy is an independent form of experience and the conception of philosophy as the reflective self-consciousness of other primary forms; and it is this tension which is resolved, in the *Essay on Philosophical Method,* by regarding "experience" and "philosophy" as successive stages on a scale of forms (philosophical self-consciousness being itself the "experience" on which a higher level reflects), and ultimately by crossing the T of the dialectical levels of consciousness. But in the early writing we find the explanation of why "religion" lost its central importance in the *Essay on Philosophical Method* and after, how the importance of history grew, and how the conception of philosophy changed.

In *Religion and Philosophy,* Collingwood's first and only pre-dialectical book, philosophy is identified with religion "on its intellectual side" as concerned with the universe as a whole, and both are contrasted with science, which is concerned with the parts and details of the whole (RP, 19–20). At the same time, philosophy is intimately connected with history (RP, 51) by the argument that although philosophy deals with the abstract and history with the concrete, neither abstract nor concrete is real or intelligible apart from the other.

That religion, and not just on its intellectual side as theology, is concerned with the world "as a whole" is a view which Collingwood never changed. In *Speculum Mentis* (1924), it is this characteristic which distinguishes Religion from the "monadism" of Art. It reappears two years later in his essay on "Religion, Science and Philosophy," [1] and again in 1928 in his pamphlet *Faith and Reason:* "The proper sphere of faith is everything in the collective sense—everything as a whole. The proper sphere of reason is everything in the distributive sense—every separate thing, no matter what." [2] And it recurs, almost as an aside, in *The Idea of History,* where theology is said to differ from history and other inquiries because it deals with a "single infinite object" (IH, 5).

But while this conception of religion did not change, it became irrelevant. It could not be carried over in the change we have traced from the dialectic of experience to the dialectic of concepts. The "living unity and adoration" which religion seeks belongs to the description of experience, not to the logic of concepts. Collingwood may have kept to the end the view expressed in *Faith and Reason* that the sphere of reason falls within the sphere of faith as the finite falls within the infinite. His eloquent defense, in the little travel book called *The First Mate's Log* (1940), of the monks of Santorin against "protestantism, secularism and utilitarianism" suggests that this may be so.[3] But in any case the infinite could embrace but not enter the finite. Once Collingwood began to think of philosophy as a conceptual method, he could no longer think of it as identical with or even as the self-consciousness of the religious attitude.

At the same time, the sophistical identification of philosophy with history underwent a different fission. The key step in this process occurs not in *Speculum Mentis* but in a little-known essay of 1928 on "The Nature and Aims of Philosophy of History."[4] The constitution of the kingdom of knowledge drawn up in that essay is mainly the one codified in *Speculum Mentis;* history differs from art as knowledge from imagination, from science as particularizing from universalizing, from philosophy as the "world of fact" from the knowing mind. But almost by the way he adds another distinction which completes the abandonment of the earlier identification of history with philosophy: philosophy is said to be self-referential, history not. The philosophy of history is reflection not on the facts and patterns of facts of historical reality but on the historian's effort to attain truth; "the philosopher's object is at once himself and his world, and hence philosophy and the philosophy of philosophy are identical."[5]

In the series of constitutions which Collingwood drew up between 1916 and 1933—to repeat all their details would only obscure their outcome—there is a shift from the emphasis on similarities (often called "identities," as in *Religion and Philosophy*) to an emphasis on differences. The fields allocated to science and history hardly change, but philosophy is increasingly distinguished from religion, whose function becomes more existential as it becomes less cognitive, and from history as philosophy itself comes to be recognized as uniquely self-referential. Yet Collingwood is accused of having only a few years later abandoned philosophy by assimilating it into history. The claim that he underwent such a change will be less persuasive, I think—and the parts of the *Essay on Metaphysics* and *Autobiography* on which it is based more intelligible—if we look at the principles of Collingwood's philosophy of philosophy which survived into his last days and ideas.

3 · Collingwood's Philosophy of Philosophy

All of Collingwood's attempts (after 1924) to characterize philosophy can be brought under five main theses:

a. Philosophy is systematic.

b. Philosophy is self-referential.

c. Philosophy is "criteriological," i.e., philosophical thinking is both descriptive and normative.

d. Philosophy is an activity of thinking about the activity of thinking itself, as distinguished from thinking about objects and processes in the external world or about imagined or constructed objects.

e. Philosophy elucidates what in some sense we already know; there are, in the strict sense, no philosophical discoveries.

These brief statements are neither independent nor complete; in discussing them separately I hope to exhibit them as severally representing the same complex idea regarded under different aspects, and at the same time to indicate how the meaning of some of them (particularly the first and fifth) changed over time as their connection with other ideas and arguments developed.

a. *Philosophy is systematic.* In an age of philosophical analysis which in its extreme form consisted of putting forward a solution to a philosophical problem without regard to what one had said or would want to say about any other problem, Collingwood maintained the interconnectedness of all philosophical problems, concepts and fields. His belief in systematic philosophy survived all changes in his accounts of the particular nature of systematic relations. In an early popular lecture on John Ruskin (in part an act of filial piety, since his father had been Ruskin's neighbor and friend), Collingwood argued that Ruskin, although he "did not dissect his own mind to find out what his philosophy was," nevertheless could be said to have a "philosophy" because his thought reveals a "nucleus" or "ring" of ideas or principles "to which everything [else] is attached." [6] And this may be taken as a description of Collingwood's own later philosophy, although inexact in a specific way. A constellation of absolute presuppositions, or the levels of the theory of mind, can be regarded as a "nucleus" but not at all as a "ring"; for absolute presuppositions change under strain, and by the crossing of the T the fourth level of consciousness is open toward the future. Dialectic opens the ring.

Classically, the notion of philosophical system has two main features: the idea of a single structure of conceptual implication or relevance, and the ideal of completeness. Apart from the perversion of the latter ideal, which led Kierkegaard to complain that whenever he asked an Hegelian a question the reply was that the System was not quite complete on that point but would be finished by Saturday afternoon, one can still say that the classical ideal of philosophical system was a set of doctrines which would contain or imply an answer to every nonfactual question (including the question whether a given question is factual or nonfactual).

Of these two aspects of interconnectedness and completeness, the former is dominant and the second recessive in Collingwood's thought—so recessive in fact, that it soon vanished completely, leaving behind it only a smile for those who through ignorance or inattention have dismissed Collingwood as a minor adherent of the school of "absolute idealism." We have already seen how Collingwood allied philosophy with religion as different attitudes toward the same object—the "whole of reality." And as this alliance gives way, philosophy becomes allied with science as different methods of inquiry in the process of asking and answering questions. To distinguish philosophy from science as conceptual methods, rather than to complete a system, is the problem of the *Essay on Philosophical Method*.

But the other meaning of "system"—the idea of a unified conceptual structure—remains; and throughout the series of attempts at elucidating the specific elements and relations of a philosophical system—from the "forms of consciousness" in *Speculum Mentis* to the "absolute presuppositions" in the *Essay on Metaphysics*—he was always perfectly definite about the fact that the idea of system in philosophy stands opposed to the kind of philosophical analysis which would treat problems piecemeal, discussing each without regard to others, or which would divide philosophical inquiry into specialized fields—logic, ethics, metaphysics, etc.—which can be pursued independently of each other. Collingwood's view remained that "the different parts of philosophy are so related among themselves that none of them can be discussed without raising problems belonging to the rest" (EPM, 7). This had been asserted as early as *Religion and Philosophy:* "All philosophical problems are interconnected, all problems whatever" (RP, 124); and it was repeated as late as *The Idea of History* and *The Principles of Art:* any "addition to the body of philosophical ideas alters to some extent everything that was there already" (IH, 6); but "an erroneous philosophical theory . . . cannot be dissected into true statements and false statements; every statement it contains has been falsified"—by a distortion which is "thoroughgoing and systematic" (PA, 107).

The precise point at which the "ring" is opened, I believe, is in the chapter on "The Idea of System" in the *Essay on Philosophical Method.* The concept of philosophy, Collingwood points out there, is itself a philosophical concept; hence by the principle that the species of a philosophical concept are not mutually exclusive but overlap, the parts of philosophy, or the "different philosophical sciences" will themselves belong to a scale of forms. What are these "parts of philosophy"? Hegel might have said: Logic, the Philosophy of Nature, and the Philosophy of Spirit. Following *Speculum Mentis* we might guess: Philosophy of Art, Philosophy of Religion, Philosophy of Science, Philosophy of History, and Philosophy of Philosophy. Collingwood suggests (EPM, 194) that he has in mind the traditional division of metaphysics, logic, ethics, "and so forth" (the "and so forth" is his, not mine). But in fact the conception of the "parts of philosophy" is so vague that it *liberates* him to move, within the overarching rubric of a scale of forms, from thinking of the specialized branches of *a* philosophical system to thinking of one philosophical system succeeding another to form a history in which "all the philosophies of the past are telescoped into the present, and constitute a scale of forms, never beginning and never ending [here the ring has opened], which are different both in degree and in kind, distinct from each other and opposed to each other" (EPM, 195). The dialectical scale of forms, in other words, is sufficiently general to model both the logical statics of *a* philosophical system and the dynamics of the process of systematic change. The apparent completeness and finality of the former evanesces as the real incompleteness and lack of finality of the latter come into view. But the systematic connections of structure remain.

b. *Philosophy is self-referential.* No one would deny that some philosophical propositions are instances of their own meaning, viz., "All universal statements are hypotheticals," or "Nothing is certain." But it might well be denied that self-reference is unique to philosophy—grammarians use grammar in discussing it, and there are histories of historiography, which might even discuss themselves —or that it characterizes any but a small and special part of philosophy—discussions of morality are not themselves moral or immoral. For Collingwood, however, self-reference properly understood is a unique and ubiquitous mark of philosophical thought. This is not a doctrine about philosophical *propositions.* The Logic of Question and Answer rules out the possibility of giving meaning to propositions lifted from the process of inquiry to which they belong. Nor is it a doctrine about self-consciousness in general: certainly I can become aware of my process of breathing as I can of my process of thinking. What distinguishes the one kind of self-awareness from the other? Becoming aware of breathing is categorically different from breathing, but becoming aware of thinking is itself a kind of thinking. By self-reference Collingwood means the self-awareness of a form of activity which in its self-awareness is not essentially different from its awareness of other things. I can think about a moral problem without becoming critically aware of the type and order and assumptions of my thinking. But I cannot think about it *as* a moral problem—that is, as a case or example, rather than as the direct presence of circumstances and imminence of decision—without at least being able to recognize that some of the same standards and principles govern both my thinking about the problem and my critical thinking about that thinking. To characterize philosophy as self-referential is evidently connected with the fourth thesis (that philosophy is thinking about thinking). To emphasize self-reference, however, helps to clear up some of Collingwood's most opaque and puzzling claims: I am thinking particularly of his defense of the Ontological Argument in the *Essay on Philosophical Method,* and of his notorious outbursts against psychology in the *Autobiography* and the *Essay on Metaphysics* (A, 92–95; EM, chs. XI–XII).

The Ontological Argument (called by Collingwood the "Ontological Proof") finds itself introduced in the following way: Collingwood is distinguishing between scientific thinking as hypothetical (to assert that all cases of tuberculosis have certain characteristics is not to assert that there are any such cases) and philosophical thinking as *categorical,* i.e., necessarily asserting the existence of its subject-matter in every statement made about it. In all philosophical thinking, therefore, Collingwood detects the principle of Anselm's argument, that in a special case "the distinction between *conceiving* something and thinking it to exist is a distinction without a difference" (EPM, 125). Now although the "special case" or "unique object" to which this principle applies is identified as the *ens realissimum,* classically the object of metaphysical thought, Collingwood immediately says that "this means the object of philosophical thought in general" (EPM, 127); and, as subsequent argument makes clear, this is not a transcendent object but rather experience organized as a whole by principles which (implicitly) run through it. The "conclusions" of philosophical thinking and the "experience" on which they are based "are names for any two successive stages in the scale of forms of philosophical knowledge" (EPM, 172). That the self-referential character of philosophical thinking explains why the principle of the Ontological Argument holds *for it* is especially supported by the fact that the only examples given of categorical thinking in philosophy are from logic and ethics: the propositions of which logic consists must conform to the rules logic lays down, "so that logic is actually [although not exclusively] about itself" (EPM, 129); moral philosophy, which like logic is both descriptive and normative, gives an account of the moral ideal as how people think they ought to behave, and this cannot be "conceived as a mere thought wholly divorced from existence" (EPM, 132–33). The argument is a good one in the case of logic, a poor one, as stated, in the case of moral philosophy. But the point of the argument can be put more simply: since the data for any given level of thinking are provided by experience at a lower level (cf. EPM, 172), thinking about thinking *must* presuppose the actuality of its object in a logically peculiar but simple sense. That object is not what thought at a lower level *refers* to (*its* object) but the lower-level thinking including its intended reference. Kant's critique of the Ontological Argument is inapplicable to thoughts; one can think about nonexistent *thalers,* but not about a non-actual experience of thinking. If I think about Plato's "thoughts," for example, I may well be mistaken in thinking that they were Plato's but I cannot be mistaken in thinking that they are thoughts. (Consider the cartoon of the psychiatrist who says to his patient, "Perhaps you just imagine that you're imagining these things.") The implicit point of Collingwood's adoption of the Ontological Argument, therefore, is to call attention to the fact that the epistemic gap between thought and object does not exist—*cannot* exist—in the special case of self-reflective thinking. And all philosophical thinking contains an element of such self-reference.

Collingwood's animus against any psychology which claims to

be the science of thought (rather than a "science of feeling") is based on the claim that such a psychology exempts itself from the accounts it gives of thinking; it rules out the possibility of self-referential thought while covertly engaging in it. Although psychology claims truth for its theories about thinking, it cannot as an empirical science distinguish between *reasons* for a belief and non-rational *causes* of a belief. So "psychology is refuted by the psychology of psychology" (SM, 276). The main point of this argument must, I think, be granted. Suppose that a psychologist were to investigate the question why people make errors of simple reasoning and were to explain such errors as "correlated with" their emotional approval or disapproval of the conclusions. No one doubts that non sequiturs are often accepted as valid arguments because their alleged conclusions are already believed, or that valid arguments are often called "illogical" because of antipathy to their conclusions. But no psychologist could call such responses errors unless he already knew, or claimed to know, whether the test arguments were logically valid or not; and he could not discover this as a result of any *empirical* inquiry. Thus in his own practice he appeals to principles of logic while treating his subjects as if they were totally explicable in terms of causes of behavior. Or, to put it in a different way, either he distinguishes between reasons and causes, or he does not. If he does not, the appropriate question to ask of his theory is not whether it is true, but how his acceptance of it is causally connected with something nasty he saw long ago in the woodshed. If he does, then he must do so on some basis other than empirical observation and analysis. Nothing in empirical procedure requires that he make himself a subject for observation; but he must, in giving reasoned arguments, acknowledge that any theory of thinking which he propounds refers to and should be consistent with his own rational processes in accepting and defending it. What inspired Collingwood's contemptuous anger at some psychological claims (and that this was not merely a symptom of the illness of his last years is indicated by the discussion in *Speculum Mentis* referred to above) was the spectacle of self-reference presupposed in denials of it, of rejections of the relevance of philosophy themselves based on arguable philosophical assumptions.

c. *Philosophy is "criteriological"*—neither, that is, purely descriptive nor purely normative nor a conglomerate of propositions, some descriptive and some normative. This is not put forward by Colling-

wood as the most important characteristic of philosophy; he introduced the term itself in the *Essay on Philosophical Method* and referred to it again only in *The Principles of Art* (PA, 171 n.) But it is
useful to state it as a separate characteristic, because it connects and
brings out certain features of the description of philosophy as self-
referential and the description of it as thinking about thinking.

As we have just seen, Collingwood alludes to the Ontological
Argument as the principle of his claim that philosophical statements
are categorical, necessarily asserting the existence of what they are
about. In this sense, philosophical statements are descriptive. And he
castigates the empirical psychology of thinking for being unable to
account for the criteria and standards of its own intellectual processes, i.e., philosophical principles which are normative. But in
thinking which self-referentially instances its own principles, descriptive and normative cannot be separated, even though they may
be distinguished as aspects. "Criteriological" inquiry is in fact the
study of thinking, and *only* that, because "in order to study the nature of thinking it is necessary to ascertain both what persons who
think are actually doing and also whether what they are doing is a
success or a failure" (PA, 171 n.; cf. EM, 107–111).

In Chapter 5 the conclusion about the Logic of Question and Answer was that this "Logic" is actually a theory of inquiry and not, as
it sometimes purports to be, a program for a novel propositional
logic. A similar distinction may help in understanding the intended
sense of "criteriological." It is very doubtful whether the thesis that
every philosophical *proposition* is both normative and descriptive
can be sustained. Collingwood's argument is that an ostensibly normative proposition is the outcome of a process of reflection on an actual experience of thinking. But although it may in that sense *reflect*
or be derived from an actual experience, it does not, as a proposition,
refer to it; it is the latter, however, which is the condition of regarding a proposition as descriptive. It is more revealing, therefore, to regard not propositions but the activity of thinking as "criteriological."
One can then restate the point as follows: activities in general can be
judged as better or worse, successes or failures. Some activities—like
dancing gracefully—can be carried through without any acknowledgment or awareness by the agent of the criteria of judgment. A
peacock's courtship display may in fact fail or succeed, but it is not
(we think) governed as it develops by criteria of better and worse
execution. Almost all of the activities of animals, and human activi-

ties which are involuntary, habitual, imitative or impulsive are of this sort: one can completely describe the activity without referring to the standards by which it is judged. However, activities of a second class, such as solving a problem, learning a language, painting a picture, or fighting a battle, are guided at each step of their development by awareness of the criteria which determine success or failure. They are, Collingwood would say, *thoughtful* activities if not strictly activities of thought. Finally, there are activities which consist of the reflection on activities of the second class: analyzing the process by which the problem was solved, criticizing the choice and execution of tactics and so on. In some such cases, the criteria of judgment will be identical with the criteria which guided execution (or were acknowledged as the criteria by which it should be guided); in other cases they will differ. A general may evaluate from a strategic standpoint an action carried through according to tactical principles. ("Another victory like that and we are lost.") But, as we saw in the last section, in self-referential thinking some of the same criteria apply both to first-order and to second-order thought. What Collingwood apparently wishes to say is that all those and only those activities of thinking are "criteriological," and hence philosophical, which have as their object thoughtful activities of the second class and which appeal in judgment to the same criteria involved in the activity reflected upon.[7] But this is already to state the fourth characteristic of philosophy.

d. *Philosophy is thinking about thinking.* Of all the *dicta* of which Collingwood's philosophy of philosophy is composed, none is announced so early nor repeated so often and so late as this one. In *Religion and Philosophy* he referred to it as "common doctrine" and drew from it the conclusion that philosophy "has no methods of its own at all" but is "the free activity of critical thought," "applicable to any problem which thought can raise" (RP, 16). And as late as *The New Leviathan,* he observes that "sciences of mind teach men only what they had already reflected on as features of their own consciousness" (NL, 1.77, 34.15).[8] But by far the most extended discussion of the principle is in the *Autobiography,* where Collingwood presents his conclusions as those of a *philosopher* reflecting on his experience of *historical* thinking. One example will suffice: it is in the *Autobiography* (4, 29–31) that he describes his meditations on the aesthetic disaster of the Albert Memorial—"mis-shapen, corrupt, crawling, verminous"—which he passed daily while living in London. The *first*-order thinking in this case was: Why is it so bad? Did Scott have some aim in view which he failed to realize, or was he on the contrary perfectly successful in realizing an aim which he would have done better never to have conceived? The *second*-order thinking is: first-order thinking proceeds by formulating and answering questions; and in turn, when considering the aesthetics of even a grossly ugly monument, it must treat an artifact as if it were an attempted solution to a problem posed by the architect to himself. In the first instance one thinks about the monument; in the second instance one thinks about one's process of thinking, seeking to elucidate its principles and in fact making explicit something like a regulative principle in the Kantian sense (in this case, the principle that meanings must be interpreted by reconstructing the questions to which they are answers). But one has not invented such a principle but only recognized it as already operative in his thinking. Of course, one might very well use the principle without ever becoming explicitly aware that he was doing so.

No one can doubt that Collingwood has described at least *some* instances of philosophical thinking. Yet one might say, "Surely philosophical thinking is more than reflective preoccupation with one's own processes of thought, even if it is sometimes that or even always partially that." We may remember that Collingwood said of "criteriological" or philosophical inquiry that it seeks "to ascertain both what persons who think are actually doing and also whether what they are doing is a success or a failure" (PA, 171 n.). "Thinking about thinking" is vague: does it mean thinking about *one's own* thinking, or about the thinking of *others* ("what they are doing") or both? Collingwood sometimes suggests the former, as in the *Autobiography,* sometimes the latter, as in the *Essay on Metaphysics*— where metaphysics is called the historical study of what other thinkers have absolutely presupposed—and often, as in each of these cases, he seems to imply that it cannot be both.

We already know enough of Collingwood, however, to recognize that the problem is specious. One can, in a sense, think only about one's own thinking, but that may be either enacted (like Collingwood's about the Albert Memorial) or re-enacted (as in ours about his). Nor is it a trivial truth that we cannot think about the thinking of others without re-enacting it, since in order to do so we may have to come to understand it in terms of absolute presuppositions which differ from our own; and that is something at which we may succeed or fail. In any case, the self-criticism of thought does not take place *in vacuo* but assimilates its own past in order to move on into its own future. Yet, if philosophy is thinking about thinking, it can claim at most to make explicit what is already implicit in thinking itself; and thus we arrive at the fifth, and final, characteristic of philosophy.

e. *Philosophy elucidates what in some sense we already know.* This Socratic thesis is already present in germ in the doctrine of *Speculum Mentis* that Philosophy is not a specialized form of experience but the self-consciousness of experience in general (SM, 247, 256). In the development which we traced in Part I from the dialectic of experience through the dialectic of concepts to the dialectic of mind, the thesis does not change its formulation but its meaning becomes more complex and its applications more various as it comes to describe that development itself. A firm grasp of this thesis illuminates many of Collingwood's more obscure passages and paradoxical dicta in the same way as seeing that the pattern of "implicit-explicit" in levels of consciousness is the conceptual armature of Collingwood's thought. The doctrine of *Speculum Mentis* reappears quite clearly in the *Essay on Philosophical Method* as the doctrine that the "conclusions" of philosophical thinking and the "experience" on which they are based are names for any two successive stages on a philosophical scale of forms. But it underlies as well Collingwood's rejection of the conception of experience as a one-dimensional flow of perceptions and ideas, a conception which he finds to disqualify the theories of history of such otherwise diverse philosophers as Bradley, Bergson, Oakeshott, and the "positivists" (IH, 141, 152, 188, 287–92); and it also underlies such apparently casual remarks as the comment that in presenting his theory of presuppositions, "I shall not be trying to convince the reader of anything but only to remind him of what he already knows perfectly well" (EM, 23). Socrates might have said the same thing of Meno's slave.

Thus in philosophy there are no discoveries either in the sense of finding for the first time a novel empirical fact, such as an egg-laying mammal or a quasar, or in the sense of discovering a "new" theorem or a contradiction in an existing logical or mathematical system. A theorem or contradiction is already "implicit" in the postulates of such a system in the sense that it is entailed by them even though no one has yet constructed its proof. Before that construction no one *knows* the theorem. But a philosophical conclusion elucidates a concept or principle which already informs thinking as an actual process, and in the process of making it explicit makes us know it not for the first time but in a different and more connected way. "Normally," Collingwood says in *The Idea of Nature*, "a person who is said to 'make a philosophical discovery' in, say, his fortieth year would tell you, if you asked him, that he had known for a long time, perhaps all his life, the thing which he is said to have discovered; and that what he did in his fortieth year was not to discover it but to see for the first time, or to see more clearly and steadily than before, the connexions in a new light, as useful or clarifying connexions, having seen them hitherto as irksome and confusing connexions" (IN, 59–60). There is a striking similarity between this account and recent conceptions of philosophy which owe nothing to Collingwood but are virtually indistinguishable from his when summarized. An explanation of philosophical thinking by Stuart Hampshire, for example, includes all of the five characteristics heretofore discussed except self-reference, and is manifestly not incompatible with that: "The kind of missing connection that a philosopher wishes to uncover is between concepts; it is not a connection between already identified classes of events, which is the kind of connection that an experimental scientist seeks. . . . Wherever there is a gap in our understanding of the conceptual scheme, a gap that we cannot close by the discovery of a middle term, there is an unsolved philosophical problem. We close the gap when we bring to light an unnoticed overlapping between the conditions of application of one concept and the conditions of application of another, an overlapping that we had hitherto overlooked. Then the puzzling illusion of contingency disappears, and we understand why we *must* at this point think and speak as we do. . . . But it is only a truly philosophical curiosity, if the irritating gap in the conceptual scheme occurs at a crucial point in systematising a whole set of concepts according to some uniform principle. As philosophers, we want to see, in a single survey, the full range of our complex concept of mind in all the connections of its parts. . . ." [9] It is evident that Hampshire's statement, too, is an example of "thinking about thinking," that it shares Collingwood's view of philosophy as systematic (". . . in all the connections of its parts . . ."), as criteriological (". . . why we *must* at this point think and speak as we do . . ."), and as an elucidation of something already implicitly known (". . . when we bring to light . . ."). It differs, however, in not historicizing the concept of mind (or concepts generally). The characteristics of philosophy we have already noticed might almost be said to be the philosophy of philosophy implicit in the *philosophia perennis*. What gives them especial force in the case of Collingwood is that the understanding of them is systematically changed and supported when one interprets them in terms of the dialectical history of mind.

Why do philosophers disagree? If philosophical thinking is the elucidation of principles and conceptual connections normatively present—that is to say, a priori—in thought, as Collingwood and Hampshire agree, it would seem that elucidation should be cumulative, a gradual approximation to Hampshire's "single survey" of the full range of our conceptual scheme or schemes. For if there are ways in which we *"must* think and speak," those ways are not open to falsification by experience or, it would seem, to systematic correction in any other way. Yet philosophers do disagree, and the very point and manner of their disagreements change over time. Moreover, the discussion of philosophical problems displays the phenomenon so elegantly described by William James as the classic stages of a theory's career: first "it is attacked as absurd; then it is admitted to be true, but obvious and insignificant; finally it is seen to be so important that its adversaries claim that they themselves discovered it." [10]

Now Collingwood's philosophy of philosophy explains not only the systematic nature of philosophy but the reasons for philosophical disagreement and change; and it explains these *philosophically,* not just psychologically or sociologically. One could, in the latter ways, regard James's "classic stages" as indicating no more than lack of perspicaciousness and resistance to change and novelty, combined with vanity and insecurity. Intellectual innovations, to be sure, are resisted, just as technological, political, and artistic innovations are resisted, and often for the same reasons. But that some new ideas are resisted as *absurd* is exactly what one would expect on Collingwood's theory of the function and change of absolute presuppositions as a priori conceptual systems. A statement uttered from the standpoint of even a partially novel constellation of absolute presuppositions does seem from the standpoint of the old to be an absurd and insouciant refusal to admit the obvious. From the standpoint of the new, it relieves certain "strains" in the old; from the standpoint of the old, however, especially to someone whose sensibilities have not been irritated by those strains, it merely sets up new and unnecessary ones. From the standpoint of an historical reconstruction of the passage from the old to the new, each is right in its way; the adventure into the new could never have been undertaken without neglecting for the time being the force of the difficulties generated by partial change, for the sake of the partial clarity achieved. And as the adventure continues (if it does), there is progressive conceptual consolidation and an accretion of new recruits to puzzle over the new problems. And more and more the old system of absolute presuppositions comes itself to seem alien and absurd, except to those who can interpret what has happened as a process of historical development rather than as the fortuitous replacement of prejudice and superstition by clear thinking and good sense.

Conceptual change does not take place according to rules or by applying an effective method. It takes place in puzzlement and struggle, and cannot even be correctly described while it is going on. For the new standpoint from which it *will* be possible to understand it is not yet constructed. *Contemporary* elucidations of new concepts (e.g., absolute presuppositions) are necessarily a pastiche of old and new; they stand on the old while feeling around for a foothold in unknown territory. Only when the second foot has been planted can the first be withdrawn; yet while the process is going on the description of it cannot possibly be given which *will* be possible retrospectively from the standpoint of the new conceptual connections achieved.

Now Collingwood's philosophy of philosophy is retrospectively self-referential in just this way. Looking backward from the standpoint of the dialectic of mind and the theory of absolute presuppositions, one can see the *Essay on Philosophical Method* as a stage of the process—including its paradoxes and exaggerations—by which Collingwood moved from the traditional view of *Speculum Mentis,* that "philosophy is the self-consciousness of experience" through the theory that a philosophical concept comprises a scale of forms, to the point where he crossed the T of the levels of consciousness and spread out the fourth level of mind over a temporal dimension of historical development. Collingwood's thinking about dialectic was itself a dialectic of thinking.

In the end, therefore, there can be said of Collingwood's thought what he came to understand as his own contribution to the problem of twentieth-century philosophy—it does indeed "reckon with twentieth-century history," that is, with the conceptual scheme of the historical consciousness. Established structures of ideas serve out their days as scaffoldings within and around which men in their puzzlement and hope build up new ones and eventually dismantle the old —as for centuries the Romans quarried from their ancient buildings the stones for the ever-renewed city.

NOTES

CHAPTER 1

1. H. A. Hodges' definitive study *The Philosophy of Wilhelm Dilthey* (London: Routledge & Kegan Paul, 1952) concludes with an extended comparison of Dilthey and Collingwood, in which their points of agreement are found to be less significant than their differences.

2. John Dewey, *Logic, The Theory of Inquiry* (New York: Henry Holt and Co., 1938), p. 507.

3. Karl Jaspers, *Reason and Existenz,* tr. William Earle (New York: The Noonday Press, 1957), pp. 49–50.

4. Alan Donagan, *The Later Philosophy of R. G. Collingwood* (Oxford: The Clarendon Press, 1962), p. 262.

5. Although it has come to my notice too late to have accelerated the process of drawing my own conclusions, Lionel Rubinoff's essay, "Collingwood and the Radical Conversion Hypothesis" (*Dialogue,* V [1966], pp. 71–83), argues convincingly and I believe for the first time in print for the essential continuity of development of Collingwood's views. This article, together with a later article by Rubinoff, "Collingwood's Theory of the Relation Between Philosophy and History: A New Interpretation" (*Journal of the History of Philosophy,* VI [1968], 363–80), both prevision a forthcoming book on Collingwood's philosophy of mind to be published by the University of Toronto Press. Rubinoff's interpretation of Collingwood, although wholly independent of mine in origin and development, is so remarkably similar to mine in outline and detail as to convince me that we must both be right—no doubt because, unlike any previous critics, we have both simply undertaken to understand Collingwood's thought as exemplifying his own conception of dialectical philosophy.

6. Plato, *The Republic,* 532; tr. F. M. Cornford (New York: Oxford University Press, 1945), p. 252.

CHAPTER 2

1. In addition to *Speculum Mentis* and the *Essay on Philosophical Method* the major discussions of the classification of knowledge are in *Religion*

and Philosophy, the articles "Croce's Philosophy of History" (1921), "Are History and Science Different Kinds of Knowledge?" (1922), "The Nature and Aims of Philosophy of History" (1925), "Religion, Science and Philosophy" (1926), and *Faith and Reason* (1928). After 1933, the important discussions are in *The Idea of History* (written ca. 1936), where there is interestingly no attempt to define philosophy, and the *Essay on Metaphysics* (1939), which is concerned exclusively with philosophy and history.

2. The pentagonal organization of knowledge is repeated, with only minor changes of emphasis, in "The Nature and Aims of Philosophy of History" and *Outlines of a Philosophy of Art,* both of which appeared in 1925, the year after the publication of *Speculum Mentis.*

3. Why no single noun will serve in all five cases is an interesting question, to which a possible answer may be that we do not, or our language does not, regard these modes of experience as coordinate species of a single genus. But that they are not is also an explicit and central doctrine of Collingwood's. They are related, not as exclusive alternatives, but as transformations of each other.

4. "Aesthetic," in *The Mind,* ed. R. J. S. McDowall (London: Longmans and Co., 1927), p. 227.

5. The analogy between perception and "historical thought" was never repeated by Collingwood after *Speculum Mentis* and was soon contradicted by reinstating the analogy between perception and science which in *Speculum Mentis* is denied. Perception is not mentioned in the summary of *Speculum Mentis* which appears in Chapter 6 of *Outlines of a Philosophy of Art* (published a year after *Speculum Mentis*), nor in "The Nature and Aims of Philosophy of History" (1925), where history is said to differ from science as individual from universal and as categorical judgment from hypothetical judgment. In the *Essay on Philosophical Method* (1933), he makes much of the fact that the data of science, unlike those of philosophy, are "individual facts . . . apprehended by perception" (169)—no mention here of abstract and concrete facts; and in *The Historical Imagination* (1935, reprinted as § 2 of the Epilegomena to *The Idea of History*), he says that the object of history, like that of perception, is individual but differs in being *past.*

There is a natural enough explanation for these contradictions, however. In the later works, Collingwood uses terms like "science" and "history" in a way which comes closer to a description of the activities usually called by these names. In *Speculum Mentis* they are given a more stipulative definition as ideal types of thought not *necessarily* exemplified in practices called by the same name (thus Plato is the only named representative of Science).

It seems that Collingwood went through a discernible and not capricious process of change in his views on what is *denoted* by certain terms while keeping their *connotations* firmly fixed, at least in part. Thus theology is identified first with religion, then with science, then with philosophy. But once this is understood the difficulty is not serious and quibbling over terms is not necessary. It is the logical connection among types of thought, and not their proper names, which is Collingwood's continuing concern.

6. There is a recent history of the ideas and changes of ideas revealed in

the series of Presidential Addresses to the American Historical Association. If this is followed by other interpretations there will presumably eventually be a history of the histories. And then of course there will be—the mind boggles.

7. Collingwood, himself deeply religious, had no sympathy with the "philosophy of religion." One statement gives something of the flavor of his attitude: "Philosophers drag in the idea of God when they are conscious of coming to the end of their tether, and not before: so that the entry of God into a philosophical system marks unerringly the point at which the system breaks down" (SM, 269).

8. Cf. *Essay on Philosophical Method,* pp. 213–15, and *The Principles of Art,* pp. 296–99.

9. Cf. *Speculum Mentis,* pp. 48, 220, 231, 299; in this book, of course, one must always distinguish between what Collingwood is asserting *in propria persona* and what he is describing as the point of view of a certain level of dialectical process. But although he concludes that "History" cannot grasp the "whole" which it comes to recognize as its object, the recognition is itself an achievement which survives the transition from History to Philosophy, which *can* grasp the "whole" although in a way different from that to which History can only hopelessly aspire.

10. The examples are not Collingwood's; but I do not apologize for suggesting more illuminating illustrations than he provided. This is only a natural consequence of the attempt to understand him better *now* than he understood himself *then.* We have, as he did not, the record of his later books, and the privilege of genetic explanation.

11. Collingwood notes that we can say, "He is not himself today" (RP, 108), and that it would be nonsense to make such exceptions unless we assigned meaning to a wider and concrete sense of "self."

12. DeQuincey, trans. (*The London Magazine,* October, 1824), Prop. IX. Collingwood's first mention of Kant's *Idee* is in the pamphlet *The Philosophy of History* (1930), where he accuses attempts at universal history of distorting facts in order to show the recurrence of the same abstract forms. In terms of the dialectic of forms of experience, Collingwood would regard the Kantian notion of universal history as belonging to the transitional stage between Science and History: it has attained to the recognition of history as a single whole but has not yet left behind the abstractness of scientific concepts and hence seeks laws of history strictly analogous to laws of nature. Exactly the same accusation is made of contemporary "philosophers of history" like Spengler and Toynbee (cf. IH, pp. 159–65 and 181–83; and "Oswald Spengler and the Theory of Historical Cycles," *Antiquity,* I [1927], pp. 318 ff.).

13. Collingwood is here referring to utilitarianism in the generic sense, not exclusively to that specific form of it for which Bentham succeeded in converting the general term into a proper name. Utilitarianism is the view that the rightness or wrongness of an action is derivative from the goodness or badness of the consequences of the action, and from nothing else. The "Utilitarians" additionally identify "good" and "bad" with pleasure and pain; but other states could be and have been regarded as good or bad even if not

pleasurable or painful. Collingwood correctly remarks that "theological ethics is notoriously a form of utilitarianism" (although this is not true of "religious" ethics, which neither justifies nor calculates). This is a neatly symmetrical analogue to the classification of theology not with Religion but with Science.

<h2 style="text-align:center">CHAPTER 3</h2>

1. Cf. T. M. Knox, *Proceedings of the British Academy*, XXIX (1943), p. 8; and Preface to *The Idea of History*, p. xxi.

2. E.g., p. 92: "The doctrines of classification and division, as contained in traditional logic, . . . have been framed with an eye to the peculiar structure of the scientific concept, and must be modified in certain ways before they can be applied to the philosophical. . . . [And] the same is true of definition."

3. This claim by Collingwood would not even seem to apply to a logic of *statements* as distinguished from a logic of judgments or propositions. One can define molar and molecular statements, for example, so that there is no overlap. Collingwood would no doubt reply that this is a scientific, not a philosophical, classification, a reply with which most logicians would heartily agree as showing that the distinction is unnecessary to begin with. However, Collingwood is talking about the genus *thought,* and *statements* are not species of this genus. If logicians do not care to introduce this concept, they cannot very well prescribe qualifications for those who do.

4. In his lectures on moral philosophy and in his article, "Economics as a Philosophical Science" (*Ethics*, XXXV [1925], 162–65), Collingwood made sharp distinctions between philosophical and empirical concepts in the course of discussing economics and political science. The ground of his distinction was that empirical concepts (e.g., money, credit, production, and consumption) apply only to the special field of economic facts, while philosophical concepts (e.g., wealth, labor, utility) not only apply to specific kinds of action but tend to expand to cover rational action in general. In politics, the concept of state is empirical and the concept of law philosophical. Collingwood held that there can be a *theory* of "philosophical elements" but only a *history* of "empirical elements." The philosophical concepts in economic and political theory are "universal and necessary characteristics of rational action as such"; this Kantian language indicates that he was thinking of such concepts as a priori. This explains why they tend to "leak or escape" from attempts to define them as applying to specific types of actions: they are presupposed in the identification of anything as a rational action at all, and are not corrigible descriptions of characteristics possessed by some but not all of such actions.

5. It is obvious that Collingwood has in mind, among other things, the classical theory that evil is the privation or absence of good, a theory which he accepted with reservations in *Religion and Philosophy* (135–44) and in his early essay, "What is the Problem of Evil?" (*Theology*, I [1920], 66–74). One ought not, however, accuse him of surreptitiously trying to rationalize an

argument which appears as an ad hoc defense of theism. What is relevant to his point is not that the neo-Platonic explanation of evil is *cogent* but that it is, for better or for worse, *philosophical*.

CHAPTER 4

1. Collingwood lectured at Oxford on moral philosophy annually from 1919. What changes there were between 1919 and 1933 I do not know, apart from his statement (A, 149) that the lectures underwent "constant revision." If there should come to be a field of Collingwood studies, questions may yet arise which can be answered only by attempting to reconstruct this period; but at present these questions cannot be predicted, and my purpose here is to disclose the continuity of his thought between 1924 (*Speculum Mentis*) and 1933 (*Essay on Philosophical Method*), and between 1933 and 1941 (*The New Leviathan*).

2. In *The New Leviathan* Collingwood defines "love" somewhat differently, as the appetite to overcome loneliness (NL, 8.16); and in general his earlier leitmotif of the "ideal" is replaced by the theme of the "social." This interesting difference, a critic of Collingwood might claim, suggests that the whole theory of lower levels of consciousness is simply a projection onto hypothetical states of just those characteristics which Collingwood wishes to find in more specific forms at the higher levels. But on Collingwood's behalf it can be replied that if there are lower levels of consciousness, they cannot be precisely described but only indicated and evoked. We do recognize from time to time the occurrence of highly indeterminate kinds of experience—the peculiar but unidentifiable feeling of unease on entering a room, for example, or the twilight experience between sleep and waking, or the experience known —to a higher level of consciousness, which always transforms it in the process of describing it—as déjà vu. Ordinarily we describe such experiences in the language of "as if": "It was as if something important were missing," "It was as if even the articles of furniture were menacing and malevolent"; and the like. Now each person will fill the blanks after "as if" with images borrowed from his own idiosyncratic fears, frustrations, wishes, and preoccupations, and with whatever vocabulary and command of nuance he possesses. But it does not follow that there is not a common element in such feelings. The description is more determinate than the experience itself, and the experience may sustain different "as if" statements, but the blanks after "as if" cannot be filled in just any way. Collingwood's theory does not depend, I think, on the specific characterization of the elements of appetite, but on the claim that they are links in the genetic connection between feeling on the one hand and the most complex processes of rational deliberation on the other. And this claim is independent of the intrinsic difficulties of describing what states of consciousness are like in themselves when any example can be described *only* as something already attended to by a higher state.

3. The "third form of goodness"—whose name is reminiscent of Spinoza's "third kind of knowledge"—is in *The New Leviathan* called "duty." In his *Autobiography*, Collingwood called it simply "morality," as distinguished

from "economicity" (utilitarianism) and "politicality" (regularianism) (A, 148–49).

4. The importance of this principle in Collingwood's thought can be fully recognized only in considering his theory of historical knowledge. In sum, the argument of *The Idea of History* is that the subject-matter of history is *res gestae*, or actions in the sense discussed above; and such actions can be understood only by reconstructing the way in which they were conceived by their agents. Collingwood's well-known principle that "history is the re-enactment of past thought" therefore depends on the very special meaning he gives to "thought" as belonging to fourth-level consciousness in the dialectic of mind. This is discussed in greater detail in Chapter 6, below.

5. Collingwood's summary of his own view in *The New Leviathan* is, characteristically, provocative but misleading. He defines knowledge there as "the conviction or assurance with which a man reaffirms a proposition he has already made after reflecting on the process of making it and satisfying himself that it is well and truly made" (NL, 14.22). The definition itself is open to many criticisms, primarily the objection that it confuses logical certainty with psychological certitude. Opinions which are not only false but ungrounded may, we know, be held with the greatest conviction, and while a true believer may be willing to say that *"I* am convinced that such-and-such is the case" is equivalent with *"I* know that such-and-such is the case," no one, it is clear, would be willing to say that *"He* is convinced that the earth is flat" is equivalent with *"He* knows that the earth is flat." The latter expression entails, as the former does not, that the earth *is* indeed flat.

But such an objection is beside the point unless Collingwood were undertaking to represent the feeling of assurance as the ubiquitous and infallible mark of knowledge; and he is not. His purpose is not to state a criterion by which knowledge may be distinguished from error but to show that knowing, as an activity, results from reflection on opinion. The reference to "conviction or assurance" is also a way of making the point that in the development from feeling to reason emotions are not eliminated or made irrelevant but rather are vested in the order of forms of thought which increasingly control but do not replace the emotions. As an *activity of consciousness,* there cannot be knowledge without conviction (this is why it is odd to say "He knows it but he doubts whether it is so"). At the same time there can be conviction without knowledge; this occurs at a lower level of consciousness (and is why it is not odd to say "He believes it and it is in fact the case, but yet he doesn't know it.")

6. The conception of art as "monadic," which appears in *Speculum Mentis* (Ch. III, § 3) and *Outlines of a Philosophy of Art* (pp. 23–26), is repeated without significant variation in *The Principles of Art,* attributed to imagination on pages 252–53 and to art on pages 288–89.

CHAPTER 5

1. One corollary of this interpretation is that for Collingwood there is no "dialectic of nature," although there is a dialectic of concepts of nature and

of scientific theories. Another way of putting this point is that dialectical analysis applies only to processes which are actually or potentially self-referential; and any such process is for Collingwood a process of *thought*. Whatever nature may be, it is not self-referential.

2. This of course contradicts the principle of the Logic of Question and Answer that truth and falsity are properties not of propositions but of question-and-answer complexes. It seems, however, that for purposes of argument Collingwood is accepting the usual view of propositions because he is arguing that absolute propositions are not subject to proof or disproof in the usual sense of *those* terms.

3. The quotation is from *Witchcraft, Oracles and Magic Among the Azande* (London: 1937), pp. 319–20.

4. Even those most sympathetic to Collingwood have not seen, despite his own examples (e.g., EM, 97–98), that absolute presuppositions function exactly like a priori concepts, like Kant's except for the incorrigibility of the latter. To my knowledge, the only one to have recognized this, and therefore the only one to have understood Collingwood in a way at all compatible with the present interpretation, is David Rynin, in "Donagan on Collingwood: Absolute Presuppositions, Truth and Metaphysics," *The Review of Metaphysics*, XVIII (1964), 301–333.

5. There is, however, major disagreement on the issue whether patterns of argument in different fields (e.g., law, natural science, history) can be analyzed as exemplifying the same formal rules of inference. That they cannot is the main burden, for example, of Stephen Toulmin's *The Uses of Argument* (Cambridge: Cambridge University Press, 1958).

6. William James, *Pragmatism* (London: Longmans and Co., 1912), pp. 171–72.

7. Ibid.

8. Kant, *Critique of Pure Reason,* tr. Norman Kemp Smith (London: Macmillan and Co., 1933), p. 10.

9. Norman Malcolm, *Ludwig Wittgenstein, A Memoir* (London: Oxford University Press, 1958), p. 55.

10. Thus Collingwood says in *The Idea of History* that there can be a history of politics, of warfare, of economic activity, of morals, and of religion, but no history of perception or of artistic *problems* (as distinguished from artistic achievements; artistic "problems" occur at the second level of mind, prior to third-level question-and-answer, on which fourth-level consciousness can reflect) (IH, 309–315). This repeats a conclusion Collingwood had reached many years before, although he could not then state it as a consequence of the dialectic of mind; see *Outlines of a Philosophy of Art,* 99.

CHAPTER 6

1. Mutual exclusion is a property of species of a genus for *scientific* concepts. The explicit point of the *Essay on Philosophical Method* is that species of a *philosophical* genus are not exclusive but "overlap," that is, belong to a scale of forms.

2. To be consistent, he should have said, "potentially a work of art," since, as we shall see in the following chapter, he admits that not all activity is successfully expressive, and art, by definition, is.

3. Compare the well-known difficulty in Hume's account of the origin of our ideas: a succession of perceptions is not the same thing as the perception of succession. In Collingwood's terms, the former occurs in third-level, the latter in fourth-level consciousness.

4. Alan Donagan, *The Later Philosophy of R. G. Collingwood* (Oxford: The Clarendon Press, 1962), 203.

5. In the literature concerned with the thesis of "methodological individualism," this suggestion has been advanced in defense of that thesis by J. W. N. Watkins, in "Historical Explanation in the Social Sciences," *Theories of History*, ed. P. Gardiner (New York: Free Press of Glencoe, 1959), 506. As Watkins sees, to permit the methodological individualist to refer to the *"dispositions of anonymous individuals"* [italics his] makes his position indistinguishable from the view that there are "social facts." But he then blames the advocates of that view for not defending something which he can more easily refute!

6. Each of these is discussed in Part I of *The Idea of History*. But Collingwood had criticized Spengler on similar grounds as early as 1927, in "Oswald Spengler and the Theory of Historical Cycles," *Antiquity*, I (1927), 311–25. This article is reprinted together with a sequel in the same volume, "The Theory of Historical Cycles II: Cycles and Progress" (pp. 435–46), in *Essays in the Philosophy of History by R. G. Collingwood*, ed. W. Debbins (Austin: University of Texas Press, 1965), 57–89.

7. Stephen Toulmin, *The Uses of Argument* (Cambridge: Cambridge University Press, 1958), 258. One such study is carried out in Toulmin's *Foresight and Understanding* (Bloomington: Indiana University Press, 1961), where what he calls "ideals of natural order" are acknowledged to be versions of Collingwood's "absolute presuppositions." T. S. Kuhn, in *The Structure of Scientific Revolutions* (Chicago: University of Chicago Press, 1962), has also given—apparently without any direct influence by Collingwood—an account of the history of change in the explanatory "paradigms" of natural science which can be read as a study of specific changes in constellations of absolute presuppositions.

8. The objections to such broad correspondences are not as strong as they are familiar. It might be objected, for example, that Collingwood overlooks a fundamental difference between civil "law" and natural "law." Human laws are commonly distinguished from laws of nature on the grounds that the former can be disobeyed but the latter not, or that the former are normative while the latter are descriptive. Failure to note such distinctions, it is quite correctly observed, can lead to such confusions as the belief that Nature "punishes" violations of her "laws." Collingwood's point, however, is independent of such distinctions, not a violation of them. He does not mean that there is no difference between statements of practical rules and statements of natural laws, nor that descriptive and normative statements can entail each other, nor that both are *deducible* from a common set of absolute presuppositions stateable in propositional form (since, as we have seen, absolute pre-

suppositions are not propositions but concepts); his point is rather that the conceptual system which informs, for example, the "regularian consciousness" (NL, 18.43) makes possible the conception of "law" as something independent of any particular exemplifications. This conception is common both to civil and to natural law and is presupposed whether one distinguishes or in some way equates one type of law and another.

9. F. H. Bradley, *Collected Essays* (Oxford: The Clarendon Press, 1935), I, 1–53. This essay, written in 1874, is remarkable for being the only English contribution to critical philosophy of history before Collingwood. In the landscape of British intellectual history it is a monadnock.

10. What if the "evidence" comprised by an historical narrative should turn out as a result of new discoveries to be false or inaccurate? The answer to this, I believe, is that it would not affect the intelligibility of the discredited narrative. The authentication of evidence is a different process from the characteristically historical activity of rendering it intelligible; an analogue in formal logic (the conceptual structure of "Science") is that a deductive argument may be perfectly valid even though its premises and its conclusion are false. Collingwood's point, however, is that the relation between evidence and conclusion in history is neither deductive nor inductive, and is not even in the proper sense of the term inferential. The historical conclusion is directly shown in the ordering of evidence, not inferred from it. Hence the authentication of particular facts is one problem, their conversion into evidence by being organized into narrative another. Collingwood is interested in the process by which "facts" become "evidence" rather than in the process by which putative facts become established facts. So, "genuine history has no room for the merely probable or the merely possible; all it permits the historian to assert is what the *evidence before him* obliges him to assert" (IH, 204; italics added).

CHAPTER 7

1. Cf. Vincent Tomas, "The Concept of Expression in Art," *Science, Language and Human Rights* (Philadelphia: University of Pennsylvania Press, 1952). For Tomas, a "two-termed" theory of art asserts, and a "one-termed" theory denies, that what a work of art "expresses" can be ultimately distinguished from the work of art itself. In this sense, Collingwood has a "two-termed" theory of what we call "works of art" and what *they* express (emotion), but he has a "one-termed" theory of emotion and the expression of emotion.

2. There is some truth to the saying that an artist does not paint what he sees but sees what he can paint.

3. This objection is made, for example, by Susanne Langer, in *Feeling and Form* (London: Routledge & Kegan Paul, 1953), pp. 383 ff. Such objections invariably refer to Book I of *The Principles of Art,* where Collingwood, in distinguishing "art proper" from kinds of pseudo-art and especially from craftsmanship, tends to say that works of art are "imaginary things" (PA,

139 ff.). But this is at a stage of his argument where as yet, he explicitly says, "we do not know what imagination is" (PA, 152). Even at this stage he has said nothing to imply that one could "imagine" the development of a sonata form without knowing, as a matter of technique, how to modulate through key-relationships.

4. The production of *King Lear* by Peter Brook was widely acclaimed for having recognized the play as Shakespeare's contribution to the "theater of the absurd." That conception illustrates my point; for the special feature of the theater of the absurd is that it evokes complexes of emotion which are powerful, definite, and clear until we try to say what they are, i.e., to *describe* what we experience as *expressed*.

5. This quotation is not a bad example of the way in which Collingwood achieves his directness and clarity of style by leaving to the reader the qualifications which would make his meaning more exact but would greatly complicate its statement. Of course he does not mean that an entity, whether a "lady" or the "world" can be both X and non-X; he is not denying the logic of fourth-level consciousness. What he obviously means is that second-level emotions, and the expression of them, can be felt as coherently related even though the descriptions of them are incompatible. The moral is that poetry is not primitive psychology and cannot be replaced by sophisticated psychology; poetry does not describe but expresses. Collingwood assumes that a reader will supply from context the recognition that a poet's panegyric to a lady is different from a statement that she is five feet three and one quarter inches tall.

6. Consider, for example, the raptures of self-expression traditionally aroused by the Mona Lisa. It is not unknown for teachers of "music appreciation" to exploit the power of music to serve as a stimulus for fantasy and to praise students who produce the most interesting, which is almost to say the most irrelevant, fantasies about the music. In just such an infamous case, a prize was awarded to a student whose "impression" of the fourth movement of Brahms's Fourth Symphony was a poem about "A Trip to the Zoo."

7. Review of S. Alexander's *Art and Instinct* in *Journal of Philosophical Studies* (now *Philosophy*), III (1928), 370–73.

8. *Cours de linguistique générale.*

9. Cf. Rulon S. Wells, "De Saussure's *System of Linguistics*," *Readings in Linguistics*, ed. Martin Joos (New York: American Council of Learned Societies, 1963), 1–18.

10. "Über Kunst," *Verse und Prosa aus dem Nachlass* (Leipzig, 1929).

Chapter 8

1. *Truth and Freedom*, II (1926), 3.

2. *Faith and Reason* (London: Ernest Benn, 1928), 27. Collingwood describes faith as "theoretical, practical, emotional"; he does not mean, as the contrast with "reason" might suggest, that it is irrational or non-rational.

Faith has the same forms as reason, but is directed toward the whole rather than toward the relations of parts.

3. *The First Mate's Log* (London: Oxford University Press, 1940), 145–53.

4. *Proceedings of the Aristotelian Society,* 1924–25, pp. 151–74; reprinted in *Essays in the Philosophy of History,* ed. William Debbins (Austin: University of Texas Press, 1965), 34–56.

5. Ibid., 165.

6. *Ruskin's Philosophy* (Kendal, England: Titus Wilson and Son, 1922), 6–7. The lecture had been delivered in 1919. It could not be clearer that Collingwood had not yet achieved the idea that philosophy and the philosophy of philosophy are identical.

7. This reconstruction of the meaning of "criteriological" is partly supported by what Collingwood said as early as 1924, in *Outlines of a Philosophy of Art:* "To distinguish an activity as worse or better does not imply referring it to some standard other than itself. If we suspect ourselves of having thought wrongly, there is nothing to do but to think again; thought cannot be checked except by further thought" (OPA, 19). He went on in that passage to make the foolish error of saying that "action can only be judged by reference to action," and that therefore (assuming that all activity is either thought or action) there is *never* a criterion outside the activity. Whatever it means to say that action is judged "by reference to" action, it is obviously judged *by* thought. Interestingly, however, the only mileage Collingwood tried to get from his false generalization was to deduce from it that imagination contains its own criteria. He could have reached this result just as well from the premises that thought contains its own criteria and that imagination is a form of thought. This is just what, later, he did hold.

8. Other characterizations of philosophy as thinking about thinking, or "thought of the second degree," are in EPM, 172; IN, 2–3; IH, 1–2; and PA, 167–68.

9. Stuart Hampshire, *Feeling and Expression,* Inaugural Lecture delivered at University College, London, 1960 (pamphlet).

10. William James, *Pragmatism* (London: Longmans and Co., 1912), 198.

INDEX

This index contains, in alphabetical order, a glossary of terms in Collingwood's systematic theory of mind. It should be remembered that one of the major principles of that theory is that some activities or functions occur at different levels of consciousness, so that the terms naming them will be systematically ambiguous from level to level; cf. Chapter 4, pp. 106-107.

Terms belonging to the theory of mind are indicated by small capital letters; in the explanation of each, terms which are themselves glossed are italicized. The interrelations of the glossed terms are also shown in Figure 2 on page 117.

ABSTRACTION. The activity of selective *attention,* which divides or separates features within the objective field of *consciousness* at any level; also the result of this activity. Consciousness at any level has for its first-order object the activity of the next lower level; when it abstracts from that activity, the resulting abstraction is its second-order object. The species of abstraction at different levels have no distinguishing names; but it is usually called "attention" at lower levels and "abstraction" at higher levels. In SM, "abstraction" has a quite different sense; it is regarded as an error, opposed to "concrete thinking."
37, 41 f., 47 ff., 54 f., 74, 76, 94 f., 98, 106 ff., 122, 153, 203, 224, 242

Action, 8 f., 53 f., 83, 85, 88 ff., 107, 158, 163, 168, 268; "inside and outside," 8, 20, 163, 189 f.; action and behavior, 168

Alexander, S., 226

Anaximander, 137

ANGER. One of the *passions* through which *appetite* becomes *desire,* and the chief link in this development (NL, 10.51). It is the active opposition to a not-self (NL, 10.44; PA, 232) and develops from *fear* through *shame.*
86

Anselm, 247

Anthropology, 158

APPETITE. The second level of *practical consciousness* (NL, 9.4, 9.55, 36.77), the consciousness of *feeling* (NL, 7.6) resulting from selective *attention,* or *conceptual thinking,* directed upon *feeling* (NL, 7.2 ff.). Its two forms are *hunger* and *love.*
17, 81, 83 ff., 87 f., 92 ff., 100, 102 f., 109, 114, 151, 162, 167, 262

Aristotle, 137, 165, 211

Art, 27, 30 ff., 114, Ch. 7, 241, 243; art criticism, 213 f.; art as expression, 199 ff.; art as imagination, 23, 215 ff.; art as language, 226 ff.; artistic creation, 122; monadism of art, 30, 35, 43, 114, 209, 242, 263

Assertion, 31, 34 f., 37, 114, 132

ATTENTION. In making distinctions (*abstractions*) within the here-and-now of *feeling* (NL, 4.5; PA, 204), attention is the activity of second-level *consciousness* (NL, 4.33). It is also called *imagination* (PA, 222), *conceptual thinking* (NL, 7.23) and often just *consciousness* (PA, 207).
94 f., 98 f., 108 f., 112, 122, 203

Augustine, 14

Bacon, F., 138

Beauty, 216

Beethoven, L. v., 32 f., 206 f.
Behavioral science, 158
Bentham, J., 88, 260
Berenson, B., 231
Bergson, H., viii, 46, 253
Berkeley, G., 155
Biography, 43, 159
Bipolarity, 99 f., 102 f., 114, 203
Botticelli, 205
Bradley, F. H., 2, 78, 183, 253, 266
Broad, C. D., viii f.
Brook, P., 267
Brouwer, L. E. J., 45

Caesar, J., 166 f., 184
Cage, J., 220
CAPRICIOUS CHOICE. See *Choice*
Carroll, L., 145
Cezanne, 231
Chaplin, C., 208
CHOICE. The generic characteristic of fourth-level *practical consciousness* or *will*. Its two forms are capricious choice and rational choice; the three forms of the latter are *utility, right,* and *duty*.
81, 84 f., 88, 91, 114, 152; capricious choice, 85, 94, 105, 115, 170; rational choice, 85, 94, 115, 116, 170
Chronicle, 170, 186
Classification, 37, 63 f., 261
COGNITIVE CONSCIOUSNESS. See *Theoretical Consciousness*
Cohen, R. S., ix
Columbus, C., 171
Concepts, 63 ff., 76, 94 f., 106 f., 144 ff., 152 f.; a priori concepts, 144 ff., 152; empirical concepts, 151, 261; philosophical concepts, 64 f., 66 ff., 76, 81, 95, 107, 135, 151, 206, 246, 256, 261; scientific concepts, 76, 107; self-instancing concepts, 107; transcendental concepts, 69
CONCEPTUAL THINKING. The activity of second-level (and higher) *consciousness* by which features in the objective field of consciousness are discriminated by selective *attention* (NL, 4.5, 7.2). 94 f.
Concrete, the, 11, 41 ff., 47, 49 f., 54 f., 83, 93, 242; concrete fact, 46, 55; con-crete thought, 61; concrete universal, 48 ff., 57, 76; concrete whole, 89
Confucius, 34
CONSCIOUSNESS. The generic name for mental functions regarded as activities of a given level rather than as objects for a higher level. The forms of *practical consciousness* are the activities of emotive *feeling, appetite, desire* and *will;* the corresponding forms of *theoretical consciousness* are the activities of sensory *feeling, imagination* or *conceptual thinking, propositional thinking* and *rational thinking.* (The last three terms may also refer to the corresponding levels of practical consciousness.) In NL, "consciousness" is used to refer to every level, and "simple consciousness" occasionally to refer to *feeling,* or first-level consciousness (NL, 4.22, 9.41). In PA, "consciousness" refers throughout to *imagination,* i.e., second-level consciousness (PA, 215), or to the activity in which the latter is attained.
29, 46, 53, 90 f., 92 ff., 95, 106 ff., 233 f.; first-level consciousness, 84, 92, 202, 215, see also *feeling;* second-level consciousness, 84, 87 f., 92 ff., 99, 116, 203, 209 f., 233, see also *conceptual thinking, appetite, imagination;* third-level consciousness, 84, 88, 92 f., 94 f., 99, 116, 224, 229, see also *propositional thinking, desire,* perception; fourth-level consciousness, 10, 84 f., 88 f., 92 f., 94 ff., 116, 123, 211, 228, 229, see also *choice, rational thinking*
Cook Wilson, J., 2
Copernicus, 149
"Corruption of consciousness," 11, 99, 169, 203 f., 211, 238
"Criteriological" thought, 72, 105, 249 ff., 268
Crites, S. D., ix
Croce, B., 2, 6, 13, 196 f., 218, 223, 231

Dance, 230 f.
Dante, 32, 203
Debbins, W., ix
Definition, 107, 162
Descartes, 138, 147

DESIRE. The third level of *practical consciousness,* the consciousness of *appetitive* activity and the *passions.* It is the lowest level at which *propositional thinking* takes place, hence the lowest to have a negative form (NL, 11.22), to be capable of being true or false (NL, 11.3), and to include awareness of alternatives (NL, 11.14). It is also (always) an activity of asking and answering questions (NL, 11.12).
17, 80 f., 83 ff., 86 ff., 92 ff., 103, 114, 151, 167

Determinism, 38

Dewey, J., 1, 8 f., 155

Dialectic, 16, 20 ff., 46, 60, 68, 73 ff., 78, 80, 85, 91, 92, 107, 110, 111 f., 139, 196, 203, 241, 245, 246, 256; dialectic of concepts, 23, 57 f., 59, 61, 78, 80, 82, 242, 253; dialectic of experience, 23, 27, 52, 58, 59, 61, 80, 82, 116, 197, 242, 253; dialectic of mind, 17, 20, 23, 58, 79, 80, 110, 116, 151, 197, 199, 233, 253, 256, 264; dialectic of implicit and explicit, 20, 35 ff., 45, 56, 76, 237, 253; dialectic of nature, 263; dialectic of philosophical theories, 76; dialectic of question and answer, 132 f.; dialectic of whole and part, 52

Dilthey, W., 6

Distinction, 67 f., 73; distinction of degree, 68, 73; distinction of kind, 68, 73

Dogmatism, 16, 46, 60, 74, 124

Donagan, A., ix, 15 ff., 20, 172

Double genesis, principle of, 154 f.

Dualism, 33, 91

DUTY. The third and most inclusive form of practical reason at the fourth level (rational *choice*) of *practical consciousness.*
11, 54 f., 72, 83, 96, 153, 155

Einstein, A., 19, 138

EMOTION. The generic name for the affective charge on objects of *consciousness* at every level (NL, 4.77; PA, 266-67, 293), although Collingwood refers to it specifically only as the charge on *sensation* at the level of *feeling* (NL, 4.1, 4.62). In PA, such first-level emotion (called "psychical emotion") is distinguished from second-level emotions (called "emotions of consciousness") e.g., hatred, love, anger, and shame (PA, 231-32), and the latter are distinguished from higher-level "emotions of reason" (PA, 292-99). An emotion of any level can be expressed at its own or a lower level, or transformed into an emotion of a higher level as an object of consciousness of that level (PA, 232-34).
4, 33, 85 f., 96, 97, 107, 151, 154, 158, 164, 201 ff., 215, 233 ff.; psychical emotion, 164; emotion of consciousness, 164; emotional charges, 99

Empathy, 231

Empiricism, 111 f., 215

Enlightenment, the, 176

Ethics, 53 ff., 71 f., 83, 88 ff., 96, 111, 190 f.; absolute ethics, 55

Evans-Pritchard, E. E., 143

Evidence, 160, 193 f., 266

Existentialism, 10 ff., 21, 91; existential psychoanalysis, 123

EXPERIENCE. Not used by Collingwood as a term with systematic meaning except as roughly synonymous with *"consciousness."* It usually suggests any activity of consciousness insofar as it is an object for higher-level consciousness.
13, 27, 37, 97, 102, 108 ff., 111, 146 f., 164, 204 f., 213, 216, 242, 253, 255

Explanation, 160; teleological explanation, 116; explanation by law, 116

Expression, 99, 196 f., 201 f., 204, 206 f., 208 f., 212, 215, 216 f., 236

Falsity, 100, 103, 129 f., 264

Faraday, M., 37

FEAR. One of the *passions* (NL, 3.45) connecting *appetite* with *desire.* A form of *conceptual thinking* as *practical consciousness* of a not-self distinguished from self (NL, 10.26, 10.43); develops from *love* (NL, 10.3) and through *shame* into *anger* (NL, 10.47). 86, 153

FEELING. The lowest (first) level of *consciousness* (NL, 9.4, 36.76); not distinguishable into *practical* and *theoretical.* A sensuous-emotional "here-

FEELING (*Continued*)
and-now" consisting of a sensuous element with an emotional charge (NL, 4.1; PA, 162). An "apanage" of mind (NL, 9.41), and knowledge (NL, 5.19), not a constituent.
10, 17, 46, 81, 84, 86, 93, 94, 97 ff., 103, 151, 162, 163, 168, 199, 262

Fermat, P., 226

Feuerbach, L., 34

FREEDOM. The spontaneity of *consciousness* at any level in becoming conscious of lower levels of consciousness and giving form to those activities through selective *attention.*
5, 10, 50, 106 ff., 109, 110

Freud, S., 168 ff., 210

Galileo, 179

Geisteswissenschaften, 156

Genetic fallacy, 111

Gentile, G., 196

Gibbon, E., 45

GOOD. Any object of *desire* insofar as it is desired (NL, 11.5); an *abstraction* from the activity of desiring (NL, 11.54). One form of *happiness,* i.e., happiness in relation to oneself (NL, 12.53). The other form is *power.* Before NL, the good is a genus whose species at ascending levels of *practical consciousness* are *satisfaction, happiness,* and "the third form of goodness."
17, 80, 87 ff., 95, 107; third form of goodness, 88 ff., 262 f.; good and evil, 80, 87, 95, 261 f.

Green, T. H., 2

Haig, D., 189 ff.

Hampshire, S., 254 f.

HAPPINESS (AND UNHAPPINESS). An *abstraction* from the activity of *desiring* (NL, 12.34, 12.52); its forms are *goodness* (NL, 12.53) and *power* (NL, 12.55).
87 ff., 107, 153

Harding, W. G., 229

Hegel, G. W. F., 2, 5 f., 11, 17 f., 21 f., 33, 42, 47 ff., 55, 61, 68 f., 137, 151, 196 f., 239, 246

Herder, J. G. v., 181

Hermeneutics, 131

Heyting, A., 45

Historical consciousness, 6, 49, 51, 104, 155 f., 256 f.; historical certainty, 160, 187 ff.; historical fact, 41; historical imagination, 97, 183 ff.; historical knowledge, 11, 40 ff., 69, 137; historical thought, 45 f., 138 f., historical understanding, 8, 122, 135, 241

Historicism, 20, 149

History, 14, 15, 22 f., 38 f., 41 ff., 115 ff., 149 f., Ch. 6 passim, 242 f.; "scissors and paste history," 170, 183, 187, 193; "critical history," 170, 183, 187, 193; "scientific history," 183 f., 187, 193; narrative history, 192 f.; history of art, 156, 165, 264; history of perception, 264; history of politics, 264; history of science, 39, 156.

Hitler, A., 160, 163

Hobbes, T., 80 f., 234 f.

Hodges, H. A., 258

Hume, D., 29, 101, 155, 265; theory of impressions and ideas, 71, 99, 102, 109, 215

HUNGER. The *appetite* (NL, 3.45, 7.12) to be omnipotent (NL, 8.25, 8.44); it develops into *love* (NL, 8.55) as appetite for partial and incomplete *satisfaction.*
86 f.

Idealism, 2, 57, 111 ff.; absolute idealism, 46 f., 245

IMAGINATION. The second level of *theoretical consciousness,* the result of the conversion of *feeling* by selective *attention.* Properly, consciousness, as selective *attention,* is the activity which effects the conversion, and *imagination* the new (second-level) form of feeling so converted (PA, 215). But Collingwood frequently uses the term in PA for the activity as well as the result. In view of NL 9.41, one could say that *conceptual thinking* is the form of consciousness which is the constituent of mind at the second level. As *practical consciousness,* its apanage is *appetite,* and as *theoretical consciousness* its apanage is *imagination.* But Collingwood regularly uses "appetite"

and "imagination" for second-level consciousness itself.
17, 23, 30 ff., 74, 81, 94 ff., 97 ff., 106, 114 f., 122, 151, 167, 216 ff., 235, 243, 263, 268; "a priori imagination," 140, 151, 159 f., 183 ff.
Inquiry, 8 f., 43, 63, 131, 135, 138 f., 193 f., 245, 252
INTELLECT. Not used by Collingwood as a systematic term, except in PA to refer to any form of *thought* (i.e., activities of third- and fourth-level *consciousness*) higher than *imagination* (PA, 171, 215).
33, 46, 92, 97, 103 ff., 112, 115 ff., 151 f.
Intentional fallacy, 204
Intuition, 32 ff., 74, 196 f.

James, H., 3
James, W., 7, 147, 255
Jaspers, K., 12
Jimson, G., 28
Joad, C. E. M., 1
Johnston, W. M., x
Joyce, J., 233

Kandinsky, W., 32
Kant, I., 2, 5, 6, 33, 51, 64, 67, 72, 90, 103, 146 ff., 152, 161, 180, 185 f., 216, 224, 248, 252, 264
Kepler, J., 19
Kierkegaard, S., 11, 22, 74, 245
Knowledge, 27 f., 31, 43, 46, 93 ff., 106 ff., 125, 132, 224, 241 ff.; see also *Theoretical Consciousness*
Knox, T. M., ix, 4, 14 ff., 117, 240
Kuhn, T. S., 265

Langer, S., 216, 266
LANGUAGE. Any system of bodily movements used to mean something (PA, 241; NL, 6.1). The characteristic linguistic activity is naming, but "naming" is used in such a broad sense that a shiver "names" the feeling of being cold (NL, 6.25). There are characteristic species of language at each level of *consciousness*, but they have no distinguishing names (cf. PA, 266-67). At each level, language expresses the consciousness of a lower level and is the instrument through which the higher level comes into being.
20, 35 f., 80 f., 102, 108, 215; art as language, 226 ff.
Leibniz, G. W., 30
Lenin, V. I., 21
Limited objective, principle of, 126, 161 f.
Linguistic philosophy, 146, 228
Locke, J., 41, 47, 67, 97, 141 f., 155
Logic of question and answer, 8 f., 13, 23, 81, 118, 123 ff., 162, 190 ff., 247, 250
Logic, dialectical, 61, 66, 72; formal logic, 8, 22, 61 ff., 123 f., 261; propositional logic, 121, 123 f., 130
LOVE. A form of *appetite* and also of *desire* (as *consciousness* of appetitive love, NL, 3.45). It develops from *hunger* (NL, 8.35) and into *fear* (NL, 10.3). The lowest level from which the contrast of self and not-self is an *abstraction* (NL, 8.49; PA, 232), and lowest level of Limited Objectives (NL, 8.58). *Appetitive* love invests its object as beautiful (NL, 8.44); at the level of *desire,* love regards its object as *good* (NL, 11.51).
86, 262

McTaggart, J. M. E., viii f.
Malcolm, N., 149
Marx, K., 22, 175 ff.
Marxism-Leninism, 21, 23
Materialism, 38
Matisse, H., 221
Mechanism, 38, 52
Memory, 165
Merton, T., 28
Metaphysics, 118, 123, 142, 148, 156
Methodological individualism, 159
Mill, J. S., 54, 72, 88
MIND. "A mind is nothing except its own activities; but it is all these activities together, not any one separately" (IH, 292). Mind has as constituents the forms of *consciousness* (NL, 5.91) (synonymous with "*thought,*" NL, 1.61, 4.18) and as apanages the forms of *feeling* (NL, 4.18, 9.41).
8, 16, 17, 44, 81 f., 106 f., 146, 150, 161, 162; "absolute mind," 48, 76

Mondrian, P., 212
Moral philosophy, 16, 82 f., 92, 240, 248
Mozart, W. A., 219

Naming, 80, 108, 234
Napoleon, 206
Nietzsche, F., 14

Oakeshott, M., 253
Objets trouvés, 221
Ontological argument, 247 ff.
Ortega y Gasset, 10
Overlap of classes, 17, 49, 62 ff., 70

PASSION. A modification of *appetite* (NL, 9.55) not as a separate level of *consciousness* but as the transition to *desire* (NL, 11.15). Its forms are *fear, shame* (NL, 10.5), and *anger* (NL, 10.2). The idea of alternatives (a third-level concept) is an *abstraction* from experience of fear and anger as alternative responses to a not-self (NL, 11.14).
80
Peirce, C. S., 9, 46
Perception, 92, 103 f., 147, 165, 167, 216 f., 253, 259
Periodization, 52 f.
Philosophy, 13, 15, 18 f., 20, 27, 44, 45 ff., 105, 113, 115 f., 148, 239 f., 242, 245; philosophy of history, 175, 243, 246; philosophy of philosophy, 60, 239 ff., 246, 251; philosophy of religion, 246, 260; philosophical method, 63, 75, 77
Picasso, P., 221
Plato, 5, 20 f., 34, 37, 67, 75, 77, 237, 259
Play, 53, 114
PLEASURE AND PAIN. Aspects of simple *feeling* (NL, 3.44), converted at the level of *appetite* into *satisfaction and dissatisfaction,* and at the level of *desire* into *happiness and unhappiness.*
87, 107
Political science, 158
Positivism, 175 f., 253
POWER. One form of *happiness* (NL, 12.55), as an *abstraction* from the activity of *desiring.* The other form is *goodness.*

PRACTICAL CONSCIOUSNESS. *Consciousness,* at any level above the first, which is concerned with or continuous with action. At the fourth level it is sometimes called *"choice,"* more often *"will"* (to emphasize its connection with lower levels) or *"practical reason"* (to emphasize its connection with fourth-level *theoretical reason*). Its fourth-level forms are capricious *choice* and rational *choice.*
81, 82 ff., 100, 102, 111, 115, 116, 181
PRACTICAL REASON. Fourth-level *practical consciousness;* also called *"choice"* (*capricious* or *rational*) and "will."
97, 114
Pragmatism, 7 ff., 12, 138
Presuppositions, 118, 133 f., 139 ff., 143 f.; absolute presuppositions, 6, 9, 19, 23, 82, 118, 121, 122 f., 126, 139 ff., 162, 194, 241, 244, 245, 252, 255 f.; constellations of presuppositions, 142, 145 f., 153
Prichard, H. A., 2
Proposition, 130, 144 f., 152, 264; categorical proposition, 140, 151
PROPOSITIONAL THINKING. The form of *consciousness* at the third level of *mind* (NL, 6.58, 10.51, 11.15); involved in all *desire* (NL, 11.22); the activity of asking and answering questions (NL, 11.22), but distinguished from knowledge proper (NL, 11.11 n.1, 14.22).
94 f., 97, 99, 103, 105, 114, 224
Psychoanalytic theory, 168
Psychology, 158, 248 f.

Questioning, 31 f., 95, see also Logic of question and answer

Ranke, L. v., 190
RATIONAL CHOICE. See *Choice*
RATIONAL THINKING. The form of *consciousness* at the fourth level of *mind* (NL, 6.58, 10.51). Its two forms are *practical reason* and *theoretical reason* (NL, 14.3 ff.).
94, 96, 104
Rationalism, 36, 96

Realism, epistemological, 44 f., 77, 111 ff.
Reason, 92 f., 96, 105, 149, see also *Practical Reason* and *Theoretical Reason*
Recollection, 93
Re-enactment, 8, 22, 159, 162 ff., 181 f., 190, 222, 252, 263
Regularianism, 90 f., 116, 263
Relations, external and internal, 49 f.
Religion, 20, 27, 34 ff., 38, 39 f., 114, 241 ff., 245
Richards, I. A., 227
RIGHT. The second of the three forms of *practical reason* at the fourth level (rational *choice*) of *practical consciousness.*
72, 83, 89 f., 96, 116, 153, 155
Rilke, R. M. v., 230 f.
Romanticism, 12, 31, 176, 204, 236
Royce, J., 22
Rubinoff, L., 258
Ruggiero, G. d., 13
Ruskin, J., 244
Russell, Bertrand, 1, 38, 145
Rynin, D., 264

Santayana, G., viii
Sartre, J.-P., 10 f., 91, 110
Satisfaction (and Dissatisfaction). Abstractions from *appetitive* activities recognized as having initial and terminal points (NL, 7.55); the extension of *pleasure* as an immediate quality of a here-and-now to the potential of a there-and-then (NL, 7.45).
17, 87 f., 93, 107, 109
Saussure, F. d., 228 f.
Scale of forms, 20, 49, 58, 63, 66 ff., 85, 91, 95, 107, 122, 134 f., 149 f., 162, 242, 246
Schiller, F. C. S., 7
Schopenhauer, 33
Science, 20, 22, 37 ff., 104, 114 ff., 124, 138 f., 141 f., 147; Greco-medieval science, 155; modern science, 116, 155; science and history, 40 ff., 157 ff., 259
Scott, G., 252
Self, concept of, 84, 152 f., 260
Self-consciousness, 36, 39 f., 44, 46 ff., 56, 57, 96
Sensa (sense-data), 97 ff., 115, 216 f.
SENSATION. An inseparable element in the sensuous-emotional flux of the first level of *consciousness* (PA, 171, 215).
80, 86, 97 f., 101, 102, 154, 162 f., 235 f.
SHAME. The *passion* by which *fear* is transformed into *anger* (NL, 10.5).
164
Shelley, P. B., 209
Skepticism, 15
Sociology, 158
Socrates, viii, 5, 20 f., 75, 88, 94, 144, 253
Sophocles, 30, 210
Spengler, O., 175 ff., 260, 265
Spinoza, 5, 42, 67, 93, 262
Stein, G., 232
Sullivan, J. W. N., 32 f.
System, 76, 150; conceptual systems, 152 ff.; systematic philosophy, 2 ff., 16, 41, 244 ff., 254; systematic theory, 158

Tchaikovsky, P. I., 225
Thales, 65, 137
Theology, 20, 36, 40, 242
THEORETICAL CONSCIOUSNESS. *Consciousness,* at any level above the first, which is concerned with or issues in cognition; hence often called in this book (although not by Collingwood) "cognitive consciousness." It is not synonymous with *"thought,"* which also includes *practical consciousness.* At the fourth level it is called "theoretical reason"; its fourth-level forms are teleological understanding, nomological understanding, and historical understanding, corresponding respectively to *utility, right,* and *duty* as the fourth-level forms of *practical consciousness.*
81, 94, 100, 111, 115, 116
THEORETICAL REASON. Fourth-level *theoretical consciousness.*
97, 114
Theory and practice, 8, 79, 95, 110
THINKING, THOUGHT. Another name for the activity of *consciousness,* both *practical* and *theoretical,* at any level above the first. Collingwood often uses the term to emphasize that second-level consciousness (*imagination, appetite*), although not "intellectual,"

THINKING, THOUGHT (*Continued*)
contains the elements which develop into the higher and more identifiable forms of abstract and analytic (PA, 253-54) thinking, e.g., PA, 164-67, 221-24; IH, 305-306 and passim. In NL, second-, third-, and fourth-level *consciousness* are called *"conceptual thinking," "propositional thinking,"* and *"rational thinking"* respectively.
4, 8, 10, 36, 45, 79, 80, 93, 95, 108, 122, 146, 158 f., 180 f.; reflective thought, 162 ff.; "primary" or empirical thought, 104; "secondary" or thought about thought, 104, 118, 244, 251 f.
Thomism, 203
Tinguely, J., 220
Tomas, V., 266
Tomlin, E. W. F., ix
Toulmin, S., 179, 264, 265
Tovey, D., 224
Toynbee, A., 175 ff., 186, 260
Transcendental deduction, 5, 156
Truth, 100, 103, 127, 129 f., 264

Unconscious, the, 98, 99, 165, 168, 169 f.

Utilitarianism, 54, 72, 83, 88, 90, 181, 243
UTILITY. The first of the three forms of practical reason at the fourth level (rational *choice*) of *practical consciousness.*
72, 89, 90, 96, 115, 116, 153, 155

Value, 85, 87, 88, 107
Vico, G. B., 6, 174, 196, 208
Vitalism, 38

Watkins, J. W. N., 265
Wells, R. S., 267
Weltanschauungen, 12
Whitehead, A. N., viii, 6, 29, 37, 145
Whole and part, 48 ff., 57, 90
WILL. The activity of *practical consciousness* at the fourth level (NL, 36.8); its forms are capricious *choice* and rational *choice.*
17, 81, 83, 84 f., 92, 114 f., 152, 162 f.
Wittgenstein, L., viii, 146, 149, 228
World of fact, 41

Zimmerman, A., 160